V&R unipress

TRANSitions.
Transdisciplinary, Transmedial and Transnational
Cultural Studies
Transdisziplinäre, transmediale und transnationale
Studien zur Kultur

Volume / Band 7

Edited by / Herausgegeben von
Renata Dampc-Jarosz and / und Jadwiga Kita-Huber

Advisory Board / Wissenschaftlicher Beirat:
Lorella Bosco (University of Bari, Italy), Leszek Drong (University of Silesia, Poland), Elizabeth Duclos-Orsello (Salem State University, USA), Frank Ferguson (University of Ulster, Ireland), Odile Richard-Pauchet (University of Limoges, France), Monika Schmitz-Emans (University of Bochum, Germany), Władysław Witalisz (Jagiellonian University in Kraków, Poland)

The volumes of this series are peer-reviewed.
Die Bände dieser Reihe sind peer-reviewed.

Marta Tomczok

Postmodernizing the Holocaust

A Comparative Study of Chosen Novels

V&R unipress

Bibliographic information published by the Deutsche Nationalbibliothek
The Deutsche Nationalbibliothek lists this publication in the Deutsche Nationalbibliografie;
detailed bibliographic data are available online: https://dnb.de.

This publication was co-financed by the Silesian University in Katowice.

The project is co-financed from state budget funds allocated by the Minister of Education and Science under the Program "Doskonała Nauka II – Wsparcie monografii naukowych", number: MONOG/SP/0205/2023/01 (Poland).

© 2023 by Brill | V&R unipress, Robert-Bosch-Breite 10, 37079 Göttingen, Germany,
an imprint of the Brill-Group
(Koninklijke Brill NV, Leiden, The Netherlands; Brill USA Inc., Boston MA, USA; Brill Asia Pte Ltd, Singapore; Brill Deutschland GmbH, Paderborn, Germany; Brill Österreich GmbH, Vienna, Austria)
Koninklijke Brill NV incorporates the imprints Brill, Brill Nijhoff, Brill Schöningh, Brill Fink, Brill mentis, Brill Wageningen Academic, Vandenhoeck & Ruprecht, Böhlau and V&R unipress.
Unless otherwise stated, this publication is licensed under the Creative Commons License Attribution-Non Commercial-No Derivatives 4.0 (see https://creativecommons.org/licenses/by-nc-nd/4.0/) and can be accessed under DOI 10.14220/9783737016780. Any use in cases other than those permitted by this license requires the prior written permission from the publisher.

Cover image: © Monika Blidy (University of Silesia)
Translation: Jacek Mydla
Printed and bound by CPI books GmbH, Birkstraße 10, 25917 Leck, Germany
Printed in the EU.

Vandenhoeck & Ruprecht Verlage | www.vandenhoeck-ruprecht-verlage.com

ISSN 2751-8345
ISBN 978-3-8471-1678-3

Contents

Chapter 1. Postmodernization of the Holocaust 7
   The return of postmodernism 7
   The state of research abroad 9
   Research in Poland 15
   After *Tworki* 18

Chapter 2. The Siren Song and the Birth of an Alternative:
Edmond Jabès, Leopold Buczkowski, and Halina Birenbaum 23

Chapter 3. Fog and Shadows: E. L. Doctorow, Raymond Federman,
Georges Perec, Anatol Ulman 45
   The Holocaust as a Hidden Source of Politics 49
   A Blurred Holocaust: A Journey in the Other Direction 53
   Foggy Holocaust 59
   Holocaust *sous rature* 64

Chapter 4. Climate of the Holocaust: Paweł Huelle, Tadeusz Konwicki,
Andrzej Kuśniewicz, Piotr Szewc 71
   Introduction: a climate of change 71
   Working assumptions and reservations 73
   Two case studies: *Bohin Manor* and *Nawrócenie* 78
   Climate change: an ending 84

Chapter 5. Liquid Foundations: Walter Abish and D. M. Thomas 89
   Liquid foundations 91

Chapter 6. The Shadow of the Holocaust and the Hiroshima Mushroom:
Paul Auster 101

Chapter 7. Vibrating Histories: Raymond Federman and Harry Mulisch . 111
   Childhood 113
   Oblivion 113
   Searches: museums and monuments 117

Chapter 8. Allegories of the Holocaust: Marek Bieńczyk and
Ewa Kuryluk 123

Chapter 9. "They found their way home… through the rivers, through
the air": Anne Michaels 139

Chapter 10. The Babel Library of the Holocaust: Nicole Krauss 149

Chapter 11. Postmodern Narcissism and Its Functions: Andrzej Bart . . 159
   Working assumptions 159
   Photographs, screens, interfaces 162
   Mise-en-abyme 165
   Misunderstandings 167
   Narcissistic narratives 171
   "This song is written for money"? 174

Chapter 12. Styles of Reception of the Polish Holocaust Novel:
Marek Bieńczyk and Andrzej Bart 181

Chapter 13. Postmodern Realism, Abjection, Evaluation: The Benefits of
Critical Reflection on Postmodernism and the Holocaust 197

Chapter 14. *Rien ne va plus?* 207

Bibliography 211
   Primary sources 211
   Secondary sources 213

Index 225

Chapter 1.
Postmodernization of the Holocaust

The return of postmodernism

The thing that encourages a return to the study of postmodernism today is the disproportion between its spectacular beginnings, which researchers commonly place in 1960s, and its blurry, barely visible end. In his 2016 article, "The End," Brain McHale, author of the groundbreaking *Postmodern Fiction* (1987, Polish edition 2012), referred to this as the "vanishing," thus reminding us of the prophetic story "The Death of the Novel" by Ronald Sukenick (1932–2004), written in 1969. McHale came to see in this novella an anticipation of the 9/11 2001 events, when the terminally sick writer was evacuated from his flat in Battery Park City.[1] While some critics, Alison Gibbons for instance, believe that the crisis of the post-modern era was brought on by the World Trade Center attack,[2] others talk about the dissolution of postmodernism,[3] claiming that, unable to withstand the "brutality of the real,"[4] it caved in under the pressure of new materialism, post-politics, and the struggle to restore the identity of the "forgotten majority."[5] In practice, however, it means something completely different. As a recent category, postmodernism has for many humanists become a symptom of their individual past, too difficult to summarize, not easy to resolve, perhaps even identical to positions they are eager to deny today. Two examples of bypassing rather than solving the problem are worthy of notice. One is McHale's. Asked to sum up his earlier work on this topic during his stay at the University of Otago, New Zeland,

---

1 Brian McHale, "The End," https://electronicbookreview.com/essay/the-end/ [accessed 16.09.2019].
2 Alison Gibbons, *Postmodernism is dead. What comes next?* TLS online (*The Times Literary Supplement*), June 12, 2017, https://www.the-tls.co.uk/articles/public/postmodernismdead-comes-next/ [accessed 16.09.2019].
3 Andrzej Leder, *Był kiedyś postmodernizm... Sześć esejów o schyłku XX stulecia* (Warszawa: Wydawnictwo IFiS PAN, 2018), p. 9.
4 Leder, *Był kiedyś postmodernizm*, p. 9
5 Leder, *Był kiedyś postmodernizm*, p. 9.

he stated, "What did we conclude, back in June 2015 in Dunedin, about postmodernism? Nothing."[6] The other is Andreas Huyssen's, a position of questioning the earlier appreciation of postmodernism with the statement that now there is no need any more to talk about it because questioning modernity no longer makes sense.[7] Loss of faith in former apologists signals that, before postmodernism passed, it was perceived as an uncomfortable and unfavorable tradition, masking not only more serious problems, but also a possible lack of involvement of the thinkers themselves.[8]

Another way to look at the return to postmodernism is offered by the Freudian category of *Nachträglichkeit*. Commonly translated as afterwardness or retroactivity,[9] it is an effect (called retroactive) which causes a delay in the understanding of a new system, which in the case of postmodernism means at least a dozen years.[10] Referring to Frederic Jameson's interpretation of retroactivity (the "retroactive effect"), Hal Foster proposes to understand by it, not only a perspective external to postmodernism, but also its internal dynamics, which reflects "a continual process of anticipated futures and reconstructed pasts."[11] All this places postmodernism among phenomena that are extremely difficult to evaluate, due not only to its ambiguous role in the creation of culture, but also to its insufficient attractiveness, which today is recalled with a sense of disappointment rather than nostalgia.

One of the effects of not taking up the debate summarizing postmodernism in Poland seems to be the problem of postmodernism's impact on knowledge about the Holocaust. While countries like the United States and Israel have produced synthetic studies of postmodernism, in Poland, its extensive exploration seems to be underway. This suggests that discussions around methodologies that represent the so-called new humanities, such as affective and post-dependent criticism or studies on plants, animals, and material objects, may lack adequate support in critical reflection. Seen in this context, Ewa Domańska's *Historia egzystencjalna*.

---

6 McHale, "The End."
7 "Na straży różnicy. Rozmowa z Andreasem Huyssenem," Czas Kultury 17.08.2018, http://czaskultury.pl/czytanki/na-strazy-roznicy/ [accessed 16.09.2019].
8 Leder expresses a similar insight: "Of all these events the most curious is the abruptness with which postmodern narrative removed itself from the very center of the intellectual debate and into its background." Leder, *Był kiedyś postmodernizm*, p. 9.
9 Fredric Jameson, *Postmodernism, or, The Cultural Logic of Late Capitalism* (Durham: Duke University Press, 1991), p. xix.
10 Hanna Gosk's concept of interventional humanities, focusing attention on "unprocessed aspects of the past" and trying to include them "in a set of communal stories" seems to be helpful in understanding postmodernism as a recent past. Hanna Gosk, *Przemoc w opowieści. Ze studiów postzależnościowych nad literaturą XX i XXI wieku*, (Kraków: Universitas, 2019), p. 236.
11 Hal Foster, *The Return of the Real. The Avant-Garde at the End of the Century* (Cambridge, Mass. and London: The MIT Press, 1996), p. 33.

Krytyczne studium narrratywizmu i humanistyki zaangażowanej[12] [*Existential History. A Critical Study of Narrativism and Engaged Humanities*] is a notable exception.

The state of research abroad

The relationship between postmodernism and Holocaust-related literature is usually discussed in relation to philosophy. The philosophical context, on the other hand, rests on the assumption that the conclusions of thinkers such as, to name two, Jean-François Lyotard and Philippe Lacoue-Labarthe in relation to literary narratives are pre-emptive. This may not result from the actual dynamics of the development of both these areas, but may have to do with the style of literary critique adopted in academic discourse, some traditions tending to emphasize a literary work's ideological and philosophical context, others – to ignore it. Worth recalling is Hayden White's remark on how some aspects of the past can and indeed must be represented with the help of figurative poetic devices.[13] If this assumption makes the composition of some literary works into a phenomenon governed by convention and subordinated to a particular custom, we do need to disregard in principle any of the discourses involved, despite the impression one sometimes gets that only some are relevant.

The first monograph book devoted to postmodern philosophy in the context of Holocaust studies is the 1998 collection of essays *Postmodernism and the Holocaust* edited by Alan Milchman and Alan Rosenberg, lecturers at Queens College at New York's City University.[14] These researchers point out the associative and paradoxical nature of the issue in hand, as well as its transformative potential. Interested in creating a list of relevant postmodern philosophers, among the precursors they name Georges Bataille, Maurice Blanchot, and Emanuel Levinas. They include Jacques Derrida, Lyotard and Michel Foucault

---

12 Ewa Domańska, *Historia egzystencjalna. Krytyczne studium narratywizmu i humanistyki zaangażowanej* (Warszawa: PWN, 2012).

13 "[...] much factual writing is non-literary, while some fictional writing may lack any literariness whatsoever. It all depends upon the degree of artistic freeplay that enters into the composition. Certain aspects of a given past may be representable only in a poetic mode of utterance [...]." Hayden White, "Postmodernism and History." Hayden White, *Postmodernizm i historia*, p. 41. This essay was published in 2010 in French as "Postmodernisme et histoire" (in *Historiographies. Concepts et débats*, vol. II, Paris, Gallimard, pp. 839–844) and in an updated version, "Postmodernizm i historia," in *Przeszłość praktyczna*, ed. Ewa Domańska (Kraków: Universitas, 2014). The English version is quoted here and elsewhere from a manuscript shared with me by Professor Ewa Domańska, to whom I express my gratitude. Page numbers are those in the Polish translation.

14 Alan Milchman and Alan Rosenberg, ed., *Postmodernism and the Holocaust* (Amsterdam and Atlanta, GA: Rodopi, 1998).

among the first generation of postmodern thinkers, and Nancy, Lacoue-Labarthe, Marc Froment-Meurice and Sarah Kofman among the second. Yet they do not propose clear ideological and formal criteria with which to define philosophical writing. Drawing on Steven Best and Douglas Kellner, they take shelter in the statement of the indefinability of the phenomenon of the Holocaust in theory and the pluralism of points of view in practice. The essays on the Łódź ghetto (Gregory Fried's "*Inhalt Unzulassig:* Late Mail from Lodz – A Meditation on Time and Truth"), the prominent place of Arendt (Fabio Ciaramelli's "From Radical Evil to the Banality of Evil: Remarks on Kant and Arendt" and essays on Levinas by James. R. Watson, Robert John Sheffler Manning, Tina Chanter, and Helmut Peukert), Levinas and Derrida (David Michael Levin's essay on *Cinders*, "Cinders, Traces, Shadows on the Page: The Holocaust in Derrida's Writing") testify to the reconnaissance and pioneering character of this book. Tracy Fessenden's essay on Mark C. Taylor (e.g., his *Disfiguring*, 1992) is particularly interesting in this respect. A religious critic affiliated with Columbia University and a postmodern theologian,[15] Taylor was one of the first to draw a line between modernism and postmodernism in isolation from history, claiming that "in the dark light of those flames [of Hiroshima] and the avid dust of those ashes [of Auschwitz], modernism ends and something *other* begins."[16]

In their subsequent book, *Experiments in Thinking the Holocaust: Auschwitz, Modernity and Philosophy* (a Polish translation came out in 2003), Milchman and Rosenberg describe the Holocaust, after Dan Diner, as a transformative event (*das Ereignis Auschwitz*), thus emphasizing its caesura-like character and pointing to the impact that the Holocaust has had on the present.[17] The need to see the Holocaust in retrospective and prospective categories,[18] about which Milchman and Rosenberg wrote in the earlier book, returns here in the form of the concept of the Holocaust as a warning.[19] The Holocaust must be seen not only

---

15 Mark C. Taylor, *Erring. A Postmodern A/theology* (Chicago and London: The University of Chicago Press, 1987). The pejorative valuation of postmodern theology in Poland and its entanglement in nihilism, dark pessimism and axiological emptiness, on the one hand, and the resistance of the Catholic Church, on the other, have been addressed by Michał Zawadzki, among other scholars. See Michał Zawadzki, "Teologia postmodernistyczna jako szansa dla religii chrześcijańskiej", *Diametros* 2008, n. 15, pp. 97–101.
16 Mark C. Tylor, *Disfiguring. Art, Architecture, Religion* (Chicago and London: The University of Chicago Press, 1992), p. 47; italics in the original. In Poland, a similar issue was taken up by Przemysław Czapliński in "Zagłada jako wyzwanie dla refleksji o literaturze," *Teksty Drugie* 2004, n. 5, pp. 9–22.
17 Alan Milchman and Alan Rosenberg, *Eksperymenty w myśleniu o Holocauście. Auschwitz, nowoczesność i filozofia*, trans. by Leszek Krowicki and Jakub Szacki (Warszawa: Wydawnictwo Naukowe Scholar, 2003); all subsequent references are to the Polish eidtion.
18 Milchman and Rosenberg, *Eksperymenty w myśleniu o Holocauście*, p. 14.
19 I am indebted here to Timothy Snyder's *Black Earth: The Holocaust as History and Warning* (London: The Bodley Earth, 2015).

as a turning point in the history of genocides, but it must above all be kept "alive in a genocidal universe" due to the lessons it teaches.[20] Rather than deliver on the promise to reflect on the impact of the Holocaust on the present, *Experiments in Thinking the Holocaust* focuses on the Nazi roots of postmodernism, and especially on the Nazi past of Martin Heidegger. However, this angle does not exclude thinkers in whose biography such roots were noted (Maurice Blanchot, Bataille, Paul de Man). Rather, it sustains a thesis about the preventive nature of their activity, which Milchman and Rosenberg work into a scenario of the future. Their thesis, which to a large extent is a repetition of their earlier theories, is an expression of pregenocide concern, which sometimes allows free interpretations of selected systems of thought (Arendt, Foucault) with which to develop new descriptions of the Holocaust. As we read:

> What postmodernism can offer is a series of re-descriptions of the Holocaust, breaking with old paradigms and opening up new perspectives. These re-descriptions that stop the flow of preconceived arguments, provide us with new metaphors for re-facing the experience of Auschwitz, and create new ways of presenting the Holocaust – these descriptions make it possible to grasp those aspects of the "Final Solution" which have been hidden or obscured by recognized vocabulary.[21]

A much broader perspective on the relationship between postmodernism and the Holocaust was proposed in a 2004 book by Robert Eaglestone from Royal Holloway University in London. Replacing the term "postmodernism" with "the postmodern," Eaglestone has traced the development of thinking about the Holocaust in the most important works of postmodernity, from Arendt to Giorgio Agamben. He has detected the influence of postmodernism on the contemporary understanding of the Holocaust primarily in relation to postcolonial studies, narrowing down Milchman and Rosenberg's proposal, formulated in relation to new descriptions of the Holocaust, to in-depth studies of other genocides (those of Native Americans, the first Australians and the Herero in Namibia).[22] Eaglestone's proposal has also turned out to be the first to consider the possibility of abandoning the anthropocentric paradigm in Holocaust studies, which gives it a radically distinct character. Eaglestone calls postmodernism a constellation of ideas derived from the post-phenomenological

---

20 Milchman and Rosenberg, *Eksperymenty w myśleniu o Holocauście*, p. 14. The idea is borrowed from Ernst Bloch's *The Principle of Hope*. Gérard Rabinovitch has recently written a great deal on the educational aspects of the Holocaust, for instance in his *Leçons de la Shoah*, *Nauki płynące z Zagłady*, trans. From the French G. Majcher (Warszawa: Wydawnictwo Dialog, 2019).
21 Milchman and Rosenberg, *Eksperymenty w myśleniu o Holocauście*, pp. 71–72.
22 Robert Eaglestone, *The Holocaust and the Postmodern* (Oxford: Oxford University Press, 2004), p. 343.

tradition,[23] ideas which lack validation and are ridden with simplifications. As the basic among them, Eaglestone points to the mechanism of identification in literature, normalization in history and the search for boundaries, answers, and solutions in philosophy.[24]

A study cited less frequently and proposing a psychoanalytical perspective on postmodernism and the Holocaust is a 1997 book by Elizabeth Jane Bellamy from The University of Tennessee Knoxville. Bellamy singles out the psychoanalytic phenomena of mourning and melancholia, which have now permanently entered the postmodern discourse, and proposes to regard psychoanalysis as a "wardrobe" for postmodernism. She describes postmodernism as "a melancholic reaction to the 'debris of history'" and to modernism's loss of narrative coherence.[25] She refers to Eric Santner's insights (e. g., in *Stranded Objects: Mourning, Memory and Film in Postwar Germany*; 1990) which significantly enhance the scope of Holocaust studies, and stresses that postmodern mourning tends to be exaggerated into a bizarrely pleasurable celebration of behaviors that alienate the subject.[26]

A very different approach can be found in the works of the Israeli literary scholar from the Ben Gurion University of the Negev, Efraim Sicher, chiefly *The Holocaust Novel* (2005).[27] Drawing on the findings of Milchman and Rosenberg and Bellamy, Sicher adopts a broad criterion for defining postmodernism, devoid of clearly marked boundaries. An unquestionable advantage of his approach and a feature that brings him close to Polish literary scholars is his choice of the novel as the preferred medium for communicating Holocaust-related content. Sicher explains the novel's privileged status – a claim that requires re-evaluations of

---

23 Eaglestone, *The Holocaust and the Postmodern*, p. 340.
24 It will be noted that also Milchman and Rosenberg have defined experiment in a similar manner, following Frederick Nietzsche (a trial that brings on a change; an experience that modifies things). See Milchman and Rosenberg, *Eksperymenty w myśleniu o Holocauście*, p. 41.
25 Elizabeth J. Bellamy, *Affective Genealogies. Psychoanalysis, Postmodernism, and the "Jewish Question" after Auschwitz* (Lincoln and London: University of Nebraska Press, 1997), p. 2.
26 "[...] Eric Santner has argued compellingly that the postmodern project (as the 'death' of modernity) is obsessed with 'death, loss, and impoverishment,' manifested as 'discourses of bereavement' whose labor of mourning a lost modernity enact not a true sense of loss, but rather a kind of bizarrely playful *jouissance* celebrating the discontinuities of the alienated postmodern subject.' Here Santner astutely 'psychoanalyzes' postmodernism as enacting a kind of *Trauerspiel*, in the process revealing its own repressions of a melancholic nostalgia for the past." Bellamy, *Affective Genealogies*, p. 2.
27 In the essay "The Holocaust in the Postmodernist Era" (in the collection of essays *Breaking Crystal. Writing on Memory after Auschwitz*, ed. Efraim Sicher, Urbana and Chicago: University of Illinois Press, 1998, pp. 297–328) and more recently in his book on postmodern love, Sicher has represented multi-layered, comparative studies approach to postmodernism in American and Israeli literature (Efraim Sicher, *Postmodern Love in the Contemporary Jewish Imagination. Negotiating Spaces and Identities*, New York and Oxford: Routledge, 2022).

earlier research positions – by pointing out that fictionalization of the Holocaust is a phenomenon that, on the one hand, alleviates the ineffability of the testimony while expanding this genre's framework.[28] Fictionalization gives voice to victims otherwise deprived of it without excluding the presentation of historical material (for example, in Ka-Tsetnik's novels and Jean-François Steiner's *Treblinka*). At the same time, Sicher draws attention to the distortion of historical facts, which may be related to the handling of erotic themes in the novels. Emphasizing elements of sadomasochism in perpetrators' and victims' accounts, as in the case of William Styron's *Sophie's Choice*, results in making this type of perversion a phenomenon characteristic of the Holocaust, which is not consistent with history and does not meet the assumptions of fictionalization itself.

The task Sicher takes up in *The Holocaust Novel* is first of all that of interpreting a selection of postmodern novels which address the theme of the Holocaust: Don DeLillo's *White Noise* (1984; Polish translation in 1997 as *Biały szum*), Martin Amis's *Time's Arrow: Or the Nature of the Offence* (1991; Polish translation in 1997 as *Strzała czasu albo natura występku*), Emily Prager's *Eve's Tattoo* (1992), Sherri Szeman's *The Kommendant's Mistress* (1993), Anne Michaels's *Fugitive Pieces* (1996; Polish translation in 2000 as *Płomyki pamięci*), Raymond Federman's *The Twofold Vibration* (1982; Polish translation as *Podwójna wibracja* in 1988), *Double or Nothing: a real fictitious discourse* (1971; Polish translation as *Podwójna wygrana jak nic* in 2010), *The Voice in the Closet / La Voix Dans le Cabinet de Débarras* and *Aunt Rachel's Fur* (2001), Ian McEwan's *Black Dogs* (1992; Polish translation as *Czarne psy* in 2010), G. W. Sebald's *Austerlitz* (2001; 2007 in a Polish translation as *Austerlitz: powieść*), Bernhard Schlink's *Der Vorleser* (*The Reader*) (1995; Polish translation in 2009 as *Lektor*), and D. M. Thomas's *The White Hotel* (1981; Polish translation as *Biały hotel* in 1994). Apart from the list itself and brief comments accompanying it, however, Sicher offers little justification for his selection of the literary material, no matter how obvious it may be. Nor does he draw conclusions from the clear predominance of the novel in the 1990s or comment on the significance of transgressive themes and how these themes shifted the paradigm in new directions, such as that of posthumanism in the case of Michaels.

To conclude this section, it is worth pointing out two articles by narrative theorists well assimilated into Polish academia, Frank Ankersmit's "Remembering the Holocaust: Mourning and Melancholia" and Hayden White's "Postmodernism and History." The former is indeed a frequently quoted text; however, Ankersmit's insistence on the primacy of aesthetic over ethical categories in

---

28 Efraim Sicher, *The Holocaust Novel* (New York and Oxford: Routledge, 2005), p. 184.

Holocaust research seems much less valid today than it was several years ago.[29] Considering the recent historical research, e.g., by David Cesarani,[30] a comprehensive historical account once more becomes a challenge for the humanities. At the same time, the claim that appropriateness and talent rather than truth and moral goodness are the prerogatives for writing about the Holocaust, misrepresents postmodernism itself by reducing it mainly to aesthetics and separating it from social issues, which in fact it has not ignored. White's voice sounds fresh and restorative when heard against this background. In the idea that academic historiography should be rejected in favor of amateurish and unbounded writing about history, we can hear the desire to weaken the category of "the only kind of truth"[31] by exposing the apparently impure interests of historians, and to reclaim radical history, a history that puts forward strong statements (as opposed to a soothing, anodyne type of history[32]). At the same time, White exposes the research bias of postmodern literature and, like Sicher, values fictionalization (here: factuality), going as far as to argue that in certain circumstances history will inevitably turn into literary fiction.[33]

When we juxtapose these two texts and the respective approaches, we realize that at some point categories such as appropriateness turn into dead ends in research, since virtually all postmodern fiction – from Piotr Rawicz's *Le sang du ciel* (*Krew nieba*; *The Blood of Heaven*), through Federman's *Double or Nothing*, to Harry Mulisch's *The Procedure* – has kept pushing against aesthetic barriers and in fact successfully handled the issues of representation and expression

---

29 Frank Ankersmit, "Remembering the Holocaust: Mourning and Melancholia," in Frank Ankersmit, *Historical Representation* (Stanford CA: Stanford University Press, 2001), pp. 176–196. See also Frank Ankersmit, *Narracja, reprezentacja, doświadczenie. Studia z teorii historiografii*, ed. and introd. Ewa Domańska (Kraków: Universitas, 2004).
30 David Cesarani, *Final Solution: The Fate of the Jews, 1933–1949* (New York: St. Martin's Press, 2016).
31 "It is as if historical truth were the only kind of truth we had and any attenuation of its authority would shake the foundations of civilization itself." White, "Postmodernism and History." White, "Postmodernizm i historia," p. 45.
32 "It is true that postmodernism is skeptical of the work of professional historians, not only because it is antiquarian and anodyne, but because they seem to be indentured to special interest groups, the state, wealthy patrons, political parties, corporations, and especially the culture of the university." White, "Postmodernism and History." Cf. White, "Postmodernizm i historia," p. 39.
33 "All this means that postmodernist literature features and examines the interrelation between fact and fiction, the real and the imaginary, the truth and the illusion." White, "Postmodernism and History." Cf. White, "Postmodernizm i historia," p. 41. In this respect, the case of the Polish reception of Jan Tomasz Gross's *Sąsiedzi* [*Neighbors*], a work in many respects postmodern, seems significant due to its anti-system character, the ease with which Gross divided the environment of university historians in Poland, as well as the researcher's attitude to the definition of the scientific adopted in Poland, which differs fundamentally from the understanding widespread in American academic centers with which the author collaborated for years.

without remaining beholden to tradition and convention. At the same time, White's appeal, while it does not seem to apply to historians such as Cesarani and Raul Hilberg,[34] makes it clear that, in addition to narration, lobbyists and stakeholders should also be considered when facts are to be assessed.

Research in Poland

In an insightful 2003 review of the Polish edition of Piotr Rawicz's *The Blood of Heaven* for *Tygodnik Powszechny*, announced with the slogan "the first postmodern novel about the Holocaust," Juliusz Kurkiewicz asked the following assumption-loaded questions: "Isn't the Holocaust a perfect postmodern theme?" "Couldn't postmodern literature become an excellent medium for this topic?" The statements these questions imply are noteworthy for two reasons. To begin with, Rawicz's novel is placed at the top of the list of postmodern Holocaust-related fiction, in Poland and worldwide. Second, the reviewer marks out here an important research field, on the one hand, by comparing the transgressive *The Blood of Heaven* to Jerzy Kosiński's *The Painted Bird*,[35] and, on the other, by suggesting that it would make sense to abandon the type of radical valuation of fiction which uses the form and idea of personal and factual prose.[36] Kurkiewicz's approach was taken up two years later by Arkadiusz Morawiec, who published in *Ruch Literacki* an extensive, multi-themed article devoted to Marek Bieńczyk's *Tworki*.

Referring to the Polish edition of Milchman and Rosenberg's book, Morawiec reads *Tworki* in the spirit of Derridean insights, including the lack of a "universal referent,"[37] absence and difference, trace, and dissemination of meaning. Trying to understand the interpenetration of Bieńczyk's scientific interest in melancholy and the novel's connections with postmodernism,[38] Morawiec considers, first of all, the features he had previously found in Ankersmit: seriousness, sublimity, metaphysics, and pathos. He examines Bieńczyk's fixation on lan-

---

34 Raul Hilberg, *The Destruction of the European Jews* (Chicago: Quadrangle, 1967).
35 Juliusz Kurkiewicz, "Myszkin w czasach Zagłady", *Tygodnik Powszechny* of 7 September 2003, p. 11.
36 It will be enough to recall Henryk Grynberg's severely critical opinion of Kosiński's *The Painted Bird* and the many accusation raised against that novel's purported anti-Polishness, which surfaced on the occasion of its 2019 film adaptation. Regarding the novel, see Henryk Grynberg, "Żyd, który udawał Polaka, który udawał Żyda", in: Henryk Grynberg, *Monolog polsko-żydowski* (Wołowiec: Wydawnictwo Czarne, 2003), p. 80–87.
37 Arkadiusz Morawiec, *Literatura w lagrze. Lager w literaturze. Fakt – temat – metafora* (Łódź: Publikacje Wydawnictwa AHE w Łodzi, 2009), p. 356.
38 See Marek Bieńczyk's article "Klucz francuski," *Kontrapunkt* (supplement to *Tygodnik Powszechny*) 2001, n. 3/4, p. 12.

guage, on the category of the name and on stylistic shifts, and concludes that they are manifestations of the author's ethical concern for the memory of the Holocaust. Considering these philosophical aspects of postmodernism alone would put Bieńczyk's novel on the opposite side of Rawicz's, at the same time marking two border points for the territory which Polish literary scholars visit with a great deal of reluctance.

An opposite position was taken by Aleksandra Ubertowska in her 2007 book *Świadectwo – trauma – głos. Literackie reprezentacje Holokaustu* [*Testimony – Trauma – Voice. Literary Representations of the Holocaust*] as regards both *Tworki* and, more generally, postmodernist literature:

> From the point of view established by the literature on the Holocaust, postmodern literature, preoccupied with its metafictional character, provides examples of ontological mixing of reality with representation, or even of fatal confusion of these two orders. This brings matters dangerously close to "negationist" attitudes, i.e., attempts to deny the reality of the Holocaust, which – despite all the differences – derive from an analogous cognitive disinvolvement, from a similar cancellation of the ethical perspective in reflections on the representation of historical events.[39]

Similarly to Eagleston, Ubertowska takes a broad view of postmodernism, which allows her to "disassemble" many of its criteria, including above all the aesthetic one, all-important in some narratives yet usually devoid of critical self-commentary. At the same time, Ubertowska's is the first Polish monograph-type book on postmodernism, combining philosophical commentary (with accurate and thorough chapters on Adorno's *Negative Dialectic*, Derrida's *Cinders* or Lyotard's *The Differend*) and literary analysis (Irit Amiel, Michał Głowiński, Wilhelm Dichter, Tadeusz Różewicz, Raymond Federman, Jarosław Marek Rymkiewicz, Piotr Szewc, Marek Bieńczyk and Adam Zagajewski). Unlike other studies of similar type, Ubertowska's use of the theoretical tools has allowed her to create a completely new narrative about Polish fiction, to show it in a global context, and thus to bring Polish authors out of the shadow of the local and onto the world stage. The most serious accusation she levels against postmodernism is related to its purported weak subjectivity, a feature which arguably makes it incapable of facing the "extreme evil" of the Holocaust.[40] Ubertowska places the subject in a novel position in terms of its relation to the ideas of postmodernity and its ethical imperative. This repositioning causes the entertainment aspect of postmodernism, so widespread in Poland as to have become almost a cliché, to vanish while giving due prominence to its involvement in social issues, including

---

[39] Aleksandra Ubertowska, *Świadectwo – trauma – głos. Literackie reprezentacje Holokaustu* (Kraków: Universitas, 2007), p. 19.
[40] Ubertowska, *Świadectwo – trauma – głos*, p. 39.

class inequality, ecological disasters, immigration, military conflicts, and the breakdown of interpersonal ties.

A critique based on similar arguments has been carried out by Ewa Domańska. Her starting point in her 2012 book *Historia egzystencjalna* is a reinterpretation of the work of Ankersmit and White, which leads her to engage in a debate with the concept of a weak and melancholic subject. She then goes on to reflect on the harmful nature of this type of subject in pre-genocidal times:

> Does maintaining communities in a state of neurotic melancholy really help them survive and prevent tragic events from happening again? By supporting the melancholic contemplation of the Holocaust, for example, are we not contributing to the process about which Dawid Warszawski once wrote as he claimed that "Auschwitz is a museum – a place where we come to investigate our past. It is not a place where the present and the future stand before us."[41]

Domańska's critique focuses on the features of postmodernism that dominated the Polish humanities in the last dozen or so years (her book came out in 2012), especially the following aspects of Holocaust studies: linguistics, textuality, discursiveness, constructionism and traumatophilia.[42] Interested in a variety of categories, Domańska devotes ample space to trauma, that dark side of "neoliberal triumphalism," in the words of Andreas Huyssen. According to both these scholars, trauma weakens the subject, causing him to be incapable of making decisions and of self-defense. Meanwhile, Domańska argues,

> In the face of changes taking place in the world (new acts of genocide and mass murder, terrorism, including state terrorism, governments' disregard for human rights, the use of torture, the onslaught of global capitalism, biopolitics, biotechnological progress, increase of natural disasters), the humanities cannot afford to propagate the ideas of a weak subject, a fragmented community and the exaltation of the victim figure.[43]

Moreover, the traumatocentric approach "imprisons us in the gothic aura of postmodernism with its apocalypses of the end and of death and its affirmation of negativity,"[44] and as such poses a threat to democracy.[45] Domańska's critique

---

41 Domańska, *Historia egzystencjalna*, p. 73–74.
42 By traumatophilia I understand the abuse of the category of trauma (or wound) in the humanities of approximately the past dozen years, leading to the sterilization of the concept itself and the avoidance of new challenges in studies devoted to the past, especially those which can be described as vitalist, that is, requiring a radically different type of mobilization of creative forces and actions than fixation on suffering (martyrdom).
43 Domańska, *Historia egzystencjalna*, p. 137.
44 Domańska, *Historia egzystencjalna*, p. 137.
45 In the form of a conflict within a community related to past events that were dramatic for some of its members. In recent years, Polish society has become a field of various games aimed at establishing the trauma associated with the participation of Poles in the Second World War as a superior category and recognizing the suffering of other communities, especially the Jewish one, as a competition with Polish martyrdom. The conflict of traumas is

resounds with the need to return to vitalist foundations of the humanities, which would restore respect to relations with the past while allowing us to draw knowledge, wisdom and strength from it. We should ask, therefore, whether it is possible to make the postmodern tradition a source of inspiration for this new type of thinking about the Holocaust, one which, instead of incapacitating and inhibiting new attitudes and activities, would significantly expand the scope of the existing research.

After *Tworki*

The reception of Bieńczyk's novel may be illustrative material for anyone who would like to understand the progress of literary studies devoted to the Holocaust in Poland. Its inexpressibility, rhetoric, representation and its ethical boundaries are some of the issues addressed in the debate the novel provoked, as well as, and above all, literature itself.[46] Only in Anna Mach's 2016 book *Świadkowie świadectw. Postpamięć Zagłady w polskiej literaturze najnowszej* [*Witnesses of Testimonies. Post-memory of the Holocaust in Contemporary Polish Literature*] do we find an attempt to critically to examine these categories and to juxtapose them with history. Mach notes that a major failure of early interpretations of *Tworki* lies in depriving the novel of its most obvious (although not necessarily its simplest) feature, its contact with reality. The meaning of this novel has not evaporated, nor has its code lost its referentiality.[47] On the contrary, "Sonia, Honette and Kaltz are historical figures. The hospital in Tworki really did function during the war [...], and Eugen Honette was its director from September 1940 on."[48] According to Dr. Jan Gallus's memoirs, quoted by Mach, Zofia Kubryń (Sonia), probably handed herself over to the Gestapo "after some quarrel with her boyfriend."[49] While it is difficult to dismiss Aleksandra Ubertowska's argument that Bieńczyk trivialized the Holocaust (after all, in *Tworki*, he does not

---

an example of pathology in the conduct of historical policy, serves to strengthen nationalism, spread hatred, and is itself an instrument in the hands of the authorities.

46 See Marek Zaleski, "Jedyna instancja. O *Tworkach* Marka Bieńczyka," in idem, *Echa idylli w literaturze polskiej doby nowoczesności i późnej nowoczesności* (Kraków 2007); Katarzyna Bojarska, "Historia Zagłady i literatura (nie)piękna. *Tworki* Marka Bieńczyka w kontekście literatury posttraumatycznej," *Pamiętnik Literacki* 2008 z. 2; Piotr Marecki, "*Tworki* Marka Bieńczyka jako powieść gatunkowa," *Przestrzenie Teorii* 2012, n. 18.

47 Anna Mach, *Świadkowie świadectw. Postpamięć Zagłady w polskiej literaturze najnowszej* (Warszawa and Toruń: Wydawnictwo Naukowe Uniwersytetu Mikołaja Kopernika, 2016), p. 283.

48 Mach, *Świadkowie świadectw*, p. 281.

49 Jan Gallus, "Państwowy Szpital dla Psychicznie Chorych w Tworkach w latach 1939–1945 (wspomnienia)," *Przegląd Pruszkowski* 1983, n. 1, p. 45; qtd after Mach, *Świadkowie świadectw*, p. 283.

refer to the problem of the extermination of the entire Jewish community of the hospital, but presents one episode of its history, someone's love affair), she does not address the novel's historicity. According to the principles of evaluation of a postmodern work discussed above, we could repeat after Ankersmit, "The ultimate challenge for both historical writing and the historian is not factual or ethical, but aesthetic."[50]

Meanwhile, the problem of the Holocaust in postmodern novel requires going beyond the aesthetic horizon and taking into account actual environmental and social problems. Ubertowska indicates them in her article on *Krew nieba*, where she brings into the foreground the novel's biological and geological themes accompanying the author's reflection on the genocide.[51] In this context, postmodernism has turned out to be of little importance, as we see Ubertowska reach for Bruno Latour's philosophy, which is, in part at least, anti-postmodern.[52] However, one can construe the role of postmodernism differently, namely as a cultural style that is favorable to posthumanist and postcolonial reflection on the Holocaust. This idea animates my approach to Anne Michaels's *Fugitive Pieces*, a novel well-known in Canada and the United States,[53] in which the experience of the Holocaust is compared with the indigenous lore of Canadian Indians and Greeks from the island of Zakynthos as well as with scientific knowledge: archaeology, geology and humanist geography.

The main problem highlighted by Michaels concerns the challenge of overcoming the mourning after the Holocaust and the related concepts of trauma, emptiness, and silence in the absence of a conflict between a community or a stakeholder group over the primacy of its trauma.[54] By performing indigenous practices (feeding the spirits of the dead, bidding them farewell by the sea, and

---

50 Ankersmit, "Remembering the Holocaust: Mourning and Melancholia," p. 176. The preceding two sentences provide the context for this statement: "And it is only an aesthetic category – the essentially aesthetic category of the appropriate – that may enable us to avoid here the impasses to which the search for the merely true and the ethically good invariably will lead. Hence, when confronted with the ultimate challenge – accounting for the Holocaust – it is aesthetics, and not the categories of the factually true and the morally good, to which history should appeal" (p. 176).

51 Aleksandra Ubertowska, "'Kamienie niepokoją się i stają się agresywne'. Holokaust w świetle ekokrytyki," *Poznańskie Studia Polonistyczne. Seria Literacka* 25 (45), Poznań 2015 [issue entitled *Po Zagładzie. Narracje postkatastroficzne*], pp. 93–111.

52 See Tomasz S. Markiewka, "Bruno Latour i 'koniec' postmodernizmu," *Diametros* 2012, n. 33, pp. 101–119.

53 Anne Michaels, *Fugitive Pieces*; *Płomyki pamięci*, trans. B. Malarecka (Poznań 2000). Despite the translation into Polish, neither this novel nor Michaels's other publications seem to be well known in Poland, which explains why *Fugitive Pieces* has not been discussed by Polish literary scholars.

54 The concept of multidirectional memory provides the theoretical foundation for *Fugitive Pieces*.

accepting the enduring presence of victims in the form of ashes, air, and wind), the protagonists of *Fugitive Pieces* – a Polish Jew and a Greek archaeologist – reevaluate mourning, proposing instead a life-giving memory that allows them to draw strength from coexistence with the dead. Grounding these practices in the non-European tradition, which is alien to the history of the Holocaust itself and the familiar ways of understanding it, also allows us to understand the weakness of the traumatocentric horizon of postmodernism and its dependence on the dominant Catholicism in Europe (in contrast to the indigenous beliefs as represented by Michaels) and many political traditions.

A solution may be found in Huyssen's project of "the past's pasts" based on the joint study of the past and the future for the purpose of solving the problems of the present. The goal is to prevent the hypertrophy of memory, melancholic fixations and privileging the traumatic dimension of life. Postmodernism also requires a "weighting" of history in the sense Cesarani gave it in *Final Solution*, where he emphasizes that understanding the Holocaust must be accompanied by the study of the latest historical research and by the exchange of knowledge between scholarly publications and various manifestations of cultural memory.[55] The axis of these studies cannot be defined as an exclusively human historical event,[56] but also as a post-human event, allowing us to see the planetary dimension of the catastrophe in a way that would make it understandable also where the Holocaust did not take place, but where it was brought, as it were, by survivors, causing changes in cultures detached from Eurocentrism and the European historical tradition.

Finally, a significant and at the same time a problematic issue to address is that of the novel, the literary form that attracts the attention of scholars who study the connections between postmodernism and the Holocaust. Apart from studies that contain lists of postmodern authors, brief discussions of their work and sample juxtapositions of fiction with philosophy, there is no study devoted to the Holocaust novel. I do not mean here a study which would, once more, prioritize aesthetics, but a study that would examine the novel as a carrier of socio-political content, the type of content that accompanies fictional representations of the

---

55 Cesarani, *Final Solution*, Introduction (pp. xxv ff). Cesarani observes, for instance, that "The use of survivor testimony routinely trumps the dissemination of scholarship" (p. xxvi).
56 On the idea of the Holocaust as a/the historical event, see Hayden White, "The Historical Event," Hayden White, *The Practical Past* (Evanston, IL: Northwestern University Press, 2014), p. 46. Writes White, "There has been a great deal of discussion of late about the event in general and about the historical event specifically. In historiography, the evental status of the Holocaust is a matter of extensive debate: is or was the Holocaust an event unique to history and therefore incomparable to (or incommensurable with) other events of a similar kind? So, too, for the event now called '9/11.'"

Holocaust and creates a zone of profound influence between them.[57] For this purpose, I consider it needful to examine the real and imagined relations between individual stories from the successive decades of the twentieth century (with the main emphasis on recent Polish fiction) and to search in them for a response, consisting of different voices, to the question about the meaning of the recent past. This study will focus, not on representations of the Holocaust or on the means of producing its representations, but on the capacity of the Holocaust of drawing in other problems important for post-war civilization, among them communism, post-communism, and capitalism, poverty, wealth, waste, and the destruction of the planet by man. The problem of *accommodation*, of adapting the narrative to current cognitive needs, should not be seen as a threat to the existing knowledge about the Holocaust. On the contrary, while the Holocaust still holds center stage, now the interest is in how it affects the human subject and our biosphere, rather than in the historical event as such.

---

57 I am referring here to the exhibition *Deep impact. Stefan Gierowski i europejska awangarda lat 60.* by the Stefan Gierowski Foundation in Warsaw, on display from 14 September to 15 November 2019. The method used by the curator, Michel Gauthier, involved juxtaposing images in the process of their being created without mutual influence. The aim was to suggest unconscious parallels, primarily of social and political character (e. g., space exploration, the beginning of the construction of the Berlin Wall, etc.).

Chapter 2.
The Siren Song and the Birth of an Alternative: Edmond Jabès, Leopold Buczkowski, and Halina Birenbaum

Before the post-war discourse on the Holocaust ceased for good, books heralding a new approach to the problem had begun to appear in Polish. Yet there were too few of them to attract the attention of researchers or to create a separate trend. Many years having passed, now the situation is very different, and the trend has developed a well-defined identity. Later in the book, I refer to this trend as an alternative and explain how it has managed to carve a distinct groove. Apart from Leopold Buczkowski's novel *Pierwsza świetność*, among the representatives are Anatol Ulman's *Cigi de Montbazon* (1970s), Tadeusz Konwicki's *Bohiń*, Andrzej Kuśniewicz's *Nawrócenie* (1980s),[58] Marek Bieńczyk's *Tworki*, Ewa Kuryluk's *Century 21* (*Wiek 21*; 1990s),[59] and Andrzej Bart's *Fabryka muchołapek* (2000s). Olga Tokarczuk's *Księgi Jakubowe* (2014) seems to have brought a conclusion that might seem odd and abrupt. I propose to see this trend as, as it were, running parallel to fiction published abroad, primarily in the United States. This approach, I submit, might help us see its distinctness as well as its specific framework, established many years earlier in foreign literature. If one wanted to see it in terms of negation, one should emphasize the desire and determination to be distinguished and to stand out, characteristic of authors such as Raymond Federman. Federman and Georges Perec, another representative of Holocaust-related postmodernist fiction, sought to distance themselves from the literature of the traditional forms of personal non-fiction, rather than pursuing different trajectories of literary career. An alternative, at least in a logical sense, differs from a negation in that it gives a choice. In the sense of postmodern depictions of the Holocaust, however, the alternative seems to be a consequence of the negation of the possibilities of art in the sense of creative freedom, different from the stricture of the document. That is why the postmodernists who wrote in the

---

[58] See Marta Tomczok, "Klimat Zagłady (w perspektywie powieści Pawła Huellego, Tadeusza Konwickiego, Andrzeja Kuśniewicza i Piotra Szewca)," *Teksty Drugie* 2017, nr 2, pp. 147–165.
[59] Marta Tomczok, "Alegorie Zagłady w *Tworkach* Marka Bieńczyka i *Wieku 21* Ewy Kuryluk," *Prace Filologiczne. Literaturoznawstwo* 2016, nr 6 (9), pp. 157–170.

subsequent decades, among them Ulman and Federman, would use a technique known as "under erasure," or "*sous rature*."[60] Not being a simple form of negation, but something indirect, it allows us to see the past in terms of blurring or clouding over.[61] In the 1960s, negation played an important role as part of the mechanism of concealing the experience of the Holocaust.

When in 1963 Edmond Jabès published *The Book Questions*, a pioneering and monumental 7-volume work regarded by some as poetry, Leopold Buczkowski's *Pierwsza świetność*, which would come out in 1966, was still a project, similarly to Halina Birenbaum's memoir *Nadzieja umiera ostatnia* (*Hope Is the Last to Die*), on which she worked in Hertzliya in the years 1964–1965,[62] and which was published in 1967. Do these books have anything in common besides the fact that they came out in one decade and are related, in one way or another, to the Holocaust? Contrary to appearances, they do have a great deal in common. In this juxtaposition, Birenbaum's memoir can be regarded as a model narrative about the Holocaust, one to which those by Buczkowski and Jabès represent an alternative. In this chapter, I will outline the model of testimony that emerges from Birenbaum's autobiography and compare it with passages in *The Book of Questions* that concern the Holocaust and with *Pierwsza świetność*, with the aim to explain the role of Jabès's and Buczkowski's work as an alternative to traditional testimony.

There are at least two reasons for placing the rise of an alternative narrative about the Holocaust – which in time will develop into a postmodern form – in the 1960s. First of all, a social impulse appeared then, which in some cases was felt as an imperative to talk about the wartime past and which intensified in the decades that followed. This creates a situation in which literature becomes a consequence of events other than the Holocaust, although – in an author's personal opinion – closely connected with it. For Birenbaum, such an event will be the rumored revival of fascism in the world and attempts by the Germans to introduce a resolution on the statute of limitations for Nazi crimes in 1965. In Jabès's biography, a similar role would have been played by the graffiti he saw in 1957 in the Paris district of l'Odéon: an old and aggressively offensive inscription, "death to the Jews" in French and English, which caused the author of *The Book of Resemblances*, first to feel indignation and then to experience a wave of memories, from Jewish refugees from Germany who found themselves in Suez in 1936 to

---

60 Cf. Brian McHale, *Postmodernist Fiction* (London and New York: Routledge, 1987), pp. 100ff.
61 I write about them in reference to the 1790s work of Federman, Perec and Ulman in the the article "Postmodernistyczne wymazywanie Zagłady (Raymond Federman, Georges Perec, Anatol Ulman)," *Poznańskie Studia Slawistyczne* 2017, nr 12, pp. 299–315.
62 Cf. Halina Birenbaum, *Hope Is the Last to Die. A Personal Documentation of Nazi Terror*, trans. from the Polish by David Welsh (Publishing House of the State Museum in Oświęcim, 1994), p. 246.

German extermination camps.[63] Two years later, Jabès began work on *The Book of Questions*.[64]

Second, the goal for this non-obvious suggestion of a parallel between Jabès's French work (I hesitate unambiguously to use the term prose when referring to the *Book of Questions* series because it is also made of aphorism, essays, and poetry) with the narratives by Polish authors is to lay out a context for the literature of the 1970s. When in 1979 the first postmodern Holocaust novel was published in Poland, Anatol Ulman's *Cigi de Montbazon*, in the West and North America there already was a well-established tradition of postmodern writing about the past. Even though there was no such tradition in Poland, we can point to some earlier narrative strategies, primarily those used by Leopold Buczkowski, who loosened up the strictures of factual Holocaust testimony by means of postmodern devices. It may be worth taking a closer look at them to see that, as early as twenty years after the war, an awareness of thinking about the Holocaust emerged in Poland that was burdened with many doubts and even with aporia. However, this awareness led to a conclusion which was familiar to the authors representing the traditional trend of Holocaust writing, namely, that it was necessary to talk and write about THIS THING. In an interview with Marcel Cohen, Jabès expressed this plainly:

> After Auschwitz the feeling of solitude that lies at the core of each human being has become considerably amplified. Today, any sense of trust is doubled by an all-consuming distrust. [….] To Adorno's statement that "after Auschwitz one can no longer write poetry," inviting a global questioning of our culture, I'm tempted to answer: yes, one can. And furthermore, one has to. One has to write out of that break, out of that unceasingly revived wound.[65]

---

63 "The German Jewish refugees came sharply back to mind; my wife and I had seen them, from 1936 onward, as their boats stopped over in Suez. […] Later there were the concentration camps and what we were able to learn about them." Edmond Jabès, "… to the Book," in idem, *From the Desert to the Book: Dialogues with Marcel Cohen*, trans. Pierre Joris (New York: Station Hill, 1990), p. 41.

64 As described by Paul Auster, "Beginning with the first volume of *Le Livre des questions*, which was published in 1963, and continuing on through the other volumes in the series, Jabès has created a new and mysterious kind of literary work – as dazzling as it is difficult to define. Neither novel nor poem, neither essay nor play, *The Book of Questions* is a combination of all these forms, a mosaic of fragments, aphorisms, dialogues, songs, and commentaries that endlessly move around the central question of the book: how to speak what cannot be spoken. The question is the Jewish Holocaust, but it is also the question of literature itself." Paul Auster, "The Book of the Dead," *The Art of Hunger*, in Paul Auster, *Talking to Strangers. Selected Essays, Prefaces, and Other Writings* (New York: Picador, 2019), pp. 85–86. See also Paul Auster, "Providence. A Conversation with Edmond Jabès" (1978; originally in French, translated by Auster), in idem, *The Art of Hunger. Essays, Prefaces, Interviews and The Red Notebook* (New York: Penguin, 1993), p. 153 ff.

65 Edmond Jabès, "The Core of a Rupture," in idem, *From the Desert to the Book*. Dialogues with Marcel Cohen. Trans. Pierre Joris (New York: Station Hill Press, 1990/1980), p. 61–62.

Embroiled in a conflict between the private and the public, Halina Birenbaum's autobiography was published shortly before the freezing of the Polish Holocaust discourse, which took place in 1967.[66] We can assume that a year later she would have been unable to publish it.[67] The book *Hope Is the Last to Die* is therefore a simultaneous summary of the many years of Birenbaum's struggle with the past, preceded by several destroyed versions of the book, as well as a completion of a stage in the history of the genre of testimony. Seen from this angle, the book is a model example of the autobiography of a survivor, created precisely for the aim set by the writer. As Birenbaum expressed it: "I wish by this book to express my most fervent desire that similar crimes will never be repeated anywhere on this earth."[68]

In Birenbaum's recollection, we would be looking in vain for expressions of doubts about the supreme power of the word and its connections with reality. What Jabès calls a "broken mirror of words" (the title of one of the chapters in Jabès's *Elya*)[69] does not seem to apply to Birenbaum. In her narrative, there is no alternative to the imperative which makes us convey reality in language. Instead, there is the so-called straightforward mode of representation, which expresses and sustains its authority as representation[70] and justifies its result. The narrative thus produced looks exactly as it ought to look. Yet it might be difficult to question the conviction that its model-like character consists in its being a "common" narrative, one whose poetics is a compromise between the category (probably more imaginary than real) of model testimony (Calek Perechodnik's *Memoir* and Primo Levi's *If This Is a Man*), and what can be called an average testimony, considering that it is not the style of writing that determines the value of this type of literature, and that its cognitive value – as in the case of Birenbaum's memoir – is limited to the individual story of the survivor.

The current state of knowledge about memory and the complex ways in which it impacts artistic representations of the past inevitably makes us regard as naïve declarations like this one: "But everything, down to the most minute details, remained unerased and fresh in my memory, as though it had happened yes-

---

66 About the circumstances of working on the book and the unfriendly "atmosphere" which preceded and then accompanied this effort, see Birenbaum's recollections in *Szukam życia u umarłych* (Oświęcim: Wydawnictwo: Państwowe Muzeum Auschwitz-Birkenau, 2010).
67 As we read in a lexicon on Polish literature in Israel, "[…] this was the first and for a long time the only book of this kind published in the Polish People's Republic"; Karolina Famulska-Ciesielska and Sławomir Jacek Żurek, *Literatura polska w Izraelu* (Kraków and Budapest: Austeria, 2012), p. 36.
68 Birenbaum, *Hope Is the Last to Die*, p. 246.
69 Edmond Jabès, *The Book of Questions. Yaël. Elya. Aely*, trans. Rosmarie Waldrop (Middletown, CT: Wesleyan University Press, 1983), pp. 134–140.
70 Ryszard Nycz, *Tekstowy świat. Poststrukturalizm a wiedza o literaturze* (Kraków: Universitas, 2000), p. 330.

terday."[71] Birenbaum's entire narrative represents an attempt to recreate the perspective of someone who personally experienced the portrayed events, and she is consistent in staying within that perspective. We can see this determination in her assessment of facts, which over time not only undergoes a personal re-evaluation and which, moreover, is subject to historical verification. Here are two brief examples, one concerning a German Jewish woman, Alvira, who was a *Lagercapo* in Auschwitz, the other a political prisoner from Germany and a stoker in the camp's kitchen, doing various favors for the Jews: "Without knowing why, I always had the idea that handsome people are good, understanding and generous. Consequently I was often disappointed. All the same, pretty faces still attracted me and awoke friendly feelings in me. *Capo* Alvira contradicted this naive theory of mine. She was exceptionally kind to me and to several other children in the labor gang."[72] (1); "We felt a liking, gratitude and respect for him [a boiler-room stoker – MT]. 'He's German, yet he is suffering as we are,' we sometimes said to one another, 'this means that Germans are not all alike. They are not all like that.' Yet I could not understand why some Germans were 'like that' and others not; why some preyed on people, persecuted and killed them, while other Germans endured persecution"[73] (2).

When she crossed the gate of the Majdanek camp, Birenbaum was thirteen years old.[74] The narrative perspective that informs her recollections was thus a literal imitation of this experience, devoid of any distance between the narrator, her teenage self, and the act of representation itself. We have here, in other words, a pure story, contingent and accidental, because, like an adventure, writing brings disruption and variety into life:

> Yielding to this inner force, I set about writing down my memoirs. At first it seemed to me that I would never manage. I have a husband and children. I keep a home, and it is rare that an ordinary housewife takes pen in hand to communicate her story to others. More than once I have cried over the work, living once again through the misfortunes and tragedies of my nearest and dearest, gassed or dead in extermination camps.[75]

---

71 Birenbaum, *Hope Is the Last to Die*, p. 245.
72 Birenbaum, *Hope Is the Last to Die*, p. 189.
73 Birenbaum, *Hope Is the Last to Die*, p. 191.
74 Birenbaum, *Hope Is the Last to Die*, p. 100. "I was thirteen. The years of persecution in the ghetto, the loss of my father and my brother, and – most painful of all – the loss of my mother, had impaired my nervous system, and at a time when I should have forced myself to be as resistant as possible, I broke down completely." For a thorough reconstruction of the heroine-narrator of *Hope Is the Last to Die*, see Wanda Witek-Malicka, *Dzieci z Auschwitz-Birkenau. Socjalizacja w obozie koncentracyjnym na przykładzie Dzieci Oświęcimia* (Kraków: Nomos, 2013), pp. 301–302.
75 Birenbaum, *Hope Is the Last to Die*, pp. 245–246.

This authorial confession, "I have a husband and children. I keep a home, and it is rare that an ordinary housewife takes pen in hand to communicate her story to others." conveys an important ideological reflection that accompanies Birenbaum's writing. This writing was born from an individual, strong, and simple, and at the same time direct need to tell the world about the tragedy of the Warsaw Ghetto, Majdanek and Auschwitz. The autobiography does not allow us to assume that Birenbaum wanted to expand it in either a quantitative sense (by adding a sequel) or qualitative one (by diversifying the form of the narrative). Rather, she is uncertain whether, due to the commitment of running the household, which she had seriously neglected while writing her memoirs, she would ever want to return to writing. However, as her subsequent books of poetry and prose demonstrate, the autobiography of 1960s was in fact the beginning of Birenbaum's literary career. This must be borne in mind when juxtaposing her book with the work of Jabès and Buczkowski, authors of sophisticated pens, polished talent, and mature views on art.

Extratextual reality is therefore the most important and virtually the only novelistic matter that Birenbaum is working into a narrative in a way that is simple and frequently emotional. It is the affects that create, in *Hope*, the main source of knowledge about reality; it is out of the affects, too, that Birenbaum weaves a relatively clear network of values which she abides by in her subsequent books.[76] In addition to affective evaluation, she uses straightforward narrative devices, which include first-person narration and a biography-based arrangement of content. The narrative is continuous, with no division into chapters or into thematic or problem sections (which would make it resemble an essay or a novel, as it happens in the prose of Levi or Imre Kertész). *Hope*'s content is made up of recollections from the Warsaw ghetto and the camps at Majdanek, Auschwitz and Neustadt-Glewe. Initially, Birenbaum's memories focus on her mother, whom she loses sight of at Majdanek, never to see again. Later, the focus shifts to her sister-in-law, who dies of emaciation in Auschwitz. Birenbaum devotes ample space to the friends she made in the camp: Basia, Stasia, Polusia, Celina, and others. Typically, the people who appear in her memories have no surnames, a decision Birenbaum may have made for practical reasons (she may not have known or remembered some of the names), but also one that connotes familiarity, which helps the reminiscing narrator to maintain an attitude of kindness towards the people she once met.

In Birenbaum's autobiography, the world of those who should be remembered remains a closed one. Outside it, there are primarily the Germans. "All of them,"

---

76 This is also mentioned in the entry "Birenbaum Halina"; see Karolina Famulska-Cielska, Sławomir Jacek Żurek, *Literatura polska w Izraelu* (Kraków – Budapeszt: Wydawnictwo Austeria, 2012, p. 36).

she writes of the "uncanny" *SS* tribunal composed of Dr. Mengele and *Unterscharführer* Taube, who tried unsuccessfully to separate Birenbaum from her sister-in-law Hela, "were tall, straddling and self-assured [...]. Animals will always be animals, even if they make a gesture that seems human."[77] However, it would be difficult to accuse Birenbaum of what Andrzej Werner called particularization of evil, referring above all to the demonization of executioners and the sacralization of victims.[78] In other words, her memoirs lack that dichotomy, which was completely abolished in Tadeusz Borowski's Auschwitz stories (most notably "Farewell to Maria") and which, whenever it returned later in death-camp writing, was regarded as an ideological anachronism. We do find in *Hope* features of the materialistic worldview of the kind which Borowski insisted on, claiming that only in this way "the meaning of Auschwitz ... is perfectly easy to solve."[79] We should add that Borowski was primarily interested in a straightforward representation of the relations among the prisoners. Birenbaum's narrative is about friendships, but also, and perhaps primarily, about her loneliness, aggravated by the death of her sister-in-law: "I was surrounded by hostility, but this hostility was no one's fault – it just could not be otherwise under such conditions."[80] After some time, the situation changes. The narrator makes more friends than enemies; human kindness becomes her sustenance: "Celina often gave me a piece of bread, or a little soup. She always welcomed me affectionately and warmly. In those days I needed affection no less than I needed food."[81] "I told them briefly of my experiences, and felt an enormous relief."[82] "Basia never left my side. She and the girl from Będzin looked after me during the evenings in the barrack."[83] The simple-mindedness of these passages, bordering on serenity, unbelievable in a death camp, has another dimension, one that I would call modesty in the context of historical reflection.

Birenbaum's narrative names only the most important dates, among them: the outbreak of the war in September 1939, the Warsaw Ghetto Uprising in 1943, the epidemic of the scabies in Auschwitz in the summer of 1943 and of typhus in the autumn, and the arrival of news from the front in the spring of 1944 about the impending defeat of the German army. She usually links these dates with her own experiences but does not draw any far-reaching conclusions that would betray, as it were, her interest in the history of Europe and the world or in politics. We

---

77 Birenbaum, *Hope Is the Last to Die*, pp. 143–144.
78 Andrzej Werner, "Wstęp," in Tadeusz Borowski, *Utwory wybrane* (Wrocław-Warszawa-Kraków: Ossolineum, 1991), pp. LIII–LVII.
79 Tadeusz Borowski, "Alicja w krainie czarów," in Borowski, *Utwory wybrane*, p. 496.
80 Birenbaum, *Hope Is the Last to Die*, p. 148.
81 Birenbaum, *Hope Is the Last to Die*, p. 156.
82 Birenbaum, *Hope Is the Last to Die*, p. 154.
83 Birenbaum, *Hope Is the Last to Die*, p. 158.

surmise that in memoirs with a strong ethical foundation, narrative experiments might loosen the protocols of testimony, which must be avoided. The suspension of such rules or their loosening does not have to imply that a foundation of this kind is missing. Yet it allows the reader to see an alternative, which might seem invisible in a world where hope is the last to die.

The biography of Edmond Jabès (1912–1991), the Cairo-born author and seventeen years Birenbaum's senior, may be summed up in this sentence: the Holocaust spared him. His access to knowledge about the situation of European Jews in the 1930s was very limited. In 1935, ships with Jewish refugees, mainly from Germany, began to arrive at Port Said. Some of them had experienced the Nazi terror, but, in hindsight, that was a preparation, as it were, for the tragedy proper that would occur several years later. In a 1978 interview with Paul Auster entitled "Providence,"[84] Jabès speaks of women whose arms and necks had cigar and cigarette burns on them; he describes his experience as an observer by saying: "There was no German occupation for us, no one was deported… in some sense we were protected by the English. As early as 1935, however, we were given some idea of the atrocities of the camps from the Jewish refugee boats that stopped at Port Said."[85] The experience of historical exclusion or omission in its full complexity made Jabès realize very soon that as a Jew he was not safe anywhere, even in a place where there was no German occupation, no deportations, and protection from the British was in place.[86] Perhaps as an attempt to explain their shared situation, Auster (b. 1947), a generation younger than Jabès, used a telling comparison: "You could almost say that your situation was similar to that of the American Jews. You were aware of what was taking place, but you weren't immediately threatened by it."[87]

Far from suspecting that this statement may conceal a justification for the indifference that Jews from outside the European continent had often been accused of towards European Jews affected by the Holocaust,[88] I want to draw attention to the thus emerging difference between the prose of Jabès and Birenbaum, one that affects the narrative shape of their books. First-person narration is a particularly important feature of the memories recounted in *Hope Is the Last to Die*. The narrator assumes that there is only one way to talk about

---

84 Auster, "Providence. A Conversation with Edmond Jabès," pp. 144–169.
85 Auster, "Providence," p. 147. Jacques Derrida expressed the aporia that emerges from Jabès's writings thus: "In this noncoincidence of the self and the self, he is more and less Jewish than the Jew. But the Jew's identification with himself does not exist." Jacques Derrida, "Edmond Jabès and the Question of the Book," in Jacques Derrida, *Writing and Difference*, trans. Alan Bass (London and New York: Routledge, 2002), p. 92.
86 Auster, "Providence," p. 147.
87 Auster, "Providence," p. 147–148. Jabès calls this "a very good comparison" (p. 148).
88 Cf. for example Raymond Federman, *Wygnaniec – Żyd, tułacz, pisarz…*, trans. Piotr Kołyszko, *Literatura na Świecie* 1982, nr 12, p. 301.

herself, namely, the first person singular. Her decision, which belongs in the realm of descriptive poetics, was motivated, to some extent at least, by her personal experience. Besides, we could see what Birenbaum thought of the narrativization of experience when she spoke about the relief she felt after telling her follow women prisoners in Auschwitz about the events in the camp and the ghetto. Jabès uses the first person singular much less frequently, and, I suspect, not because his prose shuns the role of a testimony to the Holocaust. Auster's statement about the common fate of people who were spared by the Holocaust and yet felt its impact in their bodies would contradict the radicalization of such thinking. The difference between Birenbaum's and Jabès's writing comes into full view only when we compare their respective statements, Jabès's declaration: "One has to write out of that break, out of that unceasingly revived wound."[89] and Birenbaum's resolution: "While still in the camp, I decided that if I lived to see liberation, I would write down everything I saw, heard and experienced."[90] Birenbaum's attitude is total: writing should encompass as much as possible, and it is possible to convey and explain everything that has caused suffering. This attitude is not naive, but the means to this end must be simple. If one wants to talk about trauma in a coherent way, which is Birenbaum's goal, going beyond the traditional form of autobiography might be too risky.

In Jabès's *Book of Questions*, the story of Sarah and Yukel, told in the form of aphorisms or micro-narratives usually unrelated by any causal links, creates a narrative about the Holocaust which would be, almost literally, a sphere of insane peril. As Auster wrote in 1976,

> At the core of *The Book of Questions* there is a story – the separation of two young lovers, Sarah and Yukel, during the time of the Nazi deportations. Yukel is a writer – described as the "witness" – who serves as Jabès's alter ago and whose words are often indistinguishable from his; Sarah is a young woman who is shipped to a concentration camp and who returns insane. But the story is never really told, and it in no way resembles a traditional narrative. Rather, it is alluded to, commented on, and now and then allowed to burst forth in the passionate and obsessive love letters exchanged between Sarah and Yukel – which seem to come from nowhere, like disembodied voices [...].[91]

In the conversation with Auster quoted earlier, Jabès uses the term *recit eclate*, or fragmented narrative, to refer to this type of narrative, and goes on to explain that it denotes both the language and the characters. It is especially relevant for Yukel, who is both the narrator and the protagonist, but who plays these two roles differently albeit simultaneously. These few features of the poetics of *The Book of Questions* which I shall call the "shattered mirror of words" do not in any way

---

89 Jabès, "The Core of a Rupture," 62; already quoted.
90 Birenbaum, *Hope Is the Last to Die*, p. 244.
91 Auster, "The Book of the Dead," pp. 87–88.

correspond to Birenbaum's testimony. The reason is because Jabès and the author of *Hope Is the Last to Die* experienced the Holocaust in different ways. The differences between their narratives result from a materialistic worldview; while this worldview is not found in *The Book of Questions*, doubts about the meaning of God's work is the most important characteristic of Birenbaum's response to the chaos of war.

The tradition of Judaic thought, which Jabès understands in an original way, and occasionally very freely, causes in his work a clash between the already-mentioned passage in the symbolic dimension (the wound as an impulse to write) and the ecstatic language used for the description of the world. The emotional charge in the language creates a certain excess, comparable to the excess found in Birenbaum's memoirs. However, while in her autobiography there is an overflow of positive emotions, in Jabès the excess is found in the verbal representation of violent affects, as we may call it. In both these cases, we observe a violation of the principle of succinctness, which many accounts of survivors abide by. The principle of excess corresponds to that of generalization, which Jabès consistently follows in *The Book of Questions*; thanks to it, his stories become aphoristic and metaphorically dense reflections on the Holocaust and its topics. As in this case:

> Smoke, smoke, higher than the feathers of time which the hours parade in, higher than the feathers of wind and morning, than the feathers dyed with caresses of the dark. Smoke of incinerators, of faltering pain, of oblivion.
> "Look at this smoke," said Reb Yahid, "the fire threw it out, and in fleeing it maddens the fire."[92]

For the sake of comparison, below are two passages from Birenbaum's *Hope* describing the smoke from the crematorium. The depiction is less metaphorical and the reference to reality is lucid and clear:

> I saw the chimney smoking almost daily. Of all the people brought here in the trains there remained only heaps of ashes. For many months I breathed air infested with the stench of burning corpses. (125)

> A bloody pillar of fire rose from the chimneys, scattering a bitter acrid smoke and the stench of burning bones. (137)

In another passage of *The Book of Yukel*, Jabès combines general knowledge about the Holocaust (the extermination of the Jewish people) with a well-known philosophical reflection reminiscent of Adorno's thesis about the impossibility of poetry after Auschwitz. The conclusion from this combination, paradoxical and even tautological, exemplifies the sharp clashes I mentioned earlier:

---

92 Edmond Jabès, *The Book of Yukel*, in idem, *The Book of Yukel. Return to the Book*, trans. Rosmarie Waldrop (Middletown, CT: Wesleyan University Press, 1977), p. 121.

A scholar: At the beginning, the Nazis sent only useless Jews to the gas chambers. Then even the notion of uselessness vanished: all Jews were to be exterminated.
Perhaps there will come a day when words will destroy words for good. There will be a day when poetry will die.
It will be the age of the robot and the jailed word.
The misery of the Jews will be universal.
Yukel: The misery of the Jews will disarm misery.[93]

The reception of Jabès's work in Poland focused on its innovativeness as a feature resulting from its connections with the trends in philosophy of literature, deconstructionism and post-structuralism, which were extremely fashionable in 1990s.[94] The 2001 issue of *Literatura na Świecie* devoted to Jabès published commentaries by Maurice Blanchot and Jacques Derrida. Unfortunately, there were no voices – I am also thinking here of the afterword to the next parts of *The Book of Questions* – that would draw attention to the similarities and differences between this writing and other narratives about the Holocaust, from Levi's and Eli Wiesel's death camp memoirs to Raymond Federman's and Georges Perec's postmodern novels. The situation in which the enthusiasm of post-structuralists imitating Jabès's style did not turn into a reflection on the actual features of his prose style was the reason for the weak influence of Jabès's work in Poland.[95] Derrida and Blanchot unanimously emphasized that his innovativeness resulted from the withdrawal of the magazine *Austeria* to defensive positions, positions essentially related to silence. "To be a poet," wrote Derrida, "is to know how to leave speech. To let it speak alone, which it can do only in its written form."[96] What exactly is the meaning of this? Isn't this what Auster meant when he stated:

---

93 Jabès, *The Book of Yukel*, p. 61.
94 This situation was changed by Przemysław Tacik's study of the mystical-Jewish context of Jabès's work. Although the Holocaust remained an area on the border of expressiveness and inexpressibility, described on a fairly general level, it also became an idea (the author usually identifies the Holocaust with Auschwitz), "the ultimate way of expressing Auschwitz and a testimony to the impossibility of narrating the Holocaust." Cf. Przemysław Tacik, *Wolność świateł. Edmond Jabès i żydowska filozofia nowoczesności* (Kraków and Budapeszt: Wydawnictwo Austeria, 2015), p. 436.
95 A special case of "choking" on Jabès's hermetic stories is Michał Paweł Markowski's afterword to the former's *Elja*, entitled, like one of the chapters, "The shattered mirror of words." Using Stanisław Balbus's observations on intertextuality, we can say that "stylization here includes [...] all strata of the text's structure" (Stanisław Balbus, *Między stylami*, Kraków: Universitas 1996, p. 23). Balbus, however, is speaking here about the pastiche of Mikołaj Sęp Szarzyński's poetry by Kazimierz Wyka, from whom that one time no one expected a substantive theoretical commentary. Markowski's position is entirely different; as a literary scholar, he should first of all explain Jabès's work instead of duplicating its complexity.
96 Jacques Derrida, "Edmond Jabès and the Question of the Book," in Jacques Derrida, *Writing and Difference*, trans. Alan Bass (London and New York: Routledge, 2002), p. 85.

> To Jabès, nothing can be written about the Holocaust unless writing itself is first put into question. If language is to be pushed to the limit, then the writer must condemn himself to an exile of doubt, to a desert of uncertainty. What he must do, in effect, is create a poetics of absence.[97]

The trouble with Auster's and Derrida's comments was that they both mistakenly attributed to Jabès's writing, which brims with rhetorical quirks and religious references, the role of anti-literature. And yet Jabès neither doubted his own words nor looked for ways to renounce communication. He used communication to the same extent as Birenbaum, as he looked for an appropriate mode of representation for the Holocaust; except that his was a representation of a different type, point-focused rather than one in which events form a comprehensive narrative. His was a story composed of singular and self-reflexive events, a story of the type Blanchot described in 1959 in his essay "The Sirens' Song."

"The Broken Mirror of Words"[98] is, in fact, a vision of an ideal representation of reality, which in its realistic assumptions has been destroyed under the impact of the war and loss of confidence in language. If we were to use this metaphor consistently, we would have to say that the stories to which it is applied in this chapter, namely *The Book of Questions* and Buczkowski's *Pierwsza świetność* [*The First Glory*], contain a longing for realism. But it is open to interpretation whether this is a real longing or rather an imposed one, and an interpretation would go beyond poststructuralist discourse and its fascination with absence, silence, and the crisis of language. In the case of *Pierwsza świetność*, this shattering of words means yet another unknown, for we cannot rule out that this novel is about a concrete Holocaust-related story, and not just chaos, as some reviewers – chiefly Jan Błoński – would have it. What's more, this story encompasses its doubling in the novel: among the protagonists, apart from the Jewish inhabitants of Bełżec, Poles, correspondents from the West and Germans, are also actors who, after the war, are shooting a film in this area. The novel even contains within itself its own denial; indeed, this seems to be its most important feature.

On the first and last pages, we find the name of a special building that does not play any serious role: *kazamata* (or *kazamaty,* casemate(s); Buczkowski switches between the two forms of the word, *kazamata* being the singular form[99]).

---

97 Auster, "Book of the Dead," p. 93.
98 Edmond Jabès, *The Book of Questions. Yaël. Elya. Aely,* trans. Rosmarie Waldrop (Middletown, CT: Wesleyan University Press. 1983), pp. 134–140.
99 According to a Polish dictionary, both forms, the singular and the plural, are acceptable, although the latter is more common. A "casemate" is "a room under fortifications, serving as a warehouse or defensive post, formerly also as a prison," as well as "an armored room for guns, located under the deck of a ship." *Słownik języka polskiego,* ed. Lidia Drabik, Aleksandra Kubiak-Sokół, and Elżbieta Sobol (Warszawa: Wydawnictwo Naukowe PWN, 2009),

"Outside the window of the casemate, one could see a Catholic cemetery, a highway to Kiev, and on the highway warnings about lice with this preface: as long as the war lasts, the louse should be the most alert when the soldier is sleep."[100] This is how *Pierwsza świetność* opens. At the end, there is a very telling statement:

> And then we carried her [Muzajka, one of the female protagonists – M.T.] behind the casemate, to a place where the bushes grew, putting a deeper meaning into them or not planting any meaning. They will entertain us in childhood and will be doing so boldly. And suppose that all the kazamaty were nothing but figments of the imagination, a shadow of a deeper intention. For there was also a forest nearby, but the view was vague and concealed all sorts of lures.[101]

Even though primarily the narrator would like us to see in this passage the influence of the romantic theme of mystery, often associated with the dark forest which is haunted (such as Johann Wolfgang Goethe's ballads *The Alder King* and Adam Mickiewicz's *To lubię* [*I Like This*], this is conjectural. What in fact is at stake here is not the mystery of knowledge, but an alternative structure, one resulting from the simultaneous statement of a fact and its denial. The same occurs in the following scene:

> These relations are what constitutes existence, he said, putting special emphasis on "Dasein," empirical beings without any additional meanings. It is difficult to decide whether the infinite, empty space of Bełżec – which we never get to see as a whole, because it cannot be captured in the report either as empty, because we are still coming to the place, or as a complete entity devoid of content, but embracing parts through perception, through relations between realities, by grasping the right truth directly – is a thing in itself.[102]

Here Bełżec makes the impression of being an entity without content, rather than a specific place; unfinished, rather than infinite. It is like the sentence of which it is the subject, separated from itself by numerous interjections, which ultimately break the syntax. In both cases, what we are talking about is an imaginary and mapped-out world, the so-called zone, i.e., the space that can be found in some extreme examples of postmodern prose.[103] In *Pierwsza świetność*, this space creates the aforementioned alternative, not only to the so-called hard reality and its realistic representation, but also to many testimonies of this type, which treat the imperative to express and depict war experiences as the sole method of narrating the war. To observe the questioning of it, visible for the first time on

---

p. 316. See also the relevant Wikipedia articles: "Kazamata" https://pl.wikipedia.org/wiki/Kazamata_(architektura) and "Casemate" https://en.wikipedia.org/wiki/Casemate (accessed 23.08.2023).
100 Leopold Buczkowski, *Pierwsza świetność* (Kraków: Wydawnictwo Literackie, 1978), pp. 5–6.
101 Buczkowski, *Pierwsza świetność*, p. 180.
102 Buczkowski, *Pierwsza świetność*, p. 65.
103 See McHale, *Postmodernist Fiction*, pp. 43 ff.

such a scale in Buczkowski's work, is to see manifestations of postmodernism and a new type of representation of the past as erasure, haziness and lostness.[104] This is a confrontation between documentary-historical actuality, antireflexive formalism and parody, which is the basis of Linda Hutcheon's definition of postmodernism.[105]

The dispute over Bełżec and its unspecified materiality, as well as the events before the establishment of the death camp in 1942 lead to the conclusion that *Pierwsza świetność* is an attempt to restore the memory of the town's Jewish community. This intention can be understood as Buczkowski's refusal to write about Bełżec exclusively in the context of the camp, which – we need to add – does not appear in the novel at all, because the portrayed events take place in July 1941, a year before the setting up of the camp. The following passage shows how *Pierwsza świetność* gives shape to the story of Bełżec:

> And here we should note that the study of Dydona's flight over Bełżec is of great importance for those who would like to remodel it into Eucharis (fourteen years old). Unfortunately, I never discussed this fact with any of the professors. Beyzym advised me not to talk about it. In Bełżec we combined Goethe with Winckelmann; the possible with the real, with what has been confirmed.[106]

This does not imply that Dydona can be, as Stanisław Barańczak argued, a resident of the town, a monument and an actress.[107] Rather, "she" may be an airplane whose role in the novel is solely a military one, not only in the strict sense (say, a bomber), but also metaphorically (say, a surreal flight of a Jewish woman abandoning a war-afflicted town, as in Marc Chagall's paintings[108]). Buczkowski depicts this scene twice at a short interval from one another, and each time it ends differently. However, he also adds a reflection that seems to confirm that he considered the Holocaust to be at once a possible scenario and an event that is bound to happen. Hardly anyone has seen Dydona's flight. Still fewer people want to talk about it. It thus combines the possible with the real, just like the word *kazamaty*.

It seems that the documentary and report-like nature of *Pierwsza świetność*, the fact that it depicts the destruction of a town but is in equal measure concerned with an attempt to document this incident, allows us to conclude that the novel is

---

104 On Leopold Buczkowski's postmodernism, which constitutes one of the many non-exclusive reading strategies, see Bogdan Owczarek's "Próba rekonstrukcji poetyki Leopolda Buczkowskiego," in Sławomir Buryła, Agnieszka Karpowicz, Radosław Sioma, eds., ...*zimą bywa się pisarzem... o Leopoldzie Buczkowskim* (Kraków: Universitas, 2008), pp. 24–25.
105 Linda Hutcheon, *The Politics of Postmodernism* (London and New York: Routledge, 2001), p. 7.
106 Buczkowski, *Pierwsza świetność*, pp. 51 and 61.
107 Stanisław Barańczak, "Krwawy karnawał," *Teksty* (1973), nr 4, p. 63.
108 Cf. Marc Chagall, "Over the Town" (1918).

– in an ontological sense – an extension of the fate of narratives such as Halina Birenbaum's *Hope Is the Last to Die*. Birenbaum's autobiography is a document, which shows in the manner and style of conveying the truth: the use of first-person narration, coherent and based on the possibility of presenting the heroine's story from the (assumed) beginning to the (accepted) end. Buczkowski talks about a situation in which protocols of verification have been lost. "Who is going to look for these scoundrels, Gestapo and spies, if witnesses have been shot dead, notes burned and evidence destroyed?" – writes Buczkowski in *Dziennik wojenny* [*The War Diary*].[109] The problem is not so much the existence of the truth, for there is no doubt that the truth is beyond human imagination. The problem is the lack of documented evidence. "Most of the records [Pl. *protokoły*] are gone…" - we read in *Pierwsza świetność*[110]; what is left are second-hand stories, but these lack the kind literal cruelty of facts that glares at us from a document.[111] This may be a self-referential passage, where the narrator is explaining why the story he is trying to tell is so confusing. One or two decades later, in the novels by Georges Perec, Raymond Federman and Paul Auster, we encounter similar situations, except that these authors will prefer to talk about lost roots rather than records. The retrospective depiction of a lost childhood, about which no one has told them enough, especially when it comes to family history and the Holocaust, usually ends with a conclusion similar to that found in *Pierwsza świetność*. If what exists is not only the experienced reality, but also a reality that could have been experienced, then there must be ways of representing the latter. In 1970s and 1980s, defining those ways became one of the most important goals of Holocaust-related historiographical metafiction.

"The questions that should be asked will always be addressed to the concept of the questioned person. For example: Who is Dydona? Where is this town? How many people live there? How long does it take to get there? Are there any bridges? How many corals and ducats did they steal?"[112] Asking these questions, Buczkowski predicted that answers to them would be the basis for understanding *Pierwsza świetność* and at the same time for questioning its reality. So let us try first to describe that reality.

The essential part of the plot may be taking place in September 1939 during the Polish-German battle of Tomaszów Lubelski.[113] There are many indications that

---

109 Leopold Buczkowski, *Dziennik wojenny* (Olsztyn: Wydaw. Uniwersytetu Warmińsko-Mazurskiego, 2001), p. 71.
110 Buczkowski, *Pierwsza świetność*, p. 68.
111 Buczkowski, *Pierwsza świetność*, p. 68.
112 Buczkowski, *Pierwsza świetność*, p. 67.
113 I am grateful to Sławomir Buryła for the hint that Buczkowski described the battle of Bełżec. "The breakthrough attack of all forces [Colonel Rowecki's, cavalry, Boruta-Spiechowicz's group, General Sadowski's Silesian group and Lieutenant Colonel Czubryt's 3 PSP group –

one of the basic roles of the narrator of *Pierwsza jasność* is associated with September and the entry of Polish infantry divisions into the village:

> A beautiful September day at dusk. A crowd of festively dressed soldiers poured out of the garrison church and into the cemetery. Soldiers, children wrapped in baptismal swaddling clothes. Then he himself remained within walls of that small cemetery.[114]
>
> Outside the cemetery, there are trenches fitted with barbed-wire obstacles. Outside the wires, machine gun posts. Further on, artillery posts and shelters. A railway bridge. On standby, three battalions, two supply companies, three companies of sappers, two companies of fortress artillery and ten batteries. The main task of this section is to maintain the railway line in such a way that the planned movement of transports is completely secure. Then the infantry will pass by the wheat field, the sappers near the mill, the artillery near the three poplars, and that, as the order goes, they are bravely to hold on to their posts.[115]

The other scene consists almost entirely of an account of the infantry's plan of action. The last sentence is a paraphrase of the words of the battalion commander. However, the narrator-protagonist, a soldier fighting in the September campaign, speaks much more often:

> In disarray, as we were pushing back, two enemy soldiers came running towards me. When they saw me, they threw down their rifles. They thought there were more of us in that dungeon of a trench, so they surrendered to me from afar.[116]

It is not clear how this soldier turns into a guerilla fighter, busy with looting while watching the destruction of the town. However, we may suspect that after the German victory, the narrator-protagonist does not abandon Bełżec and goes on to join the guerillas. Hiding and looking for food, whenever he gets a chance he also helps those who are at greater peril than himself, namely, the Jews.

As already mentioned, July 1941 is merely one episode in the story told by Buczkowski. Even so, some critics have insisted on making it the main theme of *Pierwsza świetność*,[117] while suggesting that the novel is almost exclusively concerned with the extermination camp operating in Bełżec in the years 1941–1942.

M.T.] was planned for the night of 18 September. This was to be followed by the army's further march towards Bełżec, Rawa Ruska." Apoloniusz Zawilski, *Bitwy polskiego września*, vol. 2 (Kraków: Znak, 2019), p. 159. Zawilski also states that Tomaszów was an important road junction, controlled by the Germans, which explains the fierceness of the battles. Buczkowski represents the Bełżec situation in a similar way. His novel shows that the town was primarily a railway junction for important transports.

114 Buczkowski, *Pierwsza świetność*, p. 25.
115 Buczkowski, *Pierwsza świetność*, p. 27.
116 Buczkowski, *Pierwsza świetność*, p. 29.
117 See Tadeusz Błażejewski, *Przemoc świata. Pisarstwo Leopolda Buczkowskiego* [*The Violence of the World. Leopold Buczkowski's Writing*] (Łódź: Wydawnictwo Uniwersytetu Łódzkiego, 2005), p. 93.

We will find evidence, not only that the time of plot covers the years 1939–1944, but that it actually goes beyond this frame. In fact, the novel contains comments on both the First World War and the Austrian history of Bełżec with Franz Joseph and his engagement to the Bavarian princess Sisi, as well as on the Warsaw Uprising and on shooting a film after the war. In the most general sense, *Pierwsza świetność* narrates the many different instances of wartime turmoil visited on Bełżec and other parts of the country. Yet some aspects of this vision of the past raise questions.

To begin with, it is not clear where the action of *Pierwsza świetność* takes place. Tadeusz Błażejewski, grasping at one scene at the end of the novel, believes that the setting is a place called Tymbarka (or Cymbarka) Bełzka. However, two other places are mentioned much more often: Bełżec itself and Szmulki, a rich village, which is to "provide bread to the reserve battalion."[118] Szmulki, as the course of the story shows, is not a good defensive position: "The village has a sizeable herd, which can be put at three hundred horned cattle, six hundred pigs, some sheep and two hundred horses."[119] In addition, the novel names real places, among them Usznia and Żydaczów, both associated with the battles of the Second World War, alongside ones that are difficult to identify. Below is the entire enumeration, even though some parts of it – like Żydaczów – belong to the plane of reality, not fiction:

> Military-railway units are given enough time to work out a new transportation plan: in the Szmulki region, in the Janowiec region, in the Kamień region, in the Wisznia region, in the Żydaczów region, Zwertów, Zapytów, Zaszków, Sieniachówka, Prus, Kozina, Fragi, Biłki, Buczały, Lubeszki, Pisarówka, Majdan, Łan, Przetuki, Szklina and Wyrowa.[120]

In a similar manner, by means of enumeration, the narrator describes the downtown of Bełżec, stressing its neat lay-out:

> Sixteen streets run from the market: Będnia, Ejruf, Fludeńska (bakers), Gazłena (robbers), Hajmkołska transverse (baths and laundries), Jejcerowska (temptations), Jizkorowa (to the cemetery), Katarzyńska (police), Poruszańska (teachers), Kislewska, Sfiry (bills of exchange and a pawnshop), Sycowska (fustian and percales), Kajdaniarska, Labażska, Kaszowa, Pereca, Smolki, Samsona, Koralowa, Łokumska, Brusiłowa (the military).[121]

This accumulation of detail in *Pierwsza świetność* and Buczkowski's other novels seems to serve the basic purpose of commemorating places and events wiped out

---

118 Buczkowski, *Pierwsza świetność*, p. 49.
119 Buczkowski, *Pierwsza świetność*, p. 106.
120 Buczkowski, *Pierwsza świetność*, p. 67.
121 Buczkowski, *Pierwsza świetność*, p. 98.

by history.[122] However, the actual value of both the above descriptions is not entirely clear. An existing place may change its name unexpectedly or even disappear altogether, as the following passage suggests:

> Let an officer be warned that the older the map, the less accurate it is; for it is not uncommon that, in just a few years, whole villages disappear or emerge, or two villages merge into one, or roads change direction. Mud dries up and ponds get overgrown. Bridges appear where fords used to be.[123]

In *Pierwsza świetność*, Buczkowski uses the method of naming known as space pseudonymization, used earlier in *Czarny potok [Black Torrent]*.[124] Thus "Bełżec" and "Szmulki" may conceal the name Złoczów, where in June 1941 the NKVD executed a group of Poles, and where a month later, at the beginning of July, Ukrainians and Germans carried out a pogrom of a group of Jewish people. Both massacres are described in *Pierwsza świetność*. Złoczów, located near his hometown of Podkamień, is mentioned by Buczkowski in his *Dziennik:* "We would better avoid these half-painted landscapes – years of war, frost in my and Marian's room, escapes, hiding – the well-being of besieged bandits – the road to Złoczów – the departure and death of Józef."[125] On the other hand, in *Pierwsza świetność*, there is the already mentioned passage woven around the date of July 3, 1941:

> We spent three summer days lazing and musing, even poetizing in the middle of a burnt-out town; and in its clean fountain, at the foot of the monument of Dido, we washed our shirts. The fire was consuming Dido and her animals. She died at a young age, on July 3, 1941. Besides, she splashed around for a long time, with her arms laden with two wreaths of flowers. She wasn't sad. She came to our city in the thirteenth century, no one knows where from. She became one with the city, masked, that is, with the visor down, and I had reason to believe that she presented herself under a false name. On the third day of the fire, she could no longer open her jaws to answer us, or at least spit in the face of the officers at the headquarters of the square.[126]

In the years 1941–1942 took place other pogroms of the Jewish population mentioned by Buczkowski: in Brody (*Czarny potok*) and Mizocz/Mizoch (*Dziennik*). This allows us to assume that the images of looting and the murdering of civilians described in *Pierwsza świetność* go beyond the framework of a single historical event. Moreover, looting as a rationale for the killings seems to have a separate meaning which is difficult to comprehend. Throughout the novel,

---

122 Cf. Paweł Tomczok's analysis in Pamięć i groza w "Czarnym potoku" [manuscript, p. 4].
123 Buczkowski, *Pierwsza świetność*, p. 105.
124 Paweł Tomczok has argued that Szabasowa is in fact Brody, whose almost the entire Jewish population was transported by Germans to the Bełżec death camp and exterminated.
125 Buczkowski, *Dziennik*, p. 34.
126 Buczkowski, *Pierwsza świetność*, p. 86.

the image of the banks of the company "Szüc i Chajes" alternates like a refrain with the theft of gold rings, later packed into bags and sent no one knows where. They are a symbol of Jewish gold and must suffice in place of a complete story of the looting-motivated massacre of Jews by Ukrainians. "A community is able to survive thanks to gold, and that's a fact."[127] This economic theme plays yet another role in the novel. Just as the motif of the Bełżec romance, it may have been expected to as it were cushion the real tragedy that took place in the town, namely, by reducing it to a case of looting-motivated mass murder: "Meanwhile, the number of people killed under the bridge has increased. And since rings were the goal, nothing could be more boring than this constant business of ripping off."[128]

Buczkowski often uses the language of film to depict the massacres of Jewish people; for example: "Children kept falling behind the partition. The screenwriter arranged them in various shapes: disorderly or pointy. He checked the perspective and the folding. A veritable Myszygene bank! Optimafilm, the stamp of a joint-stock company."[129] And another example: "At the cry of 'Kids on the set,' they have to come jumping out of the gate again in the prescribed formation. Then they come out: the head of the Judenrat, the militia, the police, the odemans [Jewish ghetto officers], the swindlers, the non-commissioned officers of the square."[130] This type of representation may be fulfilling two functions. In the most general sense, by film we understand a mode of representation that brackets off the represented reality; it blunts reality's sharpness and dampens down the drama of events. Consequently, even in scenes in which the filmic mode is not explicitly mentioned and in which the cruel reality has been blurred and thinned, as it were, we can see this convention at work. Here is one example of such depiction: "This is why it makes sense to ask, Is it her? She lay dead outside the barn. When we came running to the place where the noise of the rifle had been coming from, we saw a potato field littered with girls with their legs raised as though they were kicking something."[131] And here is another: "She was running off with three children. They were moving away, leaping as it were from one hiding place to another, until someone from the opposite camp caught them. I can add that that apparition had a small hat on, with a veil attached at the back, which made her look the way heroines usually look in the cinema."[132]

Buczkowski mixes cruelty with parody, thus blurring the contours of real events and drawing his readers into some insidious game that resembles the

---

127 Buczkowski, *Pierwsza świetność*, p. 44.
128 Buczkowski, *Pierwsza świetność*, p. 37.
129 Buczkowski, *Pierwsza świetność*, p. 35.
130 Buczkowski, *Pierwsza świetność*, p. 157.
131 Buczkowski, *Pierwsza świetność*, p. 79.
132 Buczkowski, *Pierwsza świetność*, p. 112.

postmodern type of entertainment indulged in by William Gass, Vladimir Nabokov and Michael Haneke in *Funny Games*.[133] The filmic nature of a massacre, however, can be even more ghastly than that. The Germans recorded many pogroms on film. It is possible that Buczkowski is referring to this notorious tradition of documenting the Holocaust. But if so, he also remains faithful to the principle of point-focused, punctum-oriented manner of representing the past. He reminds us of this principle when he writes: "We see history in flashes [...]. There's no way we take in the whole view."[134]

The similarity between the narrations of Birenbaum, Jabès and Buczkowski, as it comes to light when we juxtapose the two last-named authors, can be captured with the help of Blanchot's comment on Ulyssess' encounter with the singing Sirens:

> This is not an allegory. Every narration secretly resists the encounter with the Sirens, with their enigmatic song whose power resides in its flaw. For such resistance Ulysses' caution – whatever human truth, mystification and stubborn refusal to play into the hands of the gods he may possess – is always exploited and improved upon. And from such resistance what we call the novel is born.[135]

The secret power of this singing comes from its defect, its resemblance to animal sounds.[136] It may seem inappropriate to suggest a parallel between this interpretation and several features of *Pierwsza świetność*, *The Book of Questions* and the memories recorded in *Hope Is the Last to Die*.[137] In fact, however, the narratives of Jabès and Buczkowski, poised, as it were, on the threshold between intelligibility/readability and chaos, seem to constitute an opposite to Birenbaum's autobiography, which managed verbally to preserve the whole of the past in words. And not only that, for it also saved the system of values, which – as Borowski and Tadeusz Różewicz were determined to demonstrate – should have been upset and demolished by the war. What in my opinion brings these authors together is the illusion that one can write on the threshold of silence and chaos (Jabès, Buczkowski) or out of total order as posited by traditional literature (Birenbaum). They seem to have embraced or followed the utopian conviction that literature can arise out of silence, once the aporia of inexpressibility has been accepted. A coherent and comprehensive picture of the past as we know it from the memoirs of Birenbaum, Jabès and Buczkowski replace by a point-focused

---

133 Cf. McHale, *Postmodernist Fiction*, pp. 191–192.
134 Buczkowski, *Pierwsza świetność*, p. 163.
135 Maurice Blanchot, "The Sirens' song," in Maurice Blanchot, *The Sirens' Song. Selected Essays*, ed. Gabriel Josipovici, trans. Sacha Rabinovitch (Bloomington: Indiana University Press, 1982), 61.
136 Maurice Blanchot, "Encountering the Imaginary," in Maurice Blanchot, *The Book to Come*, trans. Charlotte Mandell (Stanford, CA: Stanford University Press, 2003), p. 5.
137 Birenbaum, *Hope Is the Last to Die*, p. 248.

story, one which is presented in fragments, in glimpses and blurry images. The defect of these stories at once constitutes their strength. In opposition to uncritical and unreflective representation, they initiate an alternative which is combined with a mode of representation where doubt plays an essential role. I submit that a metaliterary reflection, revealing the twofold aspect of this doubt, blurring the past while brightening it, like a glimpse and a fog, is the basic feature of postmodernism in Holocaust narratives from 1960s. Buczkowski gives an excellent expression to this feature in *Pierwsza świetność*:

> Is it not strange at the same time that he finds nothing among the stuff intended to go in the Main Work which would be an authentic record of the stay of Siemuszka's battalion in the town of Cymbarka Bełzka?[138]

And so the violence which we feared so much was fiction? Just as "casemates" turn out to be "an invention"?[139] In this case, postmodernism denotes the wide range of possibilities that Holocaust-related art has it its disposal. That is, if the author chooses not to limit his or her narrative to a collection of matter-of-fact reports that convey a simple message, and pursues a challenging theoretical concept.

---

138 Buczkowski, *Pierwsza świetność*, p. 118.
139 Buczkowski, *Pierwsza świetność*, p. 180.

Chapter 3.
Fog and Shadows: E. L. Doctorow, Raymond Federman, Georges Perec, Anatol Ulman

In 1960s, as a result of the first wave of postmodernism, two books appeared that influenced several generations of writers. They were Jorge Luis Borges's *Fictions* (*Ficciones*) and Vladimir Nabokov's *Pale Fire*, both published in 1962. Larry McCaffery relates their recursive and metafictional character to the substitution of the illusion of reality for realism. He argues that both writers succeeded in carrying out this substitution so convincingly that artists such as Vonnegut, Barth, Calvino, Barthelme, Gass, Márquez, Coover, Sukenick and Katz later found it much easier to break down the barrier of art's autonomy, characteristic of modernist aesthetics.[140]

The significance of Leopold Buczkowski and his *Pierwsza świetność* for the development of alternative depictions of the Holocaust in Poland may seem much humbler in comparison with those authors and their work, and it may be difficult to draw parallels between them. Seen from today's perspective, however, the trajectories of development of Polish fiction look completely different; they look bolder and clearer. Also the role *Pierwsza świetność* played in shaping those trajectories should be regarded, not only as important, but as constitutive. The position of Anatol Ulman's novel *Cigi de Montbazon* is not very different. In general terms, without the broadening of the field of vision of the past which occurred in 1960s, the progress through the 1970s and towards 1980s would be difficult to comprehend, and we would see its meaning in terms of a single and local experiment.

The view of the work of Jabès, Birenbaum and Buczkowski in the previous chapter as a coherent though internally complex way of grasping the Second World War, which can be transferred to the formation of the trajectories of

---

[140] "These authors continued to tell stories in their metafictive works, but frame-breaking and various metafictional strategies allowed them to tell them in a more honest manner by openly breaking through the illusion of autonomy between writer and work that had been a hallmark of modernist aesthetics." Larry McCaffery, "Re-double or nothing. Federman, Autobiography and Creative Literary Criticism," in: *Federman's Fictions. Innovation, Theory, and the Holocaust*, ed. Jeffrey R. Di Leo (New York: SUNY, 2011), p. 78.

development of Holocaust-related prose in the twentieth century, results from the proximity of these authors' dates of birth. The eldest, Buczkowski, was born in 1905, Jabès in 1912, and Birenbaum in 1929. Thus, at the outbreak of the war, Jabès and Buczkowski were adults, while Birenbaum, the youngest, was transported to Auschwitz as a teenager.

The memory of the war, especially in the case of Buczkowski, had a chance to materialize in the form of a coherent narrative and well-grounded in fact. I speak of "having a chance" to stress that that is not what actually happened and that Buczkowski's work makes this assumption void. As to the authors whose books I discuss in this chapter, the combination of generational reflection and the chosen strategy of narrating the past takes on a different trajectory of articulation. Raymond Federman (b. 1928), E. L. Doctorow (b. 1931), Anatol Ulman (b. 1931), Georges Perec (b. 1936) and Paul Auster (b. 1947), thus born in the 1920s, 1930s, and 1940s, were too young and immature to remember anything certain about the war. According to Susan Rubin Suleiman, they belong to the "1.5" generation, that is, "child survivors of the Holocaust"; "too young to have had an adult understanding of what was happening, and sometimes too young to have any memory of it at all, but old enough to have *been there* during the Nazi persecution of Jews [...]."[141] This is why their memories revolve around emptiness, silence, and loneliness. Those memories are also related to lost images of childhood, which raises a problem of aesthetic nature, that of "*how* to tell the story."[142]

Unlike Suleiman, my primary interest in this chapter is in the postmodern features of this literature. I do not want to discuss the psychological aspects of the memoires and their literary expressions. While Suleiman's interest is succinctly captured by the leading metaphor of "the edges of memory,"[143] I will propose the phrase *the hazy Holocaust*, which draws on the idea of "mist" in the motto used by Perec in his *W, or the Memory of Childhood*.[144] My metaphor suggests that what Suleiman regards as a clear, even sharp, experiment, leads – as I see it – to images of a past that make it seem invisible and even ridden with contradiction, a past in which memories are irrelevant and their role has been taken over by the

---

141 Susan Rubin Suleiman, *Crises of Memory and the Second World War* (Cambridge, Mass. and London: Harvard University Press, 2012), p. 179; italics in the original.
142 Suleiman, *Crises of Memory and the Second World War*, p. 184; italics in the original.
143 Suleiman's chapter (8) on Perec and Federman has the heading "The Edge of Memory: Experimental Writing and the 1.5 Generation."
144 Perec opens Part One of his memoir with Raymond Queneau's question: "That mindless mist where shadows swirl, how could I pierce it?" Part Two starts with that same author's doubt, "This mindless mist where shadows swirl, is this then my future?" Georges Perec, *W or the Memory of Childhood*, trans. David Bellos (London: Vintage Books, 2011), pp. 1, 63.

imagination in the way that Federman describes in *Smiles on Washington Square* (1995).[145]

The postmodernism of the 1970s was in many ways a response to the conclusions that were being drawn from the narratives of the previous decade. They chiefly had to do with the belief in the role of alternative sources of knowledge, a role played by a story deriving from sources that were lost, destroyed, or in need of reconstruction. Beginning with Buczkowski, postmodernists seem to have increasingly appreciated the value of such an alternative and made it the subject of discussion about art and reality. In the case of Raymond Federman, this alternative is the basis of his philosophy of literature. At this point, I will outline his philosophy, because the general assumptions of Federman's thought will accompany me throughout the course of my further considerations in this book.

Just like Jabès, to whom he refers in *The Voice in the Closet*,[146] Federman claims that his experience related to the extermination of the Jews in 1940, when as a twelve-year-old boy he was pushed into a closet by his mother, thanks to which he was the only survivor of the family, can be described. Federman ponders the challenges of the opposite claim, i. e., that the Holocaust cannot be described due to lack of appropriate language.[147] In this way he finds himself exploring what seems to be a dead end of contemporary literature and perhaps another manifestation of realism.[148] It is realism that is the main target of his attack in *Double or Nothing*, an all-out and total attack, as one can guess, considering the form of this book. In its metaliterary section, entitled "Some Reflections on the Novel in

---

145 The main protagonist, Moinous, disregards difference between facts and products of his imagination. "Moinous is the type of young man who wallows in the disorder of his obsessive imagination. For him the chaos of imagination always supersedes the order and veracity of facts. That is the basic condition of his existence. Except that Moinous makes no distinction, in his mind as well as in his life, between memory and imagination." Raymond Federman, *Smiles on Washington Square (A Love Story of Sorts)* (New York: Thunder's Mouth Press, 1985), p. 12.

146 The Polish edition of this 1979 work was published as *Wygnaniec – Żyd, tułacz, pisarz...*, trans. Piotr Kołyszko, *Literatura na Świecie* 1982, nr 12. Cf. Raymond Federman, *The Voice in the Closet [a sad tale]*, published by The United States Holocaust Memorial Museum Library; a copy available at Internet Archive, at https://archive.org/; see also http://www.federman.com/voice.htm (sites accessed 14. 09. 2023).

147 As in this passage, "[…] expelled from mother tongue exiled from motherland tongueless he extracts words from other tongues to exact his speechlessness […]"; Federman, *The Voice in the Closet*, section 20.

148 Federman depicts his predicament thus, "[…] he wants to apprehend with fake metaphors which bring together on the same level the incongruous the incompatible whereas in my paradox a split exists between the actual me wandering voiceless in temporary landscapes and the virtual being federman pretends to invent in his excremental packages of delusions a survivor who dissolves in verbal disarticulations unable to do what I had to do admit that his fictions can no longer match the reality of my past me blushing sphinx defecating the riddle of my birth […]"; Federman, *The Voice in the Closet*, Section 11.

Our Time," arranged in two parallel columns, English and French, Federman calls into doubt the efforts of critics who seek to decompose the project of the total novel.[149] In his opinion, they fail to reduce the most dangerous evil that lies dormant in this project, realism. Federman presents a simplified version of it, based on the assumption that a literary work always reflects something different and earlier than itself. This is true even when this representation proves difficult or impossible and shifts toward what we call the "nonrepresentational" or "inexpressible." Meanwhile, literature can only describe the human subject who creates it, that is, someone who exists inside it as fiction, and, moreover, as its fictional source. Instead of trying to perform the impossible task of describing the world realistically, the writer should accept the paradox and, when describing his experiences of creating literature, should go deeper and deeper into genocidal past and yield to the process of being excluded from it, which is the inevitable consequence of past events.

In *The Voice in the Closet* Federman graphically depicts the process of the writer's collapsing into himself. We see a writer locked in a room and focused exclusively on work, listening attentively to the eponymous "voice in the closet," which, however, does not lead him to what he once experienced in the closet (or to the experience of survival in general), but to the erasure of that experience. Federman calls this erasure of the original event the truth and marks it with four (or more) crosses, in imitation of the signature of an illiterate person.[150]

My goal in this chapter is to examine how erasure of the Holocaust is a means of representing memories about it, and how it is combined with fantasies of oblivion. I will be referring to four distinct literary projects: Doctorow's (the Holocaust as a hidden source of anti-Semitic politics), Federman's (the Holocaust as blurring), Perec's (the Holocaust as haze) and Ulman's (the Holocaust as doubt). All these projects represent postmodern fiction based on similar formal assumptions, admittedly the most important being the break with narrative continuity as a result of the multiplication of the plots being told (Perec, Federman), the extension of the narrative perspective to other grammatical persons (Federman, Doctorow), the laying bare of the fictionality of the narrative (Ulman, Doctorow), and the questioning of the value of memory (Ulman, Perec, Federman, Doctorow). Equally common in this literary material are ellipses (Perec), metonyms (Federman), enumerations (Perec), and above all metalepses,

---

149 Raymond Federman, *Double or Nothing: a real fictitious discourse* (Chicago, IL: The Swallow Press Inc., 1971), p. 146 ff.
150 Federman, *The Voice in the Closet*, section no.10; "[…] the whole story crossed out my whole family parenthetically x-x-x-x into typographic symbols […]".

which Federman called frog leaps[151] and Brian McHale described as shifts between ontological levels of text.[152]

Cigi de Montbazon may be the shortest among the narratives discussed here, but it is also the most important in that, according to the assumptions of this book, it brings to the fore the postmodern discourse of the Holocaust in Poland. In 1970s, as can be seen from the novels I am discussing, this discourse ceased to be merely an alternative and became a joint project of world-class authors.

The Holocaust as a Hidden Source of Politics

The novel that revealed the far-reaching consequences of the Holocaust for the postwar world, and especially for Americans, was *The Book of Daniel* published in 1971 by Edgar Lawrence Doctorow. The political is another extremely important feature we should associate it with, a feature which Doctorow successfully combined with postmodernism, thus debunking its already established image as an entertaining literary trend.

Besides being, to some extent at least, a fictionalized version of the Rosenberg case, *The Book of Daniel* is primarily an analysis of the social relations prevailing among American Jewish emigrants in 1950s and 1960s, most of whom arrived in the new continent from Europe before the outbreak of the Second World War. While in the United States, they mostly lived in large family clusters, cultivated knowledge of the Yiddish language, and upheld communist views.

Seen against this background, the family described by the narrator of *The Book of Daniel* is a model communist family. Rochelle and Paul Isaacson, members of the American Communist Party, inculcate in their children the principles of social equality, criticize Fordism, and hold up the Soviet Union as a model welfare-state. When they are exposed as Soviet spies and executed in 1953, their children, Susan and Daniel, end up in the care of adoptive parents, the Lewins.

According to Kristina Busse, even though the Holocaust is not the novel's theme, it keeps coming up in the form of verbal associations, analogies between the world of war and the modern world, and particular expressions and phrases like "*Polizei*," arguably intended to convey a thinly concealed parallel between the war-time regime and the policies the United States adopted in 1950s and

---

151 As in this passage, "as selectricstud resumes movement among empty skins images crumble through distortions spins out lies into a false version leapfrogs infinite stories falling silently into abyss [...]"; Federman, *The Voice in the Closet*, section no. 19.
152 E. g., McHale, *Postmodern Fiction*, p. 172.

1960s towards its citizens.[153] As an example, we can look at two brief passages that contain explicit references to the Holocaust. One of them is used by Paul Isaacson in a letter to his wife, in reference to a judge and prosecutor, whom he compares to Jewish concentration camp guards:

> My darling have you noticed how many of the characters in this capitalist drama are Jewish? The defendants, the defense lawyer, the prosecution, the major prosecution witness, the judge. We are putting on this little passion play for our Christian masters. In the concentration camps the Nazis made guards of certain Jews and gave them whips.[154]

In this passage, the narrator refers to Disneyland, where he goes in search of Selig Mindish, who contributed to the death of his parents:

> [...] they drove me to Anaheim, a town somewhere between Buchenwald and Belsen, where Dr and Mrs Selig Mindish were spending the day at Disneyland. [...] Plain-clothes security personnel appear in any large gathering with walkie-talkies. The problems of mass ingress and egress seem to have been solved here to a degree that would light admiration in the eyes of an SS transport officer.[155]

In both these cases, the Holocaust is a living and painful source of reflection about the modern world. None of the protagonists refers to it directly; neither the Isaacsons nor the Lewins mention the war, although Susan and Daniel's adoptive mother is a survivor. In fact, Doctorow bestows a different meaning on the word "survival," one which, as we shall see, shows up more often in Auster's prose than in Holocaust testimonies. This meaning denotes unclear Jewish roots, as when Daniel says, "Susan and I, we were the only ones left. And all my life I have been trying to escape from my relatives and I have been intricate in my run [...]."[156]

Doctorow suggests numerous similarities between the Rosenberg case and the history of the Jews' persecutions by Hitler and the Nazis. The Isaacsons' trial takes place in a Jewish community and the evidence of their guilt which leads to it is vague at best; the protagonists are convinced that if it had not been for the unfavorable times of McCarthyism and the Cold War, and the military competition between the United States and the Soviet Union, which fueled the atmosphere of anti-Semitism, which was in its turn fueled by the activities of the American Communist Party, the court's ruling would have been different. There is a lot of cruelty of unknown origin in the family relations. In the scene in which

---

153 Kristina Busse, *Imagining Auschwitz. Postmodern representations of the Holocaust. A dissertation submitted on the fifteenth day of April 2002 to the Department of English in partial fulfilment of the requirements of the graduate school of Tulane University for the degree of the doctor philosophy*, http://www.kristinabusse.com/cv/research/diss.pdf [accessed 14.08.2022].
154 Edgar Lawrence Doctorow, *The Book of Daniel. A Novel* (London: Picador/Pan Books, 1982), p. 203.
155 Doctorow, *The Book of Daniel*, pp. 291; 296.
156 Doctorow, *The Book of Daniel*, p. 30–31.

Susan and Daniel, who are less than ten years old, bid farewell to their parents, the words in which they address their mother sound harsh: "When are they going to kill you?" Susan said. [...] "But what if they kill you anyway?" Susan said. "How will they do it?"[157] And finally, because the Isaacsons' guilt has not been demonstrated beyond doubt, Susan and Daniel live in the belief that their parents died in vain and cannot free themselves from the burden of the past.

Busse rightly points out that Doctorow's novel is not a fictionalized documentary, but, in Linda Hutcheon's terminology, a historiographical metafiction, a narrative in which the relationships between the past, the present and the future play an important role in the lives of the protagonists. Susan's memory keeps alive, as it were, the death of her parents and she dies in one version of the ending. Daniel becomes a revolutionary in the alternative ending (the novel ends with student revolts in 1968).[158] These different endings complement rather than exclude each other, and this conceptually heterogeneous retrospective, Busse's "sliding over the past,"[159] causes the realism of the narrative dissipate among the alternative stories, the number of which, however, does not affect the overall message of *The Book of Daniel*. The message is expressed in an enigmatical quotation from the biblical *Book of Daniel*, with which the novel ends:

> and at that time the people shall be delivered, everyone that shall be found written in the book. [...] But thou, O Daniel, shut up the words, and seal the book, even to the time of the end ... Go thy way Daniel: for the words are closed up and sealed till the time of the end.[160]

Book of Daniel (12; Standard American Version):

> [1] "Now at that time Michael, the great prince who stands guard over the sons of your people, will arise. And there will be a time of distress such as never occurred since there was a nation until that time; and at that time your people, everyone who is found written in the book, will be rescued. [2] Many of those who sleep in the dust of the ground will awake, these to everlasting life, but the others to disgrace and everlasting contempt. [3] Those who have insight will shine brightly like the brightness of the expanse of heaven, and those who lead the many to righteousness, like the stars forever and ever. [4] But as for you, Daniel, conceal these words and seal up the book until the end of time; many will go back and forth, and knowledge will increase."
> [5] Then I, Daniel, looked and behold, two others were standing, one on this bank of the river and the other on that bank of the river. [6] And one said to the man dressed in linen, who was above the waters of the river, "How long will it be until the end of these wonders?" [7] I heard the man dressed in linen, who was above the waters of the river, as

---

157 Doctorow, *The Book of Daniel*, pp. 249–250.
158 Linda Hutcheon, *The Politics of Postmodernism* (London and New York: Routledge, 2001), pp. 69–70.
159 Busse, *Imagining Auschwitz*, p. 91.
160 Doctorow, *The Book of Daniel*, p. 308; italics in the original.

> he raised his right hand and his left toward heaven, and swore by Him who lives forever that it would be for a time, times, and half a time; and as soon as they finish shattering the power of the holy people, all these events will be completed. [8] As for me, I heard but could not understand; so I said, "My lord, what will be the outcome of these events?" [9] He said, "Go your way, Daniel, for these words are concealed and sealed up until the end time. [10] Many will be purged, purified and refined, but the wicked will act wickedly; and none of the wicked will understand, but those who have insight will understand. [11] From the time that the regular sacrifice is abolished and the abomination of desolation is set up, there will be 1,290 days. [12] How blessed is he who keeps waiting and attains to the 1,335 days! [13] But as for you, go your way to the end; then you will enter into rest and rise again for your allotted portion at the end of the age."[161]

Originating in the Bible, the belief in the suppression of words also applies to the representation of the Holocaust. Images of the Holocaust "have been shut up and sealed till time of the end." The experience of reading *The Book of Daniel* is not, or at least need not be, a process of identifying and declassifying these images and their meaning, but may be limited, as in this case, to the observation that this indeed is the case. Although the novel is silent about the war and is concerned with what preceded it and what followed it, 1930s and 1940s, in Doctorow's view, was a period of unspeakable and indelible experiences. Even Daniel's grandmother, in a letter to the editor of an unnamed newspaper, mentions her experiences as *Ostjudin* and remains totally silent about the Holocaust:

> My dear Mr Editor, you who hear the troubles of so many, and share the common misery, permit me to say what I have to say if my heart is not to burst. Surely I do not have to tell you what my life has been: first the terrible fear of flight from the Czarist maniacs who would not let us live, and who killed us in his pogroms, and conscripted our young Jewish men for twenty-five years of slavery in the Army – from this terrible animal oppression I fled by paying the same torturers money under the table to slip across the border with only the rags on my back, from the Pale, the Pale with my poor old mother and father who felt too old to go kissing my head and blessing me […].[162]

This unknown space, whose location we can only guess, like Disneyland, is the kind of "zone" that McHale writes about. He argues that, in postmodern fiction, the geographical location of space is fictional and occurs in several variants, all directly related to Michel Foucault's concept of heterotopia. He calls them "juxtaposition, interpolation, superimposition, and misattribution."[163] By "zone" McHale understands a space which has been "erased,"[164] made only of the contours of some other space. If the "second degree" space resembles America,

---

161 Daniel 12:1–13, New American Standard Bible; https://www.biblegateway.com (accessed 12.09.2023).
162 Doctorow, *The Book of Daniel*, p. 66.
163 McHale, *Postmodernist Fiction*, p. 45 ff.
164 McHale, *Postmodernist Fiction*, p. 99, the beginning of Chapter 7, "Worlds under erasure."

the level below – according to McHale – is the land of Oz from Frank L. Bauman's *The Wizard of Oz*. In the case of the world engulfed by the First and then the Second World Wars, the role of the erased zone is played by Central and Eastern Europe. It is not entirely clear whether Doctorow connects the ancestors of his protagonist character with Russia or Eastern Galicia, but he thematizes the pre-Holocaust experiences of Jewish people in those parts of the world by bestowing on them the universal dimension of the fate of all exiles. This theme was also explored by Jabès, Federman, Perec and, above all, Paul Auster. It is a sad and incomprehensible fate, a theme for stories which Jewish emigrants repeatedly tell in Yiddish, a language that in *The Book of Daniel* is not the language of life and death, as in the Régine Robin, but the language of everyday inteactions that Jewish people use when they want to enter into intimate and secret relationships with each other.[165]

A Blurred Holocaust: A Journey in the Other Direction

Published the same year as *The Book of Daniel*, Raymond Federman's experimental novel *Double or Nothing* (1971) is, in a sense, the story of a Jewish immigrant who, upon arriving in the United States, makes a heroic (or heroicomical) attempt to tell his and his family's story. It is an attempt to organize such autobiographical material by using the style reminiscent of postmodernist games. In 1966, Federman, author of the first monograph on Samuel Beckett's early novels, received a Guggenheim scholarship to France, where he was to write "another monograph, this time on the latest trends in French poetry."[166] During the voyage, however, he began to work on a novel, which he finished two years later. For the theme of *Double or Nothing*, however, he chose a journey in the opposite direction, from France to the United States, precisely the kind of journey he had to make to settle permanently in the New Continent after the war. Mentioning it at the outset as a good subject for a novel, Federman rejects this idea and makes it the subject of a parody. It would then be difficult to read *Double or Nothing* as a story of an emigrant's hardships and misery:

> Imagine a guy. An immigrant. A Frenchman. And a Jew on top of that. Imagine. Walking along the streets of Detroit. Imagine the first two or three weeks. In Detroit. Imagine what's going on in his mind. And you have a typical situation for a good story. Imagine

---

165 Régine Robin, "Gratok. Langue de vie et langue de mort," *Meta: journal des traducteurs / Meta: Translators' Journal*, vol. 40, n° 3, 1995, p. 482–487, in: https://www.erudit.org/revue /meta/1995/v40/n3/003964ar.pdf [accessed: 16. 08. 2022].
166 Jerzy Kutnik, "Tłumacz po słowie," in Raymond Federman, *Podwójna wygrana jak nic. Prawdziwy fikcyjny dyskurs*, trans. Jerzy Kutnik (Kraków: Ha!art 2010), p. vi.

how he feels. Imagine how closed in he feels. Closed up. It takes years. Five. Maybe ten. To get used to that kind existence. And sometimes a guy never gets used to it. And eventually he kills himself or if he doesn't have the courage to kill himself he asks somebody to do it for him. WHAT A STINKING STORY![167]

Explaining the reasons why Federman did not find himself in the strict canon of Holocaust literature together with Primo Levi, Jean Améry, Tadeusz Borowski, Charlotte Delbo, Jorge Semprun and Elie Wiesel, Susan Rubin Suleiman points to the postmodern character of his testimonies, which infringes their documentary character. She also observes that, unlike his parents and two sisters, Federman was not deported to Auschwitz and thus eluded the fate of Levi or Wiesel. Everything Federman could say about the Holocaust had to be related to the closet, which allowed him to survive the encounter with the French police.[168]

Nevertheless, it is still puzzling why Linda Hutcheon chose not to include Federman among postmodernists. In her *A Poetics of Postmodernism: History, Theory, Fiction* (1988), she puts Federman, side by side with Sukenick, among writers who share an affinity with the authors of the French new novel, Robbe-Grillet and Ricardou. In Federman's "extreme metafiction,"[169] Hutcheon detects the romantic and modernist assumptions about which he was to speak with a confidence unparalleled in postmodern discourse.[170] According to Suleiman, Hutcheon deprived Federman and other "surfictionalists" of a rightful place in the postmodern canon because their writing lacked historical character. Terms such as "late modernist extremism" and "autotelic reflexivity" used by the author of *Narcissistic Narrative: The metafictional paradox* became, according to Suleiman, a kind of invective, which simultaneously scratched Federman's writing off the Holocaust and the postmodern canon.

Meanwhile, Federman's writing conveys the experiences of many who survived the Holocaust as children, and its experimentality, according to Suleiman, is within the limits of survivor testimony. In the essay "When Postmodern Play Meets Survivor Testimony" (2011), Suleiman compares Federman's early work with the testimonies of other survivors belonging to the world canon, and points out that its formal originality results from the way the author experienced trauma and can be described with the help of the theories of Sigmund Freud, Donald Woods Winnicot and Jacques Lacan, especially relevant being the concept of *fort-da*, which explains a child's behavior in response to separation from the mother. Federman's creative and sophisticated imagination transformed the narrative

---

167 Federman, *Double or Nothing*, p. 95.
168 Susan Rubin Suleiman, "When postmodern play meets survivor testimony," in: Di Leo, ed., *Federman's Fictions*, p. 216.
169 Linda Hutcheon, *A Poetics of Postmodernism. History, Theory, Fiction* (New York and London: Routledge, 2010), p. 52.
170 Hutcheon, *A Poetics of Postmodernism*, p. 52.

voice, which, divided and multiplied into minor voices, remains at once a consequence of that childlike separation from his mother. As an example of this type of narrative device, Suleiman cites the protagonist-narrator in *Take It or Leave it*, appearing as Me and MOINOUS. The latter name literally denotes the relationship of "Me" over "We", or "me" and "you [pl]", which in Federman's biography denotes himself and the family killed in Auschwitz.[171]

According to Suleiman, Federman's experiments – by which she understands not only concrete prose and the multiplication of narrators, but also linguistic paradoxes, specific humor, and bold sex scenes – are an expression of his early childhood trauma. It is this trauma, like that of Perec, another representative of the "1.5" generation among French-Jewish authors, that led Federman towards an "oblique" and indirect representation of the Holocaust.

Suleiman's psychoanalytic approach has caused her to see in Federman's early paradoxes attempts at expressing what he wanted at once to hide and show in his biography ("saying while not saying").[172] The most famous example of this contradiction is the four "X's" placed side by side in *Take It or Leave It*, which represent the murdered parents and sisters. Another is the Star of David composed of sentences that make up a narrative. Brain McHale called these ideograms of the Holocaust.

> The dilemma is by now a familiar one, though no less intractable for being so familiar: how is a writer who has survived the holocaust to write about the mass death that he himself so narrowly escaped? One of Federman's solutions is *not* to write about it at all, but to let the blank spaces in the text – or the X's or zeroes or other typographical icons – speak for him. [...]
>
> It is the gaps that convey the meaning here, in a way that the shattered words *juif, cremation, lampshade, Auschwitz, responsabilité*, and so on, could never have done had they been completed and integrated into some syntactical continuity. Visually, the effect is that of a tombstone (a defaced tombstone?). This shaped passage, it seems to me, serves to prove (if proof were needed) that concrete prose can be a good deal more than just a trivial joke.[173]

To reinforce the seriousness of the ideograms Suleiman describes them as "hole in reality," resulting from the death of someone close (a loved one).[174] Gaps in the text and the visual representation of the Holocaust indicate Federman's reluctance to fill this void. Enumerations, verbal games, and repetitions create the opposite effect, one associated with the Freudian concept of *fort-da*. Therefore,

---

171 Suleiman, "When postmodern play meets survivor testimony," p. 219.
172 Suleiman, "When postmodern play meets survivor testimony," p. 220.
173 McHale, *Postmodernist Fiction*, pp. 186–187.
174 Suleiman, *Crises of Memory*, pp. 106–131; cf. Jacques Lacan, Jacques-Alain Miller and James Hulbert, "Desire and the Interpretation of Desire in Hamlet." *Yale French Studies*, No. 55/56, Literature and Psychoanalysis. The Question of Reading: Otherwise. (1977), pp. 11–52.

the essence of paradoxes, which are scattered between several layers of the narrative, consists in capturing the intention simultaneously to blur and reveal the past, this intention being an echo of childhood trauma.[175]

In *Crises of Memory and the Second World War* (2006), Suleiman juxtaposes the biographies of Perec and Federman and their two novels I am interested in, *W, or the Memory of Childhood* and *Double or Nothing*. Despite many similarities, they differ in the concept of the gap. While Perec sees emptiness where the past should be, Federman describes the Holocaust in terms of excess, combining it with a specific sense of humor and pornography.[176] Suleiman uses the term paralipsis to refer to the specific narrative predilection found in *Double or Noting*, the desire to show the excess and void associated with the experience of the past. It is a figure of speech that is internally contradictory in that it consists of affirmation and negation, avoidance and disclosure, amnesia and remembering at the same time. A paralipsis means an accurately remembered situation or experience (in *Double or Nothing* these are typically related to extermination camps), which the narrator does not talk about, using instead various other terms associated with it.

> The paradoxical combination of "saying while not saying" that characterizes the figure of preterition – with its attendant figures of suspension, postponement, digression, juxtaposition, and metacommentary – is […] emblematic of experimental writing about childhood trauma, in particular the experience of childhood loss.[177]

Using Charles Pierce's terminology, Suleiman calls the survivor and his experience an index; like a survivor, an index does not speak, and therefore needs to be interpreted. The indexical character of Holocaust literature – which I have discussed elsewhere in terms of metonymy[178] – stems from the general belief that accompanies all of Suleiman's statements about Federman and, more generally, the role of imagination in Holocaust literature. Citing Federman's statement in *Smiles in Washington Square*, Suleiman argues that fictional writing is, as it were, a natural upshot of witness literature. She cites two novels in this context, Anne Michaels's *Fugitive Pieces* (1996) and Sebald's *Austerlitz* (2001), both based on experience that is at once fictional and truthful. Both, too, though written by authors who were not directly affected by the Holocaust, are examples of fiction that imitates and creates opportunities for testimony.

According to Sue Vice, the 1979 novella *The Voice in the Closet*, published eight years after *Double or Nothing*, combines two narrative forms, testimonial and

---

175 Suleiman, "When postmodern play meets survivor testimony," p. 223.
176 Suleiman, *Crises of Memory and the Second World War*, p. 202.
177 Suleiman, *Crises of Memory and the Second World War*, p. 208.
178 Marta Cuber, *Metonimie Zagłady. O prozie polskiej 1987–2012* (Katowice: Wydawnictwo Uniwersytetu Śląskiego, 2013).

experimental. Two competing voices of the narrator are responsible for this splitting, one belonging to a boy who last saw his mother when he was fourteen, the other to an adult writer who observes and describes that child. This duality causes two distinct representations of the past: the child's flamboyant language and the adult's metaphors; yet both these modes of expression meet in obsessive images of confinement strewn throughout Federman's work.[179] Vice compares these images to Bakhtin's chronotope, which in both cases, Federman's and Dostoevsky's, signifies a borderline space, a space of renewal, epiphany, as well as danger.[180] The helplessness of the adult in the face of the experience of the Holocaust by a child is indelible. The adult succumbs to memories of past experiences, quoting and interpreting this helplessness. The two voices, the child-narrator's and the narrator-author's, mix and intertwine. Vice tries to tell them apart, yet sometimes it is impossible to do so, as the following passage shows:

> I register the final absence of my mother crying softly in the night my father coughing his blood down the staircase they threw sand in their eyes struck their back kicked them to exterminate them his calculations yes explanations yes the whole family parenthetically xxxx into typographic symbols...[181]

Federman writes about the shifts between the current and virtual narrative person, most often changing the subject and the narrative, which from first-person becomes third-person, which in turn leads to changes within the testimony. It will be recalled that in Birenbaum it was precisely this aspect of testimony, connected with the autobiographical narration, that constituted his inviolable good.

Suleiman's remarks on Federman's prose can be extended to include the game with testimonial narration. The narrator of *Double or Nothing* does not follow the autobiographical pact that he previously established between himself and the reader. Instead, by changing the names of the characters, the details of their biography, and above all the story itself, he exposes the testimony as a petrified and schematic narrative mode. It can be broken down and dismantled, if not by the truth, because it cannot be proved ("but in fact what did really happen that is the most important question WHAT REALLY HAPPENED?"[182]), then by excess. One form of such an excess in both *The Voice in the Closet* and *Double or Nothing* is masturbation. In the fictional story of Boris, a Jewish fugitive from a transportation, Federman devises a scene in which the protagonist is taken in by a farmer and, just after entering the room, "[...] the first thing he did when he got

---

179 Sue Vice, *Children Writing the Holocaust* (New York: Palgrave Macmillan, 2004), pp. 55–62.
180 Vice, *Children Writing the Holocaust*, pp. 59–60.
181 Raymond Federman, *The Voice in the Closet* (Hamburg: Kellner, 1989); section 10 (pages not numbered).
182 Federman, *Double or Nothing*, p. 156.

in the room, after he looked around, a bit scared, was to jerk off, or at least he was starting to do it, holding on to it with his left hand, when he saw himself in the mirror, and that's when the shock came, the shock of not recognizing himself [...]."[183] There is a scene of masturbation at the beginning of *The Voice in the Closet*:

> here now again selectricstud makes me speak with its balls all balls foutaise sam says in his closet upstairs but this time it's going to be serious no more masturbating on third floor escaping into the trees...[184]

Only a detailed description, repeated several times. of sexual intercourse between Boris and a black American woman makes us aware of Federman's attachment to the postmodern story of the Holocaust. This kind of story enables him time and time again and perpetually to fantasize about the past. This fantasizing, on the one hand, plays the role of self-therapy, while, on the other hand, it offers a solution to the dilemma of how to talk about the death of one's parents. The narrator does not shrink from associations which may be seen as inappropriate and even obscene:

> One of the faces he sees quite vividly in the little black triangle between the girl's legs in the subway is his father's face. Can't tell from where he's sitting if it's his real father or if it's only the face of his legendary invented father. The mythical father he started making up after the war.[185]

The blurring of the Holocaust, which seems to be where Federman is headed, is visible, often literally so, in the narrative's figural arrangements characteristic of the concrete novel, but also in explicit declarations.[186] However, they are not the only type of reflection on the extermination of the family in *Double or Nothing*. Equally important are the narrator's attempts to recreate and understand the situation of confinement experienced by teenage offspring. I deliberately avoid calling those experiences recollections, because apparently the protagonist-narrator does not remember them, or refuses to recollect. And if he is doing anything other than recreating the material base of sustenance, as he is getting ready to stay locked in for 365 days, it is imagining an extreme situation from the remote past.

Indeed, the intention that motivates the experiment of locking oneself away in an empty apartment, equipped with writing instruments, noodles, and toilet paper as his sole company, seems to be to recreate for oneself the situation from

---

183 Federman, *Double or Nothing*, p. 136.
184 Federman, *The Voice in the Closet* (section 1).
185 Federman, *Double or Nothing*, p. 158.
186 As described by Federman in a self-reflective comment, the main topic of his writing was not to depict the fate of the deported and exterminated but the erasure of that fate. Cf. Raymond Federman, *Wygnaniec – Żyd, tułacz, pisarz...*, Literatura na Świecie 1982, no. 12, p. 306.

years ago. Although that one was an extreme situation of a different kind and a different type of confinement, Federman seems to be saying that that it is impossible to recreate that otherness today, because we try to understand it in conditions that contradict that type of existence. Paradoxically, when moving away from the "originary event," the author of *To Whom It May Concern* approaches it; just as he did, when he boarded a ship from America to France and wrote a novel about a journey in the opposite direction.

Foggy Holocaust

In his 1975 autobiography, Georges Perec is not using Federman's method of describing a war-related hiding place from a contemporary position, constructed in the shape of verisimilar fiction. Perec's recollections are simpler and limited to a single plane, seemingly devoid of a postmodern dimension. These, however, are merely deluding appearances, for in *W or the Memory of Childhood* Perec has created a story about the past that is intricate and unobvious, motived by the belief that IT must be told, but that one must not write at length about IT.

> I have no childhood memories. Up to my twelfth year or thereabouts, my story comes to barely a couple of lines: I lost my father at four, my mother at six; I spent the war in various boarding houses at Villard-de-Lans. In 1945, my father's sister and her husband adopted me.[187]

According to Susan Suleiman, the formal experiment of *W or the Memory of Childhood* differs from the formal extravagance of *La disparition* from 1969, a novel devoid of "e," the most common vowel in French. In the latter novel, doublings, discontinuity, lack, and absence are imbued with childhood trauma and separation from parents.[188] Not only did its publication surprise Perec's readers; it completely changed the image of his work. He dedicated *W or the Memory of Childhood* to those hidden behind the letter "E," that is, his parents, at the same time revealing all that he wanted to conceal in *La disparition*. From now on, the Holocaust became inseparably linked with his work and its numerous formal experiments.

One of them directly concerns the title of the 1975 book. The letter "W," especially in English, is suggestive of doubling, and therefore of double representation. Suleiman associates it with the tradition of titling eighteenth-century tales, for instance *Candide: or, The Optimist* and *Tartuffe, or The Impostor*. In the case of Perec's memoires, yet another meaning of the letter "W" is relevant: a

---

[187] Georges Perec, *W or the Memory of Childhood*, trans. David Bellos (London: Vintage Books, 2011), p. 6.
[188] Suleiman, *Crises of Memory*, p. 185.

mysterious space for events reminiscent of sports competitions in ancient Sparta, for which Suleiman finds a parallel in Jules Verne's stories. It will be recalled that the other story, a parallel and alternative one, one that creates a postmodern game and dystopia at the same time, has its beginning in the meeting of the protagonist with Gaspard Winckler, who claims to have known a boy of the same name and surname. The mysterious appearance of Winckler and the disappearance of that boy, the female singer's sickly son, who during a cruise probably disembarks to leave his mother and never to return – these are the threads that Perec associates with the story of the island of W. The Spartan discipline which binds its inhabitants gradually comes to resemble Nazi terror, until we finally recognize in the Athlete, the anonymous hero of history, a concentration camp prisoner:

> A W Athlete has scarcely any control over his life. He has nothing to expect from the passing of time. Neither the alternation of days and nights nor the seasons' round will come to his aid. The fog of winter will nights, the icy rain of spring, the torrid heat of summer afternoons afflict him equally.[189]

Perec's story ends with a poignant fantasy about Jewish property:

> When someone gets in one day to the Fortress he will find first of all nothing but a sequence of dim, long, empty rooms. [...] but he must keep on going until he discovers, deep down in the depths of the earth, the subterranean remnants of a world he will think he has forgotten: piles of gold teeth, rings and spectacles, thousands and thousands of clothes in heaps, dusty card indexes, and stocks of poor-quality soap ...[190]

Perec's sporting fantasy, set on an island reminiscent of Tierra del Fuego,[191] was derived from David Rousset's *A World Apart* [*L'Univers concentrationnaire*] and the opinion expressed there on the similarity between sport and forced labor. However, the significance of this fantasy can hardly be reduced to a development of some of the themes of Rousset's book. Perec wrote an alternative story which, together with the fragmentary and "faded" memories concerning his family narrated in the first part, creates a postmodern representation of the Holocaust. Based on a complex understanding of the past, this representation contains reflections on the inefficiency of literature and memory as well as a great deal of memories recounted in ways that defy the linearity which characterizes Birenbaum's book. According to Philippe Lejeune, Perec, the author of *Life: A User's Manual*, was the first to write a retrospective narrative "edited" in this peculiar manner. However, this "gluing" together of fiction and autobiography

---

189 Perec, *W or the Memory of Childhood*, p. 159; italics in the original.
190 Perec, *W or the Memory of Childhood*, pp. 161–162; italics in the original.
191 Perec, *W or the Memory of Childhood*, p. 164.

was for Perec a necessity rather than a manifestation of the ambitions of an experimental author. There simply was no other way of doing it.

What Lejeune, in reference to *W or the Memory of Childhood*, called a critical autobiography could also be called a postmodern autobiography. It consists of a personal part of Perec's memoirs, written in 1959, and a science fiction story, mentioned above, published in *La Quinzaine Littéraire* in 1969.

In essence, a critical autobiography, however, does not consist in various narrative strands stitched together as so many raw materials. Rather, it consists in the parallel coexistence in it of a life-story and a reflection deconstructing that story. In the case of Perec, this autobiography is a hyperbolic reflection on the lack of childhood memories accompanied by attempts at their reconstruction. The whole project makes us think of the Federman paradox known as "saying without saying." Suleiman associates this paradox primarily with the uncertainty about how to write about the Holocaust, an anxiety that seem to accompany all the authors whose works we are discussing. In her opinion, the most obvious example of this specific authorial uncertainty is the ellipsis or suspension between the first and second part of the memoir, the dots metonymizing the Holocaust, or, alternatively, the unsayable of the Holocaust. Warren Motte regards the reader's decision of what to make of this ellipsis "the key statement of [Perec's] book."[192]

Let us dwell for a moment longer on the postmodern features of *W or the Memory of Childhood*. As science fiction, Perec's story is what McHale has called "*the* ontological genre *par excellence*"[193] as he compares science fiction to the detective novel, which played a similar role in modernism. There is a degree of interference between the two genres in Perec's autobiography, which causes them to remain in relation to each other in a relationship of metaphor or metonymy.[194] It is also worth remembering the "crisscross web," that is, parallels between the first and second part of the book, which Suleiman refers to by different terms, including those of "recursion" and "chiasms."[195]

The key paradox of *W or the Memory of Childhood* can also be regarded as the postmodern predicament of proclaiming the need to write in the absence of words and memories. It is emphasized by the content of Chapter VIII, which combines a supreme documentary value with an unmatched critical potential.

---

192 Suleiman, *Crises of Memory*, p. 189; after Warren Motte's "Georges Perec and the Broken Book" (1995).
193 McHale, *Postmodernist Fiction*, p. 59. "We can think of science fiction as postmodernism's noncanonized or 'low art' double, its sister-genre in the same sense that the popular detective thriller is modernist fiction's sister-genre."
194 Suleiman, *Crises of Memory*, p. 202. Suleiman does not specify which figure of speech in particular she has in mind.
195 Suleiman, *Crises of Memory*, p. 192.

Perec returns in it to early descriptions of his mother and father; marked in bold and set in the main body of the text, their meaning is then commented on in new footnotes, some of which correct the names and supplement dates missing from the main text, while others make up distinct stories.

Perec writes very little about his father, Icek Judko, who had been apprenticed to a Warsaw hatter before 1926 and whom Perec lost when he was four years old. He was helped in deciphering the past by the only surviving photograph. For example:

> I thought up various glorious deaths for my father. The finest had him being cut down by a burst of machine-gun fire as he was bridging to General Soandso the dispatch containing news of victory.
> I was rather silly. My father died a slow and stupid death. It was on the day after the armistice. He had got in the way of a stray shell.[196]

Perec had even less information about his mother, despite five surviving photographs. He makes the following assumptions: "I shall therefore say that I suppose my mother's childhood to have been squalid and straightforward. Born in 1913 [in Warsaw – M.T.], she could not avoid growing up in the war. And she was Jewish and poor. She must have been clothed in the hand-me-downs of six siblings; she must have been left pretty much to herself [...]."[197] This is the reason why Perec decided to cleanse his memories of the cruelty, previously introduced in the form of a hypothesis, and to show his mother "in a pale glow" years later, combined with motifs from Hans Christian Andersen's "The Little Match Girl" and Victor Hugo's *Les Misérables:*

> When I think of her, I imagine a twisting ghetto street in a pale, sickly light, maybe snow, and dingy, poverty stricken shops with endless, stationary queues. And my mother is in the midst of all that, knee-high to a grasshopper, a wee chit of a thing, wrapped four times round in a knitted shawl, hauling a great black shopping bag twice her own weight.[198]

The moment indicated by these conjectural recollections seems to be crucial when seen from the perspective of the representation of the times of the Holocaust in the postmodern prose of the seventies: an author born in 1936, orphaned in his early childhood, defines the challenge of describing the past in a way that radically defies our expectations. Perec is not struggling with the task of narrating the Holocaust, because the Holocaust is not something that he has directly experienced. Rather, his are struggles with what happened, as it were, around the Holocaust, on the verge of it, a few years before it began or as it was

---

196 Perec, *W or the Memory of Childhood*, p. 29; in bold type in the original.
197 Perec, *W or the Memory of Childhood*, p. 30; in bold type in the original.
198 Perec, *W or the Memory of Childhood*, pp. 30–31; in bold type in the original.

about to begin. This hazy and pale Holocaust, in the light of Perec's memories, is like a paradox; it seems to be an image through which appears a barely visible picture of loved ones. One of them died in 1940, and to the other Perec, then a young boy, said goodbye in 1942 at the age of six: "As the train moved out, I caught sight of her, I seem to remember, waving a white handkerchief from the platform. I was going to Villard-de-Lans, with the red cross."[199]

Memory being the main theme of *W*, it is also commented on in Chapter VIII, where Perec examines his memory and is trying to decide what he actually remembers about his parents and what has been irretrievably lost. He confirms the initial statement, as already quoted, in which he admits that he has "no childhood memories": "Up to my twelfth year or thereabouts, my story comes to a barely a barely a couple of lines: I lost my father at four, my mother at six; I spent the war in various boarding houses at Villard-de-Lans. In 1945, my father's sister and her husband adopted me."[200] This verification of loss or lack is primarily based on the following statements: "My father was a soldier for a very short time. Nonetheless, when I think of him, I always think of a soldier."[201] "The memories I have of my father are not many."[202] Then there are the following deliberations concerning the mother:

> These more or less statistical details, which are of fairly limited interest to me, are all that I have considering the childhood and youth of my mother. Or rather, to be more precise, all that I can rely on. The rest, although it sometimes seems that someone told it to me, and that it comes from a trustworthy source, is probably ascribable to the quite extraordinary imaginary relationship which I regularly maintained with my maternal branch at a particular time in my brief existence.[203]

This recollection about the mother is then negative in its conclusion: "I don't see my mother growing older. [...]. So they left. I don't know when or how or why. Was it a pogrom that drove them out, or did someone bring them over?"[204]

Passages like these make us see that the theme of Perec's memoirs is the opposite of memory; it is the absence of memories. His narrative is hypothetical and tends to concentrate around crucial points. Essentially, this narrative is like memory, which often cannot be made to respond, simply because it lacks content; it is void. It seems that only looking at photos and a few dubious scraps of information from the family is all that allows Perec to go on with the story. But this narrative is primarily focused on limitations as its main theme; we may think

---

199 Perec, *W or the Memory of Childhood*, p. 32; in bold type in the original.
200 Perec, *W or the Memory of Childhood*, p. 6.
201 Perec, *W or the Memory of Childhood*, p. 27; the whole section in bold type in the original.
202 Perec, *W or the Memory of Childhood*, p. 28; the whole section in bold type in the original.
203 Perec, *W or the Memory of Childhood*, p. 30; the whole section in bold type in the original.
204 Perec, *W or the Memory of Childhood*, pp. 31–32; the whole section in bold type in the original.

of them as sealed memories. They are fantasies which the writer grasps so as not to remain silent while being unable to speak, as shown in the passages about the mother.

Perec resists the temptation to search for more information or indulge in more fantasies. He refuses to produce a type of writing that would not be difficult, we assume, if he were so inclined.

> I do not know whether I have anything to say, I know that I am saying nothing; I do not know if what I might have to say is unsaid because it is unsayable (the unsayable is not buried inside writing, it is what prompted it in the first place); I know that what I say in blank, is neutral, is a sign, once and for all, of a once-and-for-all annihilation.[205]

The greater number of pronouns in this passage ("what," "it") suggests that, like Federman, Perec has found a surrogate way of talking about the past. However, unlike the former's, his method is neither an experiment nor a substitution of a symbol (*preteritio*) for the thing referred to. If Perec is more restrained than Federman, that the restraint is verbal, not emotional. In what he ultimately says he does not follow any particular rhetorical strategies, a consequence demonstrated by Federman's *Take It or Leave It*. The one exception being the paradoxical statement that ends Chapter Eight: "Their [the parents'] memory is dead in writing; writing is the memory of their death and the assertion of my life."[206]

Holocaust *sous rature*

The third edition of Anatol Ulman's *Cigi de Montbazon* was published with an introduction by Krzysztof Uniłowski. Although the Holocaust is not the subject of the whole novel, but of a short, several-page-long passage, let us refer to this critic's statement, written as a general and introductory commentary. Uniłowski is speaking here about the extermination of the Jewish population and its literary representation:

> Impotence? Lack of legitimacy? But that is why it is necessary to tell instead of being silent! When the world turns out to be opaque [...], then storytelling takes on a special role. It reveals no truth. It delivers no knowledge. It teaches no useful skills. It does not commemorate anything. Ulman derides all these old illusions and aspirations. But he also shows that in such a situation a story becomes the only proof – or at least a piece of

---

[205] Perec, *W or the Memory of Childhood*, p. 42.
[206] Perec, *W or the Memory of Childhood*, p. 42. A separate issue and one that requires deeper reflection is the similarity between Perec's memoir and Michał Głowiński's *Czarne sezony*, unreliable memory being their common theme. Głowiński seems to have preserved many more memories, and his descriptions are more accurate and disciplined than Perec's. Perec's notes, on the other hand, could be called effusive; thy are more imaginative and critical of the cruel reality, which the author refuses to describe.

circumstantial evidence – of the existence of the world and the one who is doing the telling.[207]

In the light of the statements made by Perec ("I know that I am not speaking") and Halina Birenbaum ("I wish by this book to express my most fervent desire that similar crimes will never be repeated anywhere on this earth."[208]), Uniłowski's seems to sound like heresy. We need to remember, however, that he is not speaking about a particular historical event, and thus my verdict is merely hypothetical. As can be seen from my earlier remarks on the literature on the Holocaust, a story has a factual and reporting value. It refers (directly or not) to real events. It can be used as evidence of a crime. And above all, it can bear the burden of someone's life. If it is a first-person narrative, it bears the burden of the life of the survivor. However, Uniłowski seems to suggest that a story not only does not carry any burden, but that is does not concern reality at all. A story is a self-constituted proof. Uniłowski outlines another possible understanding: a story can be called an empty metonymy. A story can create an illusion of representation, but will be nothing but an illusion, confusing and empty inside. In fact, a story does not refer to anything. It does not reveal anything. It does not imply that narrative has the form of a shell concealing a drama which is conveyed to the reader through some means of indirect expression. Uniłowski's position may sound radical due to its questioning the social role of literature. Indeed, if we apply it to the Holocaust, this statement will strike us as excessively harsh, underpinned by a concept of postmodernism as a trend that is devoid of social involvement. Meanwhile, I want to argue that in his 1979 novel Ulman developed a radical way of talking about the past, one composed not only of hypotheses, but, more radially and straightforwardly, of denials.[209] These denials, however, do not belong in literally understood testimony; much less in one that purports to represent the Second World War.[210]

Uniłowski's introduction to *Cigi de Montbazon* in a number of points resembles Raymond Federman's essay "Surfiction – Four Propositions in Form of an Introduction," which opens a book published in 1975.[211] Writes Federman,

> And so, for me, the only fiction that still means something today is the kind of fiction that tries to explore the possibilities of fiction beyond its own limitations. [...]

---

207 Krzysztof Uniłowski, "Wstęp" [Introduction], in Anatol Ulman, *Cigi de Montbazon* (Koszalin: Millenium 2001), p. 5.
208 Birenbaum, *Hope Is the Last to Die*, p. 246.
209 As Uniłowski put this, "Yet in *Cigi de Montbazon* we have a type of narration which keeps questioning and negating itself." Krzysztof Uniłowski, "Opowieść znaleziona na śmietniku (*Cigi de Montbazon* Anatola Ulmana)," *Twórczość* 1998, nr 6, p. 52.
210 Uniłowski wrote about this in his essay published in *Twórczość* (see previous footnote).
211 Federman's essay "Surfiction: A Postmodern Position," was originally published in 1975 as "Surfiction: A Position." A Polish translation was published in 1983.

> This I call SURFICTION. However, not because it imitates reality, but because it exposes the fictionality of reality. Just as the Surrealists called that level of man's experience that functions in the subconscious SURREALITY, I call that level of man's activity that reveals life as fiction SURFICTION. [...]
> To create fiction today is, in fact, to transform reality, and to some extent even to abolish reality, and especially abolish the notion that reality is truth.[212]

The story of a thirteen-year-old boy called Franciszek,[213] covering the times of war, from September 1, 1939, to the outbreak of the Warsaw Uprising, and the history of his closest family are related in a special way to a magic garden.[214] This garden constitutes a kind of bulwark that protects the inhabitants from the influence of history. The story features the figure of Mr. Bełt and his children. Bełt is an episodic character of minor significance, which perhaps is why Uniłowski, who takes note of this, does not develop his statement about the "non-Aryan origin" of Franciszek and limits himself to a puzzling paraphrase. The narrator refers to a wealthy Jewish bank clerk, his wife and two twins, whose games are the object of Franciszek's fascination and envy:

> A boy, Arkadiusz (for some time I wanted to have such a name, used in the garden), brought me a book in which there was an illustration depicting Kronos devouring his own children... [...] I saw next to him [Mr. Bełt] children I never had, or children riding bicycles in the street [...]. In the garden, with the exception of Mr. Bełt's estate, no apricots or peaches grew. I don't think that Mr. Bełt's wife would have been willing to give me even one of the few fruits... .[215]

Krzysztof Kłosiński has commented on both these affects in his interpretation of *Cigi de Montbazon*. Reflection on desire, however, has led him to a place where we can hear Maurice Blanchot's statements about how it lies in the nature of language to replace reality:[216]

> Desire turns out to be, when analysis arrives at its logical conclusion, desire for annihilation. Its logic knows only the logic of the hangman and the victim. The only way out may lie in deviation, and the universality of this exit consists in a metaphorical game. By substituting a representation for the object of desire [...] deviation at once offers up the

---

212 Raymond Federman, "Surfiction: A Postmodern Position," in Raymond Federman, *Critifiction. Postmodern Essays* (Albany N.Y.: State University of New York Press, 1993), pp. 37–38.
213 The protagonist-narrator gives his approximate age in a way that suggests that we are dealing with a story fabricated by a much older person. We can thus assume that *Cigi de Montbazon* is a fictional story that imitates a genuine memoir, and therefore a story in which these two orders meet and overlap.
214 The topos of the garden is discussed by Uniłowski in "Opowieść znaleziona na śmietniku," pp. 53–54.
215 Ulman, *Cigi de Montbazon*, p. 104.
216 Cf. Maurice Blanchot, *Wokół Kafki*, trans. into Polish K. Kocjan (Warszawa: Wydawnictwo KR, 1996), pp. 28–29.

Holocaust *sous rature*

dying of the victim as a process which is concentrated in the representation [...] and extended indefinitely.[217]

To be sure, Kłosiński refers here to photographs of naked women and not to the Holocaust. However, he connects his interpretation of the passage about Mr. Belt's children with the problem of desire. Like language, desire must destroy its object if it wants to keep it. Yet since desire wants to stay with the object as long as possible, then, through a series of statements and denials, it destroys and re-creates the object indefinitely. In a similar way, Ulman creates a convenient opportunity to turn the story into a narrative laboratory of sorts, one in which fiction and reality are subjected to various tests and examinations. This is particularly evident in the following passage:

> On the bough of the apple tree [...] hung a factory-made swing, and the girl's swinging drew arcs like time's pendulum, and unripe fruit fell from the old tree and rotted, gathering a brown sediment. Over this wasting of apples, Zuza made regular returns in the air to the place abandoned a moment ago. Thus she existed not only in the projection of her father, but also in space, at some point of space, on this curve invented by geometry. A curve like that is only a concept, so [she existed] at some point of the concept and in a moment. This leads to no self-evident statements, especially because Zuza tended to get nauseous from the swinging, which is why she never actually sat on that thing ... .[218]

In this image, Ulman seems to negate everything: starting from the unripe apples that are about to rot, through the curve described by the swing's movement, to the very existence of Zuza, who is her father's projection and, above all, something that exists somewhere between the narrator's fantasy and memory. This momentary negation of existence, stretched between "bringing forth into existence" and "bringing back to life," i.e., creation and reproduction, refers us to the deletions known from the work of Martin Heidegger and Derrida as *sous rature*, used in postmodern fiction as a literary device. It seems, however, that in the case of *Cigi de Montbazon* we can detect more than a mere trick. We can say that Ulman's "supplanting of illocutions by suggestions"[219] points to the Derridean emptiness left by the present and experience.

It may be worth pausing at this point to ponder a conundrum, to ask this breakneck question: What are the differences in the literary ways of erasing the past between Federman, Perec and Ulman, on the one hand, and Heidegger and Derrida, on the other?

---

217 Krzysztof Kłosiński, *Eros. Dekonstrukcja. Polityka* (Katowice: Wydawnictwo Naukowe "Śląsk", 2000), p. 129.
218 Ulman, *Cigi de Montbazon*, pp. 104–105.
219 Uniłowski, "Opowieść znaleziona na śmietniku," p. 55.

Let us start with Perec, who, like Ulman, chooses a house as the site for a lesson on erasures of the Holocaust. His reflection is brought on by a recollection of his aunt Esther and her house. It was near that place that the author, then a teenage boy watched a man saw wood using a wooden saw-horse, "made of a pair of up-ended parallel crosses, each in the shape of an X (called a 'Saint Andrew's Cross' in French), connected by a perpendicular crossbar, the whole device being called, quite simply, an x" (W 76). He explains, "My memory is not a memory of the scene, but a memory of the word, only a memory of the letter that has turned into a word, of that noun which is unique in the language in being made of a single letter [...]" (W 77). He goes on to reflect that "it is also the sign of a word deleted (the string of x's crossing out the word you didn't mean to write) [...]" (W 77). The image of crossed bars making up the only letter "that has turned into a word," causes Perec to think about the Holocaust-related meanings hidden in symbols, "the major symbols of the story of my childhood" (W 77), the swastika, the SS sign, and the Star of David.[220] However, Perec puts them in a place where he could simply indulge in the story of his Jewish family under Nazi rule or the wartime history of the Jewish nation in general. Here symbols replace reality, and so to some extent they are reality's metonymy (to stay with the terminology I have repeatedly used here). But they can also be that "instead-of" of language, in so far as:

> Not only does it [language] strip existing things of their ontological reality, but it also seems to lack the ability to bring back the meaning of things which are now lost in the well of the past. It is incapable of preserving what it turns into the object of the representation, what it turns into an image or a metaphor. Talking about something, naming something equals blurring, destroying the presence of that something as the object of our speech.[221]

Therefore, instead of stories, there are in Perec's work – which in this respect is akin to Blanchot's thought – several empty symbols that seem to be devoid of any reference to reality. As part of language, a symbol tends to obliterate and eradicate reality; "Their memory is dead in writing [...]" (W 42).

Federman's prose, deletions in serve the task of masking reality. Thus, they create a ssituation in which the readers are to be deceived by the erasing of the original event and then surprised that that event is accompanied by a story which is constantly multiplied and repeated. "[T]he whole story crossed out my whole family parenthetically x-x-x-x into typographic symbols while I endure my

---

[220] He observes in passing that "Charlie Chaplin, in *The Great Dictator*, replaced the swastika with a figure that was identical, in terms of its segments, having the shape of a pair of overlapping Xs [...]" (W 77).

[221] Marek Zaleski, *Zamiast. O twórczości Czesława Miłosza* (Kraków: Wydawnictwo Literackie, 2005), p. 204.

survival from its implausible beginning to its unthinkable end," wrote Federman.[222] The figure called *praeteritio* was for Federman a perfect way simultaneously to erase and to write. *Praeteritio* is defined as a cunningly applied elision. "It may indeed be an omission of unimportant things, but when an omission has been announced and declared, [...] it becomes a form of irony."[223] Federman uses this figure on the very first page of *Double or Nothing*:

> his parents (both his father and mother) and his two sisters (one older and the other younger than he) had been deported (they were Jewish) to a German concentration camp (Auschwitz probably) and never returned, no doubt having been exterminated deliberately (X * X * X * X), and that, therefore, the young man who was now an orphan, a displaced person, who, during the war, had managed to escape deportation by working [...][224]

It would be difficult to refer to the information about the extermination of the author's loved ones in terms of erasing. After all, it is conveyed here despite the parentheses and the printing symbols, their role not limited to separating the general (the Holocaust) from the specific content (the death of the Federman Family); or to the loss of meaning. Parentheses and typographic signs attract the reader's attention and make her alert to the absolutely unambiguous meaning of the event (despite the ambiguous symbols!): four among the millions of other people who died in Auschwitz. This truth remains both visible and legible.

Ulman's solution is more complicated and consists in using, instead of typographic signs, a story made of statements and denials, reminiscent of Brian McHale's concept of an erased world. Here McHale differentiates this concept from Derrida's practice of *sous rature:*

> Of course, postmodernist fictions [...] place under erasure [*sous rature*] not signifiers of concepts in a philosophical discourse, but presented objects in a projected world; and their purpose is not, as with Derrida, that of laying bare the *aporias* of western metaphysics, but rather that of laying bare the processes by which readers, in collaboration with texts, construct fictional objects and worlds.[225]

But how are we supposed to relate the erasure of fictional worlds to the portrayed reality, that of the Holocaust? Defending Ulman's aesthetic sensitivity, Uniłowski argues that the author goes beyond modernist argumentation and, instead of exposing the shortcomings of literature and dwelling on the topos of inexpressibility, shows its inherent performative potential. Residing in motifs and

---

222 Federman, *The Voice in the Closet*, Section 10.
223 Jerzy Ziomek, *Retoryka opisowa* (Wrocław, Warszawa, and Kraków: Ossolineum, 2000), p. 232.
224 Federman, *Double or Nothing*, p. 0.
225 McHale, *Postmodernist Fiction*, p. 100.

plot formats, this potential also offers the author a means to express his ontological skepticism.[226]

However, if we regard *sous rature* as a mechanism related to the style of reception, we must admit that deletion not only hinders reading, but, by the very fact of the existence of additional signs, increases the reader's curiosity to discover what has been crossed out and to bring the thus blurred existence back to life, and then to understand why someone may have fiercely tried to negate life. *Sous rature*, as well as the series of denials and statements we encounter in *Cigi*, are part of the active reading that Federman talks about in the "Surfiction" essay.[227] This kind of story is not a story about "nothing," as Uniłowski would have it, as he follows the narrative thread.[228]

Images of blurred, hazy or crossed out memories of the Holocaust, which can be found in the post-modern narratives of the 1970s, are a *residuum* of the struggle for the articulation of the genocide. Its outcome is not a foregone conclusion, because each of the authors who decided to convey a representation of the past, which in itself seems doubtful, uses a paradoxical strategy of at once negating and confirming reflections on that past. If one wanted to show the differences between these authors, one would have to say that Perec, Federman and Ulman built their war-related work on denying its presence, stating its existence and doubting it. First and foremost, Perec's memoirs seem empty and devoid of designation. The paralyzing need to remember, most strongly developed in this author, leads to a sad conclusion: forgetfulness is stronger than love. The writer succumbs to it, trying not to go too far beyond what he has managed to recall from his childhood. Federman on the other hand expands his memory endlessly, using a variety of narrative techniques, foci, grammatical persons, and even the identities of the characters. In turn, everything we read in *Cigi de Montbazon* is an alternative. The story of Mr. Belt as part of surfiction can also be read as a Polish witness account (as indicated by the author's date of birth), or as a story of a person who at once observes the events of the war but is also a participant and an actor.

---

226 Uniłowski, *Opowieść znaleziona na śmietniku*, p. 56
227 "All the rules and principles of printing and bookmaking must be forced to change as a result of the changes in the writing (or the telling) of a story in order to give the reader a sense of free participation in the writing/reading process, in order to give the reader an element of choice (active choice) in the ordering of the discourse and the discovery of its meaning." Federman, "Surfiction: A Postmodern Position," p. 40 (section "Proposition One – The Reading of Fiction").
228 Uniłowski, *Opowieść znaleziona na śmietniku*, p. 55.

Chapter 4.
Climate of the Holocaust: Paweł Huelle, Tadeusz Konwicki, Andrzej Kuśniewicz, Piotr Szewc

Introduction: a climate of change

Telling the story of post-war Polish Holocaust literature, Bartłomiej Krupa uses a metaphor that is surprisingly close to the environmental history of the Holocaust. Calling the 1980s "the third phase in the treatment of Jewish topics in Poland" and a "discursive re-emergence,"[229] Krupa, like other researchers,[230] considers the most important and start-up event the broadcast of Claude Lanzmann's film *Shoah* on Polish Television in October 1985 and the publication of Jan Błoński's essay "Biedni Polacy patrzą na getto" [Poor Poles Look at the Ghetto] in *Tygodnik Powszechny* two years later.[231] The year 1987 brought "a veritable avalanche of publications,"[232] and, as Krupa puts it, it turned out to have

---

229 Bartłomiej Krupa, *Opowiedzieć Zagładę. Polska proza i historiografia wobec Holocaustu (1987–2003)* (Kraków: Universitas, 2013), p. 57.
230 Cf. Michael C. Steinlauf, *Bondage to the Dead: Poland and the Memory of the Holocaust* (Syracuse, NY: Syracuse University Press, 1997) pp. 110ff (Polish translation by Agata Tomaszewska as *Pamięć nieprzyswojona: polska pamięć zagłady* was published by Cyklady in 2001). See also Przemysław Czapliński, "Zagłada – niedokończona narracja polskiej nowoczesności," in: *Ślady obecności*, ed. Sławomir Buryła and Anna Molisak (Kraków: Universitas, 2010), pp. 341–345. Piotr Forecki, *Od "Shoah" do "Strachu". Spory o polsko-żydowską przeszłość i pamięć w debatach publicznych* (Poznań: Wydawnictwo Poznańskie, 2010), pp. 115–165.
231 Jan Błoński, "Biedni Polacy patrzą na getto," *Tygodnik Powszechny* (1987), nr 2, pp. 1, 4.
232 Bartłomiej Krupa, *Opowiedzieć Zagładę*, p. 60. Przemysław Czapliński was the first to use the phrase "rusza lawina" (an avalanche is on) to refer to the return of Jewish topics in the mid-1980s. Cf. Przemysław Czapliński, "Prześladowcy, pomocnicy, świadkowie. Zagłada i polska literatura późnej nowoczesności," in: *Zagłada. Współczesne problemy rozumienia i przedstawiania*, ed. Przemysław Czapliński and Ewa Domańska (Poznań: Wydawnictwo "Poznańskie Studia Polonistyczne," 2009), p. 155. The metaphors of storm (Pl. *burza*), explosion (Pl. *eksplozja*) and spring (Pl. *wiosna*) in reference to the same set of issues were used by Anna Mach in her book *Świadkowie świadectw. Postpamięć Zagłady w polskiej literaturze najnowszej* (Warszawa and Toruń: Fundacja na rzecz Nauki Polskiej, 2016), p. 115. However, the statements she makes later in this book, based on a limited choice of sources, undermine the relevance of the metaphors she uses, chiefly due to the fact that, in Mach's representation, the 1980s was a period with no new narrative and derivative in its use of "ste-

produced more than a harvest of important books, to be discussed ever since. It also brought an landslide of statements about the Holocaust, in which the researcher intuitively sees history and geology as a whole. In the light of my considerations – focused on the relationship between the Holocaust and the natural environment – this encounter between history and geology has important social and intellectual consequences.[233]

Krupa's geological metaphor, in which I would like to see more than just a witty phrase, covers numerous publications from the year 1987, including Henryk Grynberg's *Kadisz*, Andrzej Kuśniewicz's *Nawrócenie*, Piotr Szewc's *Zagłada*, Roman Zimand's *Piołun i popiół* and Ida Fink's *Skrawek czasu*[234] – all of them books which in just one year significantly enriched the Polish library of post-Holocaust literature. At the same time, this metaphor seems to deprive them of deeper connections and relationships. I would like to look more closely at one such connection, a common motif in four novels from the years 1986 and 1987 concerned with the environmental history of the Holocaust. The change in intellectual climate, which occurred in the 1980s decade as a result of the "thawing" and the subsequent "warming" of Jewish themes in Polish film, literary, political and journalistic discourse, was – in a metaphorical sense – recorded in four different variants in Tadeusz Konwicki's *Bohiń* (henceforth *Bohin Manor*), Andrzej Kuśniewicz's *Nawrócenie*, Piotr Szewc's *Zagłada* (henceforth *Annihilation*) and Paul Huelle's *Weiser Dawidek* (henceforth *Who Was David Weiser?*). This recording corresponds, at least in part, to the development of Jewish themes in Poland after 1985, and draws the reader's attention to their rapid return, devoid at that time of the outlines of a distinct phenomenon. While, in these novels, climatic reflection makes up a metaliterary layer in the most conventional sense, two other aspects seem to be of greater importance. One concerns the use of metonymy in telling about the Holocaust, as in references to history as well as violent weather phenomena. The other concerns climate change, in and outside Poland, which since the early 1980s has been perceived as the sum of human activities and natural factors,[235] and which, since the late 1980s and early 1990s,

---

reotypical images and literary perpetuations of former, also antisemitic, representations" (ibid., p. 225).

233 Geological metaphors in reflections to the Holocaust are chiefly found in Anne Michaels's 1996 novel *Fugitive Pieces*. Cf. F. Quenette Between, "Earth Science and Language/Writing Imagery: How to Render the Workings of Memory in Anne Michaels' *Fugitive Pieces*," at: http://www.oalib.com/paper/2936515#.V4e0OfmLRhE [access: 14.07.2016]. See also Catherine Coussens, "'Secrets of the Earth': Geology and Memory in Anne Michaels's *Fugitive Pieces*," *Annals of the University of Craiova*, Series: Philology, English, year XI, No.2 (2010), pp. 73–88.

234 Krupa, *Opowiedzieć Zagładę*, p. 61.

235 *Warunki klimatyczne i oceanograficzne w Polsce i na Bałtyku Południowym. Spodziewane zmiany i wytyczne do opracowania strategii adaptacyjnych w gospodarce krajowej*, ed.

has been part of the public debate on global warming, linked to the heightened awareness of the effects of globalization.[236]

Working assumptions and reservations

Let us take a look at the scene in Andrzej Kuśniewicz's *Nawrócenie* which depicts the expulsion of a group of Jewish people from a borderland town during the war:

> Then, I distinctly remember, the shadow of a great cloud covered the sunny meadows, white Augusts and golden Septembers with a heavy coating of fog and a streak of acrid smoke. With their hands raised above their heads or folded over their necks, they left their homes, our inn, two adjacent whitewashed buildings. God-fearing people, flinching at the idea of shaving their facial hair and exposing their heads to others. Someone said loudly beside me, peeking out of the window of a pink living room, "Oh, Berek, too... And Mojsze ..." [...]. As noted that day in a pocket diary: "Foggy since dawn. Rounded up this morning, all of them, from ours and two neighboring villages [...]. Today, as it had got cold, I put on, instead of the beige trousers, the brown tweed ones, and a suede jacket to match, bought a year before the war on Koertnerstrasse in Vienna." (N 59)[237]

Even though it may read like a memoir, this narrative is a hoax. Born in 1904, Kuśniewicz spent the war away from his hometown, Kowenice near Sambor (Sambir). After a stay in France, he became a prisoner of the Nazi torture camp in Neue Bremm and the concentration camp in Mauthausen.[238] He regarded *Nawrócenie* in terms of a debt which he "owed to the people about whose fate [he] learned only at the end of the war, in a concentration camp, from newly arrived people. Those were scraps of information. Details about what happened in Poland, [he] found out even later."[239] In the narrative recreated from such "scraps," in addition to the plausible story told by a witness, the author ascribes an important role to climate. The Jewish population is leaving the town in smoke and fog, the "shadow of a great cloud" hanging over their heads. The cloud takes on

---

Joanna Wibig, Ewa Jakusik (Warszawa: Instytut Meteorologii i Gospodarki Wodnej, Państwowy Instytut Badawczy, 2012), p. 5.
236 Cf. Dipesh Chakrabarty, "The Climate of History: Four Theses," *Critical Inquiry*, Vol. 35, No. 2 (Winter 2009), pp. 197–222.
237 References to the four novels are marked in the following way: N – *Nawrócenie* by Andrzej Kuśniewicz (Kraków: Wydawnictwo Literackie 1997); BM – *Bohiń* by Tadeusz Konwicki, *Bohin Manor*, English trans. Richard Lourie (New York: Farrar, Straus and Giroux, 1990); A – *Zagłada* by Piotr Szewc; *Annihilation*, English trans. Ewa Hryniewicz-Yarbrough (Normal, IL: Dalkey Archive Press, 1999); WWDW – *Weiser Dawidek* by Paweł Huelle, *Who Was David Weiser?*, English trans. Antonia Lloyd-Jones (London: Bloomsbury, 1991).
238 Andrzej Kuśniewicz, *Puzzle pamięci. Z Andrzejem Kuśniewiczem rozmawia Grażyna Szcześniak* (Kraków: Eureka, 1992), pp. 21–25.
239 Kuśniewicz, *Puzzle pamięci*, p. 67.

the role of a witness of the Holocaust, bestowing on the event a sublime character and emphasizing its tragic dimension. At the same time, however, it removes that event into the shadows, screens it from view and covers it up. We do not know why this is happening and whether the presence of the fog and smoke can be explained by the sudden climate change accompanying the extermination. What we do know is that this change in the weather has a completely different dimension for the narrator in that it makes him put on a warmer outfit. The last sentence of the quoted passage can be read as an authorial provocation due to the way it exposes the gap between the protagonist's historical ignorance and his concern with the immediate present. Borrowing a term from Harald Welzer, we can also see here an example of "shifting baselines," or changing "reference frameworks," a phenomenon important for both environmental psychologists and historians.[240] In Welzer's *Climate Wars*, "shifting baselines" refers to both people's disorientation towards the physical environment and the historical processes. Welzer illustrates the former with the images of meadows and moors, which for contemporaries are objects to admire rather than inspiring observations on progressing deforestation. The meaning of history in the making is typically impossible to grasp there and then, as in case of an excerpt from Franz Kafka's *Diaries* (on August 2nd, 1914), quoted by Welzer, "Germany has declared war on Russia. Swimming class in the afternoon."[241]

In my opinion, the Holocaust provides examples of distinct cases of shifting baselines, allowing us to combine Kuśniewicz's view with Welzer's argument. The environmental history of the Holocaust may help us to understand how this combination works. Jacek Małczyński hopes that further research may help us to fill a gap; he points out that there are "no studies of the representations of nature in depictions of the Holocaust or of the ways of handling nature in museums-memorial sites where concentration and death camps used to be."[242] According to Aleksandra Ubertowska, taking up "the issues of nature, landscape, the world of plants and animals in their relation to the Holocaust,"[243] underrepresented in the existing reflection on the Holocaust, has essential links with the subject matter of Holocaust narratives, which tend to bestow symbolic dimensions on landscape. By considering climate in its various dimensions, from passing re-

---

240 "[…] 'shifting baselines' – that is, the fascinating phenomenon that people change their perceptions and values along with their environment, without even realizing that they are doing it." Harald Welzer, *Climate Wars. Why People Will Be Killed in the Twenty-First Century*, trans. Patrick Camiller (Cambridge and Malden, MA: Polity Press, 2012), p. 7.
241 Welzer, *Climate Wars*, p. 143.
242 Jacek Małczyński, "Polityka natury w Auschwitz-Birkenau," *Teksty Drugie* 2014, nr 5, p. 141.
243 Aleksandra Ubertowska, "'Kamienie niepokoją się i staja się agresywne'. Holokaust w świetle ekokrytyki", *Poznańskie Studia Polonistyczne. Seria Literacka* (2015), nr 25 (45), p. 93.

marks in documents to fictional depictions, we can glean a great deal of important historical information and may be able better to understand the various ways of addressing the Holocaust contained, not only in witness accounts and other first-person narratives (as in Kuśniewicz), but also in metaphors and metonyms.

To preempt objections stirred by a reflection that combines Holocaust and climate issues, let us return to Welzer and his examination of some disturbing examples. Without bestowing on nature the status of an independent subject and agent, a position considered by Richard C. Foltz,[244] Welzer posits a close relationship between natural and human (or social) disasters. For him, the model example of such interdependence is the destruction of New Orleans in 2005 by Hurricane Katrina, which, as it were, exposed to public view the backstage of society and its dysfunctionalities. Another important case considered by Welzer is that of the wars among on Easter Island tribes, a genocide that started around the tenth century, set off by the felling of palm forests. "Ecological degradation led to erosion not only of the soil but also of human culture."[245] Considering primarily the conflicts at the turn of the twentieth and twenty-first centuries, for instance in Rwanda and Darfur, may help us place the Holocaust in a new context, that of climate wars and natural disasters. Despite having published extensively on the Holocaust, however, Welzer does not offer sufficient justification for this conceptual recontextualization of the Holocaust. Nor does he name the features of the Holocaust which make this disaster similar to those he is interested in.[246]

These doubts are worth examining in the context of Welzer's reflections on the antecedence of the Holocaust and, especially, its onset, which has caused him to observe that "Causality is not a category that applies to social relations; contexts of interdependence may involve striking tensions and concentrated processes of change, but nothing like a decisive cause to which all else can be traced back."[247] Is this not something that clearly separates the Holocaust from the climate wars preceded by the warnings of a catastrophe? At the same time, is not this a feature that helps us to see Polish novels from 1986 and 1987 in a new perspective? Welzer's work makes us pose several questions with which we can also address

---

244 Richard C. Foltz, "Does Nature Have Historical Agency? World History, Environmental History and How Historians Can Help Save the Planet," *The History Teacher* 37 (2003) No. 1, pp. 9–28.
245 Welzer, *Climate Wars*, p. 56.
246 For a discussion of the Holocaust in terms of an economic and geographical catastrophe, see Kenneth Hewitt's *Regions of Risk: A Geographical Introduction to Disasters* (Harlow: Longman, 1997), esp. Chapter 12, "The Holocaust genocide and geographical calamity" (pp. 321 ff).
247 Welzer, *Climate Wars*, p. 145.

this fiction: Why would a psychologist want to consider the Holocaust in the context of climate at all? Does he suggest that it makes sense to approach the Holocaust in terms of a climate war? Did its antecedents take the form of violent climatic phenomena? Is interpreting them outside (post)catastrophic poetics at all legitimate? One strategy that suggests itself upon reading Welzer's book, in which W. G. Sebald's *Rings of Saturn* plays an important role, would be to look at the Holocaust as a natural disaster,[248] one preceded by nature's extinction and terminating in nature's end.[249] Welzer autonomizes and absolutizes the Holocaust to such an extent that it comes to resemble metonymy in the sense proposed by Eelco Runia, for whom "a metonymy is a 'presence in absence' not just in the sense that it presents something that isn't there, but also in the sense that in the absence (or at least the radical inconspicuousness) that *is* there, the thing that isn't there is still present."[250]

In this chapter I am looking for answers to the following questions: What are the purposes of images of natural disasters in selected Holocaust-related novels from the 1980s? Does their occurrence at a similar time set up a distinct literary trend and justify studies oriented towards the relations between the Holocaust and climate? Since, if we want to understand these images, we must reject the view that they are or can be part of the discourse of inexpressibility or an example of literature's inability to identify and express social needs and expectations (also those related to the natural environment), I opt for metonymy as a leading rhetorical figure. On the one hand, metonymy makes possible the fluctuation of different time planes in the literary text. Thus, in *Bohin Manor*, for example, there is the time after the defeat of the January Uprising, the Second World War and the Holocaust; and in *Nawrócenie*, the Holocaust and the post-war era. On the other hand, metonymy gives us the opportunity to look in the text for content that lies beyond the presented story or a metaphor, and, occasionally, to read a text against authorial intentions. Runia, who originated this approach, calls it a stowaway journey of historical reality through historiography, emphasizing that the goal is to identify historical discontinuities or instances of the intertwining of

---

[248] Paweł Tomczok develops this concept in his essay "Naturalna historia katastrof. O naturze w prozie W. G. Sebalda," *ArtPapier* 2009, nr 3 (123), http://artpapier.com/index.php?page=artykul&wydanie=76&artykul=1788 [accessed 8.07.2016].

[249] Cf. Aleksandra Ubertowska, "Natura u kresu (ekocyd)", *Teksty Drugie* 2013, nr 1–2, s. 42. The essential difference between Ubertowska's reading of Sebald's and Welzer's interpretation has to do with how these two scholars perceive Nature. For Welzer, Nature is little more than a foreground for human war, which is why he goes from a description of the military training ground on the Suffolk coast in *The Rings of Saturn* to the remains of the Nazi camp Mittelbau-Dora, without stopping to look at wild plants. Ubertowska, on the other hand, emphasizes the "de-semantization" of Sebald's landscape and the relieving of the text by depriving Nature of a metaphorical dimension.

[250] Eelco Runia, "Presence," *History and Theory* 45 (2006), 20; emphasis in the original.

continuity and discontinuity.[251] As a consequence, the history that has been "captured" in this way (or retained in metonymic images) – just like the dry, hot summer in *Bohin Manor, Who Was Dawid Weiser?* and *Annihilation* – generates a *Stimmung*, a mood, a climate and an atmosphere.[252] These evoke associations with a catastrophe (a storm, a gale, a flood, a plague), but above all create signs of latent states of affairs, states which historian Hans Ulrich Gumbrecht associates with post-war calm saturated with "violent nervousness."[253] Gumbrecht has examined how the war experience was "put to sleep," as it were, in post-war photos. For instance, those published in the *Life* magazine issue of December 24, 1945, show smiling young wives of American soldiers with small children. Images of this kind made Gumbrecht pause and ask: "So how, then, can we describe the strange presence of a past that did not disappear, even though it seemed to have lost its impact? Didn't something in the decade following 1945 vanish rather than 'emerge'?"[254]

In both cases – Gumbrecht's reflections on the place of war in the history of the post-war world and the climatic reflection on the Holocaust in the four Polish novels – we can speak about the kind of presence that Gumbrecht, after Runia, defines with the help of the metaphor of the stowaway.[255] Latency resembles an atmosphere or a general mood, something barely sensed and elusive, yet something that resists simple interpretation in the sense of pulling the hidden meaning out, as it were, and bringing it to the surface. The fullness of calm intensifies the experience of violence, Gumbrecht seems to suggest, as he examines some post-war photos, one of a volcanic eruption and another of a razor touching a baby's cheek. By the same token, images of a storm or a flood after a hot summer can be thought of as either accompanying representations of the Holocaust or as replacing them. Descriptions of changes in the weather in these novels are not only part of a larger discourse about history, but also an essential component of a message about the present and the future. They are ambiguous in that they may obscurely hint at the history of the Holocaust or of Polish-Jewish

---

251 "One might say that historical reality travels with historiography not as a paying passenger but as a stowaway. As a stowaway the past 'survives' the text; as a stowaway the past may spring surprises on us." Runia, "Presence," p. 27.
252 "Something like a disposition of violent nervousness permeates the seemingly quiet postwar world, which points to a latent state of affairs. I would like to employ the German concept of *Stimmung* as the basis for describing [...] this complex configuration." Hans Ulrich Gumbrecht, *After 1945: Latency as Origin of the Present* (Stanford, CA: Stanford University Press, 2013), p. 24
253 Gumbrecht, *After 1945*, p. 21.
254 Gumbrecht, *After 1945*, p. 22.
255 Gumbrecht, *After 1945*, p. 23; "In a situation of latency, when a stowaway is present, we sense that something (or somebody) is there that we cannot grasp or touch – and that this 'something' (or som3body) has a material articulation, which means that it (or he, or she) occupies space."

relations before and during the war. But they are revelatory as well, e. g., by conveying the mood prevailing in Poland towards climate change in the 1970s and 1980s, as well as the beginnings of the literary history of the environment. Finally, they do not create metaphors with no content; rather, they express the authors' concern for the climate, combining the narrative of the Holocaust with an attitude of vigilance towards changes taking place in the natural environment.

Because none of these metonymic novels is a Holocaust or post-Holocaust novel in Efraim Sicher's sense of this term,[256] I propose to use the phrases "a novel about the Holocaust" or "Holocaust-related fiction" in a very general sense. Especially in the case of Konwicki's *Bohin Manor* or Szewc's *Annihilation*, we find numerous other associations and factual historical statements. In Huelle's novel, on the other hand, the Holocaust is an important background for the biography of its protagonists, connected with the ghetto in Brody, where Dawid Weiser's parents may have died.[257] But here the main action of the plot takes place in 1957. Only in the case of the extensive retrospective passages in *Nawrócenie* can we speak of a Holocaust narrative in both the literal and metaphorical layers of the work.

Two case studies: *Bohin Manor* and *Nawrócenie*

The juxtaposition of *Bohin Manor* with *Nawrócenie*, *Who Was David Weiser?* and *Annihilation* is not a new idea. Parallels were brought up both by reviewers of the 1987 novel, for whom Konwicki's prose was a frame of reference, as well as authors of larger studies, including those by Jerzy Jarzębski and Przemysław Czapliński. However, so far there has been no attempt to reflect on climate as an angle which may show the matter of the Holocaust in a new light.[258] The ecocide described in these novels has usually been reductively treated in observations

---

256 Sicher based both these terms on obvious criteria, namely, the breadth and accuracy of the treatment of the subject and the author's biographical connection with the Holocaust. Yet he sometimes deviates from them, for example, when he refers to Jaroslaw Marek Rymkiewicz's *Umschlagplatz* (1988; *The Final Station: Umschlagplatz*, 1994), and Andrzej Szczypiorski's *Poczatek* (*Beginning*, 1988) as post-Holocaust novels. These novels "were written before the fall of the communist regime but explore the taboo relations of Jews and Poles against the background of renewed interest in Jewish culture and growing awareness of Poland's shameful past." Efraim Sicher, *The Holocaust Novel* (New York and London: Routledge, 2005), p. 41.
257 I write about this in my book *Metonimie Zagłady. O polskiej prozie lat 1987–2012* (Katowice: Wydawnictwo Uniwersytetu Śląskiego 2013), pp. 281–287.
258 Jerzy Jarzębski, *Apetyt na Przemianę. Notatki o prozie współczesnej* (Kraków: Znak, 1997), p. 44; Przemysław Czapliński, *Zagłada – niedokończona narracja*, pp. 341; 351.

related to apocalyptic and catastrophic metaphorics, as in the case of Arkadiusz Morawiec's comment on Piotr Szewc's novel:

> The novel does not show an annihilation in the first sense of the word [of the Holocaust, Pl. *Zagłada Żydów* – M.T.] directly. Hence the misunderstandings. However, it [the Holocaust] is foreshadowed by numerous signs and portents [...]. On the surface, the catastrophe does not seem to concern people; the word occurs in reference to natural phenomena – rain, flood, drought, and fire – and functions "merely" as a reference point for comparison. [...] One of the signs, a truly prophetic foreboding of misfortune, is the repeatedly mentioned meteorite that fell somewhere outside the city, also appearing in the form of a fiery ball with a smokey tail and sparks [...].[259]

Krzysztof Rutkowski writes about *Bohin Manor* in a similar fashion:

> In Tadeusz Konwicki's latest novel *Bohiń* [*Bohin Manor*], thunder comes rolling and a strange brightness radiates from the earth and the sky, unforeseen and terrifying. The end-of-summer heat reigns, hovering in timelessness among fading colors. The author's grandmother, Mrs. Helena Konwicka, hears this terrible sound. And he hears it, too, because time placed him here, on a patch of Lithuanian land on the eve of the great apocalypse, and bade him retrace and record his own life story and our common history.[260]

What brings these novels together is the image of a hot, dry summer. Writes Huelle: "The first days of July were passing by, and, deprived of the bay, in the sweltering, sultry weather the city seemed hardly able to breathe, as the fish soup grew thicker and thicker, giving the local authorities ever greater worries. [...] It was also noted that for two whole months, since the beginning of May, that is, not a single drop of rain had fallen; [...]" (WWDW 22). The protagonists of *Bohin Manor* complain about lack of "a breath of air" (BM 7) and "scorching" heat (BM 7), which are supposed to bring about a change in the weather, anticipated by swallows, gadflies, and rooks. In *Annihiation*, there is a drought in July; "[...] if the weather is fine and if it's warm, like today, the water in those tiny swaps will dry and disappear with no trace. The worm [...] will disintegrate into unidentifiable pieces" (A 27). Only in *Nawrócenie* is the heat wave interrupted by a rainless, dry storm, strong as a whirlwind. "And someone was telling us that everything that could get off the ground did, and things just flew round. A veritable whirlwind if there ever was one. A cyclone" (N 144–145). Apart from comments to the effect that the summer drought was "the hand of irate God" (N 144) or "a sign of heavenly retribution" (DW 22), the authors do not give reasons

---

[259] Arkadiusz Morawiec, *Literatura w lagrze. Lager w literaturze. Fakt – temat – metafora* (Łódź: Publikacje Wydawnictwa AHE w Łodzi, 2009), pp. 339–340.
[260] Krzysztof Rutkowski, "Tadeusz Konwicki: szósta pieczęć," *Kultura Paryska* 1988, nr 7–9, p. 207. In Polish, the word *los* (esp. in the plural form, *losy*) conveys the sense of both "life story" and "fate."

for this rich imagery of changing weather, and yet this sheer abundance is truly puzzling. In *Bohin Manor*, we constantly read about floods, storms, downpours, sounds from under the ground, comets, and meteorites. Most frequently, however, because as many as five times, occurs the motif of the storm. Even the January Uprising reminds the narrator of "a summer storm" (BM 23), one that "erupted suddenly" and then "blew over quietly." This seems to be a puzzling association due to fact that that historical event is associated with winter (Pl. *Powstanie Styczniowe*). In *David Weiser*, the prevailing images are ones of land scorched by a furious sun and, perhaps more disturbingly, of poisoned sea: "[t]housands of sticklebacks, floating bellies upwards, were bobbing on the lazy rhythm of the waves, in a belt of corpses several metres wide. Just dipping your hand into the water was enough to make their clinging scales glitter like chain mail, but it was by no means a pleasant sensation. Instead of a bathing place we had a fish soup, a sigh to make you spit with disgust. [...] Over the next few days the soup thickened, turning into a fetid, sticky sludge" (WWDW 10). And then, "One day we went to Jelitkowo to check the state of the fish soup, and what we saw surpassed all our blackest forebodings. For here in the stagnant water, [...]" (WWDW 85). Szewc tends to focus on a catastrophic flood, which can appear in a nightmare, as in this passage: "In a week or two or a month Mr. Hershe Baum, the owner of the fabric store [...] will not even remember last night's nightmarish dream, which he didn't expect or deserve. In his dream the town was flooded. Human heads floated in the water— his own, his wife Zelda's, and their five children's— surely the heads of half the people in town" (A 5). It can also have the form of water and beer spilled on a table in a tavern (Pl. *szynkwas*):

> As if to annihilate and eradicate from memory the landscape of threads and drops. (We remember: Rainstorms that raged for more than a week over the region left puddles, microscopic swamps in which water was distilled through leaves and time. Among larger clumps of grass — cocksfoot, timothy, rye. Among clusters of white clover, yarrow. In the holes left by horses' hooves.) Like the flood that drowns the town or destroys the harmony of the spring meadow . . . the drought that dries out tiny meadow swamps . . . the fire that burns everything. *Go back a few steps and turn your face away.* (A 29; italics in the original)

In all four novels, there are recurring images of a comet and falling meteorites:

> But Miss Helena did not know it was meteorites falling, nor did she know that a comet was also flying somewhere above in icy space, later to vanish in one of the Milky Way's infinite ruts. (BM 40)

> In the distance, where the meteorite fell into a field of grain, a rushing, rumbling train stops. A trail of sparks shoots up, hissing, into the darkness. (A 106)

> There were also some who'd seen a comet in the shape of a horse's head, moving in a circle over the city, and those who had seen it swore the comet would return after orbiting the earth, to fall with dreadful force. (WWDW 86)
>
> The tail of the comet sweeps the houses on the coast, the boarding houses, the hotels, the empty Strand; and a moment later, turning sideways, it glides upon the gentle humps of the waves rising and falling in a slow rhythm. (N 123)

To show how these phenomena are linked to the Holocaust, I will limit my discussion to two novels, *Bohin Manor* and *Nawrócenie*, this choice motivated, among other things, by the exceptional descriptive intensity of their images of Nature and the violence of the atmospheric phenomena they convey. Moreover, this literary material helps us to discern a twofold pattern in metonymies of the Holocaust: the Holocaust itself and its anticipations.

In Konwicki's novel, the relationship between the Jewish man Eliasz Szyra and the Polish woman Helena Konwicka seems to be latent. It has been read not only as a romance, but also as an invitation to a serious discussion on Polish-Jewish relations in the nineteenth and twentieth centuries.[261] The figure of Schickelgruber, a cannibal and a folk incarnation of Adolf Hitler, is Konwicki's symbol of the Holocaust. Schickelgruber haunts the forests of the Vilnius region and burns down Jewish villages. He is also responsible for the most violent storm in *Bohin Manor*, which everyone is anticipating as though in expectation of the end of the world. Konwicki calls it "Schickelgruber's night," who "loves to burn people. Especially Jews" (BM 140). During that night, which resembles an earthquake, Helena cries out: "Let him [Schickelgruber – M.T.] finally burn us all up, our houses, our woods, our cemeteries!" (BM 238). The beginning of the storm resembles the first moments of war:

> Flying low to the ground, the birds fled to the secret hiding places where they ride out storms; people were running from field to farm.
> The sky was flashing more all the time [...]. Those sinuous ripples of pale-blue light cut silently through the dark blue of the sky and might have seemed only the thunderless summer lightning that is so frequent on airless nights, some errant reflection of a distant storm killing other people's animals in the fields and setting other people's houses on fire.
> But then, after one of those mute flashes, a rumbling seemed to rite from the ground, and finally lightning struck somewhere near Milowidy [...].
> [...] The old trees with their black trunks had sprung to life, soughing and sighing. At times a branch or dead trunk would crack, making a miniature thunder for gnomes. Then she heard the first spatter of rain on the leaves, raindrops the size of cherries mixed in with huge hail.

---

261 Still, not all accepted this invitation. One of the most negative critical voices demanded that "*Bohin Manor* ought not to be read along the parameters defined by the fashion for Jewish themes." Cf. A.N. [Anna Nasalska] *Bogini*, in: *Kultura Niezależna* 1988, nr 43, p. 110.

[…]
[…] Her father was looking out the window at a world grown dark and gray, the little world of Bohin to which the end of the world had indeed come.
[…]
[…] He looked straight out the bare window and waited. A rose-colored glow was now spreading from the heart of the forest. A little backwater [Pl. *zaścianek*] or dying, resinous woods was ablaze. (BM 133–135)

Szyra, however, is killed not by lightning but by Helena's father, a Pole. This is not a neighborly murder, but a nobleman's. It is based on the disgrace that Helena committed when she became pregnant by a Jew. The Holocaust presented in the form of a storm unleashed by the German man-eater thus becomes a background for showing individual Jewish-Polish fates, created by situations known from the last war, such as hiding and killing Jews by Poles, the Polish contempt and haughtiness towards Jewish neighbors and the participation of Jewish people in Polish politics. However, Konwicki does not seem to be occupied here with a past to be "represented,"[262] but with what may be called "anticipatory retrospection,"[263] that is, a project in which the past is related to the future, and the present creates shifting baselines. One of the reference points is the destruction of the whole area: "[…] *and though it* [this valley] *perish, vanish, fade away, heaped over with time and history, it will yet live, borne over the earth in the particles of our, in the cells of our memory, and in the vestigial relics of our sacrilege that shall roam infinity above*" (BM 132; italics in the original). This universal destruction is being observed by the contemporary narrator, who, through a huge flood, makes it "to that other shore" (BM 4). In Konwicki, the annihilation of plants, people and animals is foreshadowed by a deep and terrifying sound, like "sighing," that comes from under the surface of the earth (BM 39). Helena hears it most often and identifies it with her "immense fatigue" (BM 171). It seems that it was in this sound that Konwicki tried to crystallize, as it were, his various fears, both ecological and political. This representation makes one think of Fred Pearce's vision of the earth as "a wild beast, ready and able to react violently and precipitously once it is sufficiently roused."[264] As Pearce puts it: "She [Nature] is strong and packs a serious counter-punch. […] Nature's revenge for man-made global warming will very probably unleash unstoppable planetary forces. And they will be sudden and violent."[265]

---

262 Runia, "Presence," p. 17.
263 Harald Welzer has borrowed this phrase from Alfred Schütz (Schütz's essay "Tiresias, or Our Knowledge of Future Events"); Welzer, *Climate Wars*, p. 169.
264 Anthony Giddens, *The Politics of Climate Change* (Cambridge and Malden, MA: Polity Press, 2009), p. 27.
265 Fred Pearce, *The Last Generation* (2007), qtd. after Giddens, *The Politics of Climate Change*, p. 27.

Kuśniewicz's *Nawrócenie* is, in a sense, a response to Pearce's warning in its representation of the Holocaust as a violent climate breakdown caused by harmful human activity. It resembles, not so much an ecocidal retaliation of irate Nature, as a kind of revenge that is incomprehensible and unjust in that it is inflicted on Jewish people only. The protagonist-narrator's former Jewish acquaintances, residents of Kowenice and Sambor, urge him to describe his pre-war memories of the Jewish population:

> I look around – and no one here. As if swept away. The dust only swept away by a sudden gust circled, rose to the height of the town hall tower. A veritable whirlwind. And down below danced various cigarette butts, apple cores, old train tickets, nay, lottery tickets [...]. The wind blows from the city towards the fields and the river. From the narrow alleys of the forbidden, closed district, called "Zarzecze." And from the vicinity of a small suspicious hotel on the corner of Berka Joselewicz Street. (N 101)

More vivid still is Kuśniewicz's description of the pogrom of the Jewish population of Sambor. These people die from the plague caused by the "low cloud of Shoah"[266] (N 118):

> Well, all because of... that great plague. Their mouths and noses are clogged with cotton wool and rags. These rags are saturated with some yellow oil, to offer as much protection as feasible from the venomous breath. This evil breath, this poisoned air – say those who know – usually creeps close to the ground. Most often just above the corpses piling up everywhere, soon to be cleared away [...]. Bad smells, poisoned particles of the air also seep through cracks in the planks which have been used to board up window frames in empty apartments on the upper storeys. (N 118)

Submitting the finished novel for publication long before 1987, Kuśniewicz could not have foreseen the consequences of the Chernobyl nuclear disaster which had occurred a year earlier. In particular, he could not have known the effects of the radioactive cloud, which, moving towards Scandinavia, stopped over the Opole region, causing radiocesium concentrations in the vicinity of Olesno and Łambinowice, which was one hundred times higher than the average contamination in Poland at that time.[267] However, knowing the consequences of that event, allows us to see in the "Shoah cloud" more than a product of authorial fantasy. The metonymy of the Holocaust reveals to the reader two catastrophes simultaneously: one that actually affected the Jewish population of Sambor and one that could have affected that population, although it affected other people at a completely different time.

One could ask why Kuśniewicz presents the Holocaust as a windstorm, a whirlwind, or a hurricane destroying everything, and whether his narrative re-

---

266 This spelling in the original.
267 Anna Grudzka, "Co nam zostało po Czarnobylu," http://www.nto.pl/magazyn/reportaz/art/4166081,co-nam-zostalo-po-czarnobylu,id,t.html [accessed 10.07.2023].

duces climate change to a metaphor. The frequency with which gusty winds and hurricanes occur in it allows us to assume that Kuśniewicz understands the Holocaust as something entirely different than the end of the human world. After all, the devastating storm also destroys the ecosystem, including plants and animals, leaving behind devastation and harvest failure. This seems to be suggested by a scene which, as it were, accompanies the pogrom of the Jewish community and depicts a massacre of birds: "It was said that even birds were hurled sideways and from top to bottom, their wings breaking, their beaks pried open and hoarse with screaming" (N 153). At the same time, it is difficult to agree with the statement that the metonymy of the Holocaust prevented Kuśniewicz or Konwicki from speaking about Polish-Jewish relations before, during and after the war. What *Bohin Manor* shows on the example of the drama of several people, Kuśniewicz's novel presents in the form of bold statements and generalizations, making him, next to Roman Zimand, the author of the 1987 novel *Piołun and Popiół*, one of the harshest critics of both Polish anti-Semitism and Jewish polonophobia. It is in *Nawrócenie* that we find the following passage: "If it had not been for the active participation of the authorities, but not only, because society was not blameless, Drancy would not have been possible, or mass deportations to Auschwitz, handing people over to the Germans, round-ups organized with the participation of various Légion and fascist youth organizations" (N 190). And it is also here that we find the remark that ties *Bohin Manor*, a novel about a Jewish insurgent, with Kuśniewicz's novel: "And what about the many Jewish patriots in the January Uprising?" (N 191).

Climate change: an ending

Temporal fluctuations that make up metonymies open up another possibility of understanding them, close above all to the authors themselves: the possibility of expressing in images of the Holocaust concerns about the climate and its changes in Poland in the 1980s. When asked about it directly, Piotr Szewc did not rule out this possibility, although he considered it unlikely. However, he stated that, at the time when he was writing *Zagłada* (1981–1983), the winter of the century in the late 1970s was very much alive in his memory.[268] Meanwhile, both the publications of the Polish Institute of Meteorology and Water Management and the works of Antony Giddens and Naomi Klein show that although climate change, most often associated with warming, made itself felt only in the 2000s, some of its effects began to appear as early as the 1980s. Until 1988, air pollution in Poland

---

268 The author's comments made during a private conversation on July 5th, 2016.

stayed at a very high level.[269] According to Krzysztof Klejnowski, Wioletta Rogula-Kozłowska and others, "in the 80s, the economic losses Poland sustained as a result of air pollution amounted to about 5% of national income."[270] To get a better picture, it is worth comparing this with the achievements of environmental leaders. From the early eighties, Sweden began to use nuclear and hydropower, while reducing the import of fossil fuels, and in 1980 it held a referendum among its citizens, the results of which forced the country to "phase out nuclear power."[271] In Germany, the shutting down of many nuclear power plants and a significant increase in the production of electricity from renewable sources, making this country the world leader in the area of wind and solar energy, was the result of decisions from the early 1980s.[272] In 1988, the United Nations International Panel on Climate Change (IPCC) was established. Its experts estimate that an increase in global temperature exceeding 3°C will cause "the Greenland ice pack" to melt, "a process which, once it gets under way, would be impossible to reverse."[273] This handful of data should make us realize that 1980s – not only globally, but also for Western Europe – saw the first serious measures undertaken to handle and slow down global warming.

IMGW analyses show that the 1980s in Poland was a warm and, above all, dry period. The year 1980 was an exception; next to 1956, it was the coldest year in Poland in the years 1951–2008.[274] On the other hand, "the lowest average area rainfall occurred in 1982 and was the result of an 11-month drought (lasting from February to December)."[275] Droughts, which in Poland had the character of a weather anomaly, occurred intermittently from 1982 to 1984, causing destruction and difficulties, primarily in agriculture.[276] A strong minimum of the average area annual degree of total cloudiness was recorded in 1982. In turn, the years 1980–

---

269 Krzysztof Klejnowski, Wioletta Rogula-Kozłowska, Barbara Błaszczak, Leszek Ośródka, Ewa Krajny, "Problemy zanieczyszczeń powietrza," in: *Zmiany klimatu a monitoring i prognozowanie stanu środowiska atmosferycznego*, ed. Michał Ziemiański, Leszek Ośródka (Warszawa: Instytut Meteorologii i Gospodarki Wodnej Państwowy Instytut Badawczy 2012), p. 111.
270 Ibid.
271 Giddens, *The Politics of Climate Change*, p. 75.
272 Giddens, *The Politics of Climate Change*, pp. 76–77.
273 Giddens, *The Politics of Climate Change*, p. 25.
274 Danuta Limanówka, Dawid Biernacik, Bartosz Czernecki, Ryszard Farat, Janusz Filipiak, Tomasz Kasprowicz, Robert Pyrc, Grzegorz Urban, Ryszard Wójcik, "Zmiany i zmienność klimatu od połowy XX wieku," in: *Warunki klimatyczne i oceanograficzne w Polsce i na Bałtyku Południowym. Spodziewane zmiany i wytyczne do opracowania strategii adaptacyjnych w gospodarce krajowej*, ed. Joanna Wibig and Ewa Jakusik (Warszawa: Instytut Meteorologii i Gospodarki Wodnej, Państwowy Instytut Badawczy 2012), p. 8.
275 Ibid., p. 18.
276 Leszek Łabędzki, Jacek Leśny, "Skutki susz w rolnictwie – obecne i przewidywane w związku z globalnymi zmianami klimatycznymi," *Wiadomości melioracyjne i łąkarskie* 2008, nr 1, pp. 7–9.

1989, especially against the background of the seventh decade of the last century, happened to be windy, with a predominance of gusty winds (mainly in 1985 and 1989).[277] It is worth noting that it was only after 2005 that the most destructive hurricanes and cyclones, such as Britta, Kyrill and Emma, reached Poland.[278] This does not change the fact that the decade in question is distinguished by significant weather changes when compared to previous decades.

Could this type of information have had any effect on the plot of the novels we are discussing here, and especially as regards their latent layer? Let us recall that it is in the nature of a complicated system of latent content, or rather a weave of meanings that does not create any system, that we can never be sure of its existence. Certainty in this respect would contradict the latent content which, according to Gumbrecht, is *not* hidden from view, which is precisely what prevents us from extracting it through interpretation.[279] In addition, the probability that Holocaust metonymies permeate climate-related content is at least as likely, if not more so, as in the case of apocalyptic-catastrophic references. There is, however, one major difference. Claus Leggewie and Harald Welzer point out that to interpret erratic climatic phenomena as supernatural occurrences was typical of pre-modern times.[280] The context for the emergence of the term "catastrophe" was primarily socio-cultural, causing its understanding to be narrowed to sudden events, e.g., an explosion or a sudden cessation. The term "climate change" has a scientific dimension in this context and indicates a gradual, often foreseeable process of growth,[281] as in the case of the effects of Hurricane Katrina, which hit New Orleans in 2005, partially described in 2001 by Scientific American.[282]

I think that it is beneficial to consider images of the Holocaust in the context of climate change, as well as to pay attention to what kind of insight about the Holocaust they convey. Moreover, this approach allows us to see in the fiction of the 1980s a new and boldly formulated thesis about how climate-oriented thinking links genocide and ecocide together, a thesis that confirms the generally accepted insights about this fiction's conciliatory and history-blurring charac-

---

277 Halina Lorenc, "Struktura maksymalnych prędkości wiatru w Polsce," in: *Klęski żywiołowe a bezpieczeństwo wewnętrzne kraju*, ed. Halina Lorenc (Warszawa: Instytut Meteorologii i Gospodarki Wodnej, Państwowy Instytut Badawczy 2012), p. 36.
278 Halina Lorenc, "Struktura maksymalnych prędkości wiatru w Polsce," p. 42. Cf. https://pl.wikipedia.org/wiki/Orkan_Britta.
279 "No 'methods' or standard procedures – and certainly no 'interpretation' – exist that permit us to retrieve what has passed into latency." Gumbrecht, *After 1945*, p. 45.
280 Claus Leggewie and Harald Welzer, *Koniec świata, jaki znaliśmy. Klimat, przyszłość i szanse demokracji*, trans. Piotr Buras (Warszawa: Krytyka Polityczna 2012), p. 31.
281 Ibid.
282 Welzer, *Climate Wars*, p. 25.

ter.[283] As noted by Ewa Domańska in reference to ecological humanities, this approach, radically different from the vision of reality in terms of a pyramidal metaphor, is embedded in such concepts as tangled relationships, networks, kinships, and communities.[284] In the case of the metonymy of the Holocaust, it is impossible to talk about a simple impact of scientific observations or the results of environmental research on literature. Rather, what I am proposing here is a vision of ecological disasters in a broad perspective, as catastrophes that bring about the erosion of culture and cultural reference systems which may be found applicable and conducive to the Holocaust as well.[285]

---

[283] As pointed out chiefly by Przemysław Czapliński, who, referring to Andrzej Szczypiorski's *Początek* and *David Weiser*, used two valuable phrases: "the melancholy of alienated and estranged Poles" ("melancholia osamotnionych Polaków") and "Jews without the Holocaust" ("Żydzi bez Holokaustu"). Anna Mach wrote explicitly about silences in the literature of the 1980s, especially as concerns *Annihilation*, putting its complexities down to the use of Aesopic language allegedly deriving from weakness and fear (of the book's author? of the times? of literature?). Cf. Czapliński, *Zagłada – niedokończona narracja*, pp. 345–355; Mach, *Świadkowie świadectw*, p. 218.
[284] Domańska, "Humanistyka ekologiczna" [Ecological Humanities], *Teksty Drugie* 2013, nr 1–2, p. 27.
[285] Leggewie and Welzer, *Koniec świata*, p. 30.

Chapter 5.
Liquid Foundations: Walter Abish and D. M. Thomas

Postmodernism of the 1980s, and not only in Polish literature, seems above all to be a hybrid. While in the United States, the experimental trend dominated the literary scene, in Poland only a few postmodern novels were being written, which in relation to the fiction of Marek Słyk and Anatol Ulman, published at the end of the previous decade,[286] can be seen as a continuation of neo-avant-garde and "new prose." After 1987, this year being the terminus of Krzysztof Uniłowski's narrative in his study of these phenomena, the character of Polish fiction changes. Four novels discussed in the previous chapter, Tadeusz Konwicki's *Bohin Manor*,[287] Andrzej Kuśniewicz's *Nawrócenie*, Paweł Huelle's *Who Was David Weiser?* and Piotr Szewc's *Annihilation*, may be said to have consecrated and preserved the Holocaust-related variant of Polish postmodernism. The narrative about the Holocaust emerging from these novels has no neo-avant-garde ambitions (with minor exceptions). Instead, it tells a story about a search for roots, which some would consider a betrayal of postmodernism.[288] Moreover, it favors traditional and single-person autobiography. In the background, one can discern a glowing if barely visible admission of longing for the departed Jewish population, bracketed off by the metonymization of the Holocaust, a feature all four novels share in common.[289] "We became the beneficiaries of this

---

[286] On this fiction in the context of the postmodernism of the 1970s and 1980s, see Krzysztof Uniłowski, "Postmodernizm w prozie a debaty krytyczne 1970–1987," in *Postmodernizm po polsku? Acta Universitas Lodziensis. Folia Scientae Artium et Litterarium*, no. 8, ed. Agnieszka Izdebska and Danuta Szejnert (Łódź: Wydawnictwo Uniwersytetu Łódzkiego 1998), p. 35–52.

[287] I regard this novel as representative of the "turn of 1987," but only for ideological reasons, while bearing in mind that it was published in 1986.

[288] Cf. Konrad C. Kęder's sharp if understandable response to the publication of *David Weisera*. The critic calls this novel a case of "mythography" and describes it in terms of "the root outgrowing the fiction." Konrad C. Kęder, *Wszyscy jesteście postmodernistami! Szkice o literaturze lat dziewięćdziesiątych XX wieku* (Katowice: FA-art, 2011), p. 103.

[289] On the melancholy longing in Huelle's book, see Jerzy Jarzębski, *Apetyt na Przemianę. Notatki o prozie współczesnej* (Kraków: Znak, 1997), pp. 44–48 and Przemysław Czapliński,

sublimity, which was underpinned by the absence of Jewish people," wrote Przemysław Czapliński,[290] referring primarily to the socially treacherous insincerity on which these plots were built, a trait both important and strongly affecting the audience.

The fictions of Walter Abish, Paul Auster, Raymond Federman and D. M. Thomas were shaped in very different ways, deprived of the feature of the kind of sublimity just mentioned, which would have supplied them with a common denominator. In the context made up by these authors' work, *Nawrócenie* shines like a shooting star, even though in Poland's latest literary history it has received less recognition than the novels by Konwicki, Szewc and Huelle.[291] In this chapter, I will be interested in those few novels which, if we focus on their manner of narrating the Holocaust, seem to make up a trend that is very distant from the sublime and the melancholy, and which can be called an eruption of the subject, as the highly controversial case of D. M. Thomas's *The White Hotel* makes particularly visible. However, the metaphor of eruption and volcanic activity in thinking about the Holocaust does not sound appropriate in relation to a number of social aspects called out by this fiction. It is these aspects, and especially the doubts about how to represent the consequences of the Holocaust to the post-war world, that remain the most important for all the writers named in this paragraph. The image of the war that emerges from their fictions published in the 1980s, I refer to, like their postmodernism, as hybrid, because the freedom of expression that this decade inherited from the preceding two, enabled a broader scope of theme and relevance. We can speak of three directions in this development of postmodern Holocaust-related fiction. Writers such as Kuśniewicz and Auster placed the Holocaust in a post-catastrophic trend, comparing it to natural disasters and the end of the world.[292] Thomas and Federman broadened the scope and possibilities of testimony, making it more and more amenable to fiction or, as Raymond Federman would have it, to "the reality of imagination."[293] Abish, on the other hand, gives us an image of post-war Europe inhabited by

---

"Zagłada – niedokończona narracja polskiej nowoczesności," in: *Ślady obecności*, ed. Sławomir Buryła, Alina Molisak (Kraków: Universitas 2010), pp. 350–355. On the metonymy of the Holocaust in *Who Was David Weiser?* see Marta Cuber, *Metonimie Zagłady. O polskiej prozie lat 1987–2012* (Katowice: Wydawnictwo Uniwersytetu Śląskiego 2013), pp. 271–292.

290 Czapliński, "Zagłada – niedokończona narracja polskiej nowoczesności," p. 355.

291 Przemysław Czapliński also omits Kuśniewicz in his analysis of the 1980s fiction in the context of representations of the Holocaust; cf. Czapliński, *Zagłada – niedokończona narracja polskiej nowoczesności*.

292 Cf. *Postmodern Apocalypse. Theory and Cultural Practice at the End*, ed. Richard Dellamora (Philadelphia: University of Pennsylvania Press, 1995); Kenneth Hewitt, *Regions of Risk. A Geographical Introduction to Disasters* (already quoted).

293 "[…] he knows that the reality of imagination is more real than reality without imagination […]"; Raymond Federman, *The Twofold Vibration* (Bloomington: Indiana University Press; Brighton: The Harvester Press, 1982), p. 24.

perpetrators shown from the perspective of a would-be victim who calls for a debunking of Western complacency and demands a conscientious reckoning for the guilty.

By taking into account the participation of these writers in the war and also simply their dates of birth we could draw several trajectories of the development of Holocaust-related postmodern fiction. With the exception of Paul Auster, born in 1947, we can talk about a generation of survivors (Abish, Federman) and witnesses (Kuśniewicz, Thomas). This distinction, however, does not reflect the subject matter or the narrative perspective. On the contrary, the accents of revealing and concealing biographical experiences are evenly distributed. In the novels of Abish and Thomas, the Holocaust becomes a metaphor for unlived experience, as we may call it, made accessible and possible by the participating and empathetic imagination. *The Twofold Vibration* revolves around the writer's biographical experiences, while *Nawrócenie*, even though it also "feeds" on biography, is, rather than a straightforward autobiographical narrative, a fairly easily identifiable contact between literature and "reality without imagination."[294] Abish and Thomas return to thinking of the Holocaust in terms of a genocide, which is why mass graves in Durst and Babi Yar play a key role in their novels. Federman is interested in the impact of the Holocaust on the survivor, while Kuśniewicz is interested in the consequences of failing to help his Jewish neighbors. The spectrum of the social relevance of Holocaust-related fiction in comparison with the literature of 1960s and 1970s is thus undergoing visible and significant expansion. It is worth noting that this development to some extent influences the Polish way of thinking about postmodernism.

Liquid foundations

In the years 1980–1981, two novels were published that announced the changes to be brought about by *Historikerstreit* and Zygmunt Bauman's *Liquid Modernity* (2000). Walter Abish's *How German Is It* and D. M. Thomas's *The White Hotel* turned out to be a diagnosis of the role that the Holocaust may have played in dismantling modernism, revealing its weakness in the face of totalitarianism (to which Abish pays particular attention when analyzing the German architecture of the twentieth century), and its transition to postmodernism.[295] In both novels, "The Holocaust [came to signify – M.T.] the tombstone of modernity and the

---

294 Federman, *The Twofold Vibration*, p. 24; see previous footnote.
295 Czapliński, "Zagłada jako wyzwanie dla refleksji o literaturze," *Teksty Drugie* (2004), pp. 9–10.

liquid foundation of postmodernity."[296] And it is literally fluid: Abish and Thomas based their fictions on scenes representing the memory of the Holocaust gushing forth like lava or the contents of a cesspool (the latter in Abish). In *How German Is It*, due to a burst sewer pipe and the stench, the inhabitants of the former Durst remember that they live on a mass grave, created from the corpses of prisoners of a concentration (or extermination) camp.[297] Thomas's novel, on the other hand, revolves around the reminiscences of the huge, mass grave of Ukrainian Jews in Babi Yar, which after the war was flooded with water, which then became "a green, stagnant and putrid lake. The dam burst; a huge area of Kiev was buried in mud. Frozen in their last postures, as at Pompeii, people were still being dug out two years later."[298] The odd combination of Freudian and hydraulic metaphorics gave both writers not only the opportunity to reflect on the role of psychoanalysis in the context of the Western bourgeoisie in the rise of Nazism. A memory that bursts like a cesspool turns out to be a very literal punishment for the sin of oblivion, drowning everything in the fetid content of the repressed. If we were to make the image of water or mud breaking out from under the ground into a symbol of narrative representation of the Holocaust in the 1980s, we might have to say that the essence of those narratives is, as already mentioned, a revolution in the scope and ways of dealing with the subject, related, according to some critics, to the growing role of pop culture. The question that arises when analyzing these excremental-eruptive images has been asked by Thomas Patrick Swinden: How did it happen that the protagonist of *The White Hotel*, Lisa Erdman, known from Freud's account of the case as Anna O., without being either Jewish[299] or Ukrainian, turned into a victim of the Holocaust? And how should we, readers, react to this mysterious makeover?[300] John Updike asked another question about Abish's novel in *The New Yorker:* "How German was the

---

296 Czapliński, "Zagłada jako wyzwanie dla refleksji o literaturze," pp. 9–10.
297 Abish does not allow the reader to be sure whether the purpose of the camp, as described in the novel, located in Germany was the extermination of Jews or of some other population. From the context, or more precisely from the way it is patterned after the DEATH TRAINS trope, it would seem that the trains did carry Jews. This, however, is contradicted by Abish's statement in an interview he gave to Sylvére Lotringe. He says there that the skeletons found in the mass grave could have been German or Jewish, and explains that he was primarily interested in a historical joke. Cf. Walter Abish/Sylvére Lotringer, "Wie Deutsch Ist Es," *Semiotext(e)* vol. IV, no. 2 (1982), p. 166. See also Sławomir Buryła, *Wokół Zagłady. Szkice o literaturze Holokaustu* (Kraków: Universitas, 2016), pp. 49–82.
298 D. M. Thomas, *The White Hotel* (London: Penguin Books, 1981), p. 222.
299 Lisa's father was Jewish; her mother – a Catholic.
300 This question is a paraphrase of Swniden's: "How Lisa Erdman, or Frau Anna G. as she is known to us in Freud's case history, was transformed from the one to the other, and how we are to react to the different stages of her transformation, is perplexing, mysterious and enigmatic". Qtd after Patrick Swinden, "D. M. Thomas and *The White Hotel*," *Critical Quarterly*, vol. 24, no. 4, p. 77.

Holocaust?"[301] These two doubts can be laid at the foundation of the 1980s Holocaust discourse and can be rolled up into one major query: Why would ordinary people turn into criminals capable of murdering their good neighbors? This can be addressed to Kuśniewicz's *Nawrócenie*, which recounts the pre-war history of the neighborly coexistence of the Polish and Jewish population, unimaginably disfigured and massacred during the war.

Arguably Thomas's greatest novelty in comparison with other authors of Holocaust-related fiction is the way in which his fiction unveils, as it were, the sexuality of the victims, as outlined in a sentence that explains the title: "The thirty thousand became a quarter of a million. A quarter of a million white hotels in Babi Yar. (Each of them had a Vogel, a Madame Cottin, a priest, a prostitute, a honeymoon couple, a soldier poet, a baker, a chef, a gypsy band)."[302] The white hotel, in fact Liza Erdman's pre-war resting place, changes in the novel's finale into a metaphor for a body trembling with desire, on the one hand, and a multi-layer tomb, on the other: "When the Germans wished to bury their massacres the bulldozers did not find it easy to separate the bodies: which were now grey-blue in colour. [...] These lower strata were, with few exceptions, naked; but further up they were in their underwear, and higher still they were fully dressed: like the different formations of rocks. The Jews were at the bottom, then came Ukrainians, gypsies, Russians, etc."[303] The description of the mass grave makes us think of an object of desire and phases of tearing off its veil. Yet even Brian McHale in his remarks on love and death in the postmodern novel does not go as far as Thomas, who, revealing the details of the Babi Yar massacre, seems to be looking through a crack in the wall into the gas chamber.[304] In Shlomo Venezia's memoirs, its interior, just after opening, looked like this: "The worst of it was at the beginning, when we had to pull out the first bodies, since we didn't have anything to help us. The bodies were so entangled and twisted together – legs here, heads there. The bodies lay in a pile more than three feet high, sometimes four feet or

---

301 The two questions pursued by Abish are: "How could the Germans have committed these unspeakable acts? How uniquely German was the Holocaust?" John Updike, "Sentimental re-education. The cerebral experimentalist gets personal." *The New Yorker*, 08.02.2004, http://www.newyorker.com/magazine/2004/02/16/sentimental-re-education [accessed 29.08.2023].
302 Thomas, *The White Hotel*, p. 221.
303 Thomas, *The White Hotel*, p. 221.
304 The comparison of the description of a ravine (the "yar") filled with corpses of Jewish people with a gas chamber comes to mind mainly because the "yar," like the chamber, is taboo in Thomas's novel. However, unlike the gas chamber, which, in literature, film, and art is usually presented with decorum, the mass grave in *The White Hotel* is a violation of the taboo; it is thus aesthetically and ethically confusing.

more."[305] Thomas's description is mainly based on the memoirs of Dina Mironovna Pronicheva, recreated by Anatol Kuznetsov in a fictionalized documentary entitled *Babi Yar*. However, there is no need to convince anyone that in that book there is no such thing as a grave with neatly arranged bodies, some dressed and some stripped naked. The metaphor that Thomas constructs stems from the fluctuation characteristic of postmodern writing. According to Brian McHale, "All metaphor *hesitates* between a literal function (in the secondary frame of reference) and a metaphorical function (in 'real' frame of reference); postmodernist texts often *prolong* this hesitation as a means of foregrounding ontological structure."[306] This use of metaphor allows Thomas to expand the field of testimony, which, according to Linda Hutcheon, can no longer be based on transparent reading of documents, but should also involve, like *The White Hotel*, reading textual traces.[307] This is especially relevant since, as Hutcheon goes on to point out, when historians read documents, they often fill them with content that is topical and may be fictitious, and it is this type of content that constitutes the boundary of historical narrative in the strict sense.[308]

Let us recall that the representation of the Holocaust in Thomas's novel is not limited to metaphor, but moves onto the area of parody, difficult as it may be to associate its effect with any kind of humor. The parody deployed by Thomas is the opposite to Linda Hutcheon's sense of this term. Instead of facilitating the task of interpreting the decoder, it makes it more difficult, making the imprinting associated with *Babi Yar* into a part of a complicated heteroglossia, and above all an unexpected finale of the protagonist's pre-war struggle with psychoanalysis.[309] It will be recalled that in the original, Dina Mironovna Pronicheva, saving herself from mass execution, does not meet anyone called Liza Erdman, and that a boy, Motya, with whom she escapes, gets shot. In Thomas's version, Liza is a distant acquaintance of Dina (the details of their acquaintance, even if it was only one-

---

305 Shlomo Venezia, *Inside the Gas Chambers: Eight Months in the Sonderkommando of Auschwitz*, trans. Andrew Brown (Cambridge, UK and Malden, MA: Polity Press in association with the United States Holocaust Memorial Museum, 2009), pp. 71–72.
306 McHale, *Postmodernist Fiction*, p. 134; emphasis in the original. "Postmodernist writing seeks to foreground the ontological *duality* of metaphor, its participation in two frames of reference with different ontological statuses" (ibid.; emphasis in the original).
307 Linda Hutcheon, *The Politics of Postmodernism* (London and New York: Routledge, 1991), p. 87. James Young has written on the broadening of the field of testimony in relations to Thomas's novel, citing Terrence Des Pres's distinction between survivors' testimony and his own commentary, on the one hand, and the difference, evident in Kuzniecov's *Babi Yar*, between the authentic document quoted in the work and the author's voice. See James E. Young, *Writing and Rewriting the Holocaust. Narrative and the Consequences of Interpretation* (Indianapolis and Bloomington: Indiana University Press, 1988), p. 58.
308 Hutcheon, *The Politics of Postmodernism*, p. 87.
309 Cf. Linda Hutcheon, *A Theory of Parody: The Teachings of Twentieth-Century Art Forms* (Urbana and Chicago: University of Illinois Press, 2000), p. 39.

sided, we never get to know), who survived Babi Yar and told his (and Liza's) story years later. There is another parallel between the two texts: the friendship between Liza and her foster son, Kolya, is reminiscent of the tragic journey of Moti and Dina. The beginning of the list of changes adopted by Thomas in metafiction in relation to Pronicheva's testimony is, according to Hutcheon, the fact that it is only part of Kuznetsov's book on a different subject. The first "parodist" of the text saved from Babi Yar is therefore Kuznetsov himself, and it is from his paraphrase that Thomas obtains consent for his parody.[310]

Taking all this into account, it seems incomprehensible to accuse Thomas of plagiarism. In a note, Thomas openly recognizes his debt: "I also gratefully acknowledge the use in Part V of materials from Anatoli Kuznetsov's *Babi Yar* (New York: Ferrar, Straus & Giroux; London: Jonathan Cape, 1970), particularly the testimony of Dina Pronicheva."[311] Meanwhile, in March and April 1982, *The Times Literary Supplement* debated the plagiarism that Thomas allegedly committed by "stealing" the text of Pronicheva's testimony from Kuznetsov. Linda Hutcheon reacted to this accusation with surprise, explaining that, if for anything at all, Thomas could be attacked for plagiarizing Freud's works. *The White Hotel* does use some tools of psychoanalysis, including case study, psychoanalytic session, correspondence between the doctor and the female patient, her notes and the analyst's comments. However, the novel is based primarily on *Beyond the Pleasure Principle*, which Freud as the protagonist is writing during the course of the plot.

Sue Vice, in an in-depth interpretation of *The White Hotel*, states that the criticism of the novel at the time brought up two issues, the sexuality of the Holocaust victims and the version of *Babi Yar* used by Thomas. His parody was based on the English edition of Kuznetsov's book with passages taken out by Soviet censorship. They include a scene on which Thomas based the finale of the fifth chapter and tells of six or seven Germans who rape and stab to death two

---

310 Hutcheon, *The Politics of Postmodernism*, p. 87. Dina Pronicheva's account covers 16 pages of the 335-page-long Polish edition and has been written, in Anatoli Kuznetsov's words, "according to the woman's words" with the use of the 3rd-person narration. Kuznetsov stresses the faithfulness of her account: "Several people escaped directly from the Babi Yar pits, and I shall relate the story told by one of them. I wrote it down myself from her words. She was Dina Mironovna Pronicheva, an actress at the Kiev Puppet Theater and the mother of two children. I shall give her story exactly as she told it, without adding anything." Anatoly Kuznetsov, *Babi Yar: A Documentary Novel*, trans. Jacob Guralsky (New York: Dell Publishing, 1967), p. 63. Elsewhere Hutcheon calls Thomas's novel historiographic metafiction, the reading of which shows how the reader, submitted to the working of history and fiction, produces meaning. Cf. Linda Hutcheon, "Subject In/Of/To History and His Story," *Diacritics* 16/1 (Spring 1986), pp. 78, 83.
311 Thomas, *The White Hotel*, p. 3.

women with bayonets, and then throw the bodies into a ravine.[312] In Thomas's novel, two Ukrainians are the rapists:

> After a while Semashko jeered at him, and Demidenko grumbled that it was too cold, and the old woman was too ugly. He adjusted his clothing and picked up his rifle. With Semashko's assistance he found the opening, and they joked together as he inserted the bayonet, carefully, almost delicately. The old woman was not making any sound though they could see she was still breathing. Still very gently, Demidenko imitated the thrusts of intercourse; and Semashko let out a guffaw, which echoed from the ravine walls, as the woman's body jerked back and relaxed, jerked and relaxed. But after those spasms there was no sign of a reaction and she seemed to have stopped breathing. [...] Demidenko twisted the blade and thrust it in deep.[313]

In her criticism of this scene, Linda Hutcheon objects to the female protagonist's passivity, exhibitionism and masochism, in contrast to the male SS units (Hutcheon does not distinguish between Germans and Ukrainians), characterized by aggression, sadism and voyeurism. In other words, the author's perspective is extremely non-feminist.[314] Hutcheon places on Thomas the responsibility for creating this portrayal of femininity. Her position has been reiterated by Vice, who additionally notes that the death of femininity in the novel turns into an elegy. Psychoanalysis, on the other hand, leads to the transformation of female sexual subjectivity into sadomasochism. Meanwhile, Thomas has described Liza's transformation as one from an individual person to an anonymous victim of the Holocaust, apparently ignoring the fact that the victim was a raped woman.[315]

The rape scene echoes another, earlier scene, which depicts Liza's childhood in Odessa. Sailors working for her father rape her because of her Jewish capitalist roots. This is the first image of this kind in the novel, which characteristically combines sexual violence against women and anti-Semitism. In neither of these scenes does the victim speak. The language of cruelty belongs to men. Different impressions notwithstanding, Thomas's novel does not deviate from the model of liberal narrative, which leaves no room for statements of the wronged, because

---

312 Discussing the missing scenes in the Russian and the Polish editions of the book, Vice names several pages added in the following English edition: Anatoly Kuznetsov, *Babi Yar*, trans. David Floyd (London: Sphere Books, 1970). Among the scenes rejected by censorship are chiefly those that depict Ukrainians assisting Germans in the carrying out of the massacre; see Sue Vice, *Holocaust Fiction* (London and New York, 2005), p. 178.
313 Thomas, *The White Hotel*, pp. 219–220.
314 Hutcheon, "Subject In/Of/To History," p. 89.
315 "The changes Thomas makes to Kuznetsov's rendering of Dina Pronicheva's account of the Babi Yar massacre effectively blot out female subjectivity as well as female life." Vice, *Holocaust Fiction*, p. 41.

Liquid foundations 97

solidarity with suffering fellow beings is only a project. Let us recall Richard Rorty's comments on this,[316] including the following one:

> pain is nonlinguistic: It is what we human beings have that ties us to the nonlanguage-using beasts. So victims of cruelty, people who are suffering, do not have much in the way of language. That is why there is no such things as the "voice of the oppressed" or the "language of the victims." The language the victims once used is no working anymore, and they are suffering too much to put new words together. So the job of putting their situation into language is going to have to be done for them by somebody else.[317]

Even though it seems facile for postmodern literature to associate pornography with cruelty, sometimes only to highlight the unreality of this relationship, it often does so in a way that is not without weaknesses. One of the issues concerns the unspeakable suffering of the victims. For instance, *Nawrócenie* makes suffering vividly intense due to the fact that the Jewish characters are mute, while from Marek Bieńczyk's *Tworki*, published a decade later, cruelty seems to be absent altogether. Walter Abish's approach is similar to that in the novels discussed previously, although, by choosing in *How German Is It* the perspective of the perpetrators and their children, he seems to be ignoring that of the victims. Yet when the perspective shifts to that side, as in the image of trains rushing towards the Durst concentration camp, then, like other postmodernists, what he discerns is only the muteness and phantom-like status of the Jewish victims:

> The only evidence of life on the passing trains was an occasional scarecrow face framed in the tiny cutout window of a freight car. A face whose eyes were riveted on the stationmaster, or on anyone who may have been watching the passing train, establishing a brief second of eye contact. Once in a while, the scarecrow face of a man or woman would be seen shaping, with its mouth a word, or several words. It could have been "Where?" or "When?" or "Why?"[318]

Let us return to the sexualization of victims, which became the reason for the harsh criticism leveled at *The White Hotel*. One of the few reviewers who in the British press of the early 1980s spoke approvingly about Thomas's representation of femininity noted that male readers were disturbed by the novel's images of lactation, the scenes in which Liza is breastfeeding adult men. Yet neither these, nor the two most pornographic parts of *The White Hotel*, which is how reviewers described the chapters "Don Giovanni" and "The Diary of Gastein," were read by Sylvia Kantaris as expressions of misogyny.[319] This critic was able to extract from

---

316 See Richard Rorty, *Contingency, Irony and Solidarity* (Cambridge: Cambridge University Press, 1999), p. 17.
317 Rorty, *Contingency, Irony and Solidarity*, p. 94.
318 Walter Abish, *How German Is It (Wie Deutsch ist es)* (New York: New Directions Books, 1980), p. 78.
319 D. M. Thomas and Sylvia Kantaris, *News from the Front* (Arc Publications, 1983), p. 54.

them the discourse of the sexual economy of the masses, suppressed by fascism. At the same time, she points to an element of morbidity in Liza, a highly individualized protagonist and a representative of the bourgeoisie, whose behavior takes on a broader social meaning. In the sexual sickness that plagued pre-war society, Kantaris sees a premonition of its tragic end, without depriving the psychoanalytic part of Thomas's book of its feminist potential. In the misogynistic scenes, she sees the liberation of the female subject, in sharp contrast to its humiliation by German and Ukrainian soldiers during the Babi Yar massacre.

Having said all the above, it is still worth considering Vice's opinion which, justifiably, reduces the role of psychoanalysis and later Nazism in Thomas's novel to a mechanism that humiliates women while being a personification of Jewry. On the one hand, Thomas accepts this personification; on the other, he deconstructs it, following the example of Dina Pronicheva, the wife of a Russian, who chiefly due to non-Jewish documents and Aryan appearance, managed to save her life. Liza Erdman's mother is a Pole, Maria Konopnicka. Like Pronicheva, this protagonist has a non-Jewish appearance, wears a cross around her neck and recites Catholic prayers. Long before the catastrophe, she confesses to Freud in a letter the truth about her complicated origins and her anti-Semitic husband. We can say that if the doctor had properly managed the patient's case, she might have parted with her Jewish father (the decision to separate from her husband was made by Erdman regardless of the therapy) and would have been reunited with the Catholic part of the family, thus increasing the chances of survival.

In the shadow of this gender-focused critique remains a scene which in my opinion is an excellent illustration of the connections between psychoanalysis and the Holocaust in Thomas's novel. It is mentioned in 1909, almost at the beginning of the novel, by one of the protagonists of *The White Hotel*, Sándor Ferenczi:

> He [Carl Gustav Jung] turned the conversation to some "peat-bog" corpses that apparently have been found in northern Germany. They are said to be the bodies of prehistoric men, mummified by the effect of the humic acid in the bog water. Apparently the men had drowned in the marshes or been buried there.[320]

In Thomas's narrative, Jung's fascination does not resonate strongly enough, because it is suppressed by his inability to tell stories. According to Ferenczi's account, Jung "became unusually talkative and high spirited"[321] and "talked on and on about it [the corpses]."[322] Why did Jung care so much about the bodies from the swamp, while Freud remained completely indifferent: "Jung continued to be carried away by his fascination with the story [...] Freud slipped off his chair

---

320 Thomas, *The White Hotel*, p. 10.
321 Thomas, *The White Hotel*, p. 10.
322 Thomas, *The White Hotel*, p. 10.

in a faint"?[323] Shouldn't we see in this contradiction, articulating the paradoxes of psychoanalysis, both the possibilities and the pitfalls of postmodern fictional representations of the Holocaust? The frame supplied by Ferenczi's memoir, together with a paraphrase of Pronicheva's account of the Babi Yar massacre, is based on the "dry" – "moist" opposition. Discussed by Jonathan Littell in *The Damp and the Dry: A Brief Incursion into Fascist Territory*, it is also present in Abish's novel, in the scene of a septic tank's content gushing forth from under the pavement. Stinky liquids, such as a swamp, the contents of a septic tank or mud, bring associations with the analyses of Klaus Theweleit, who, in a chapter of volume 1 of his *Male Fantasies* talks about the role and meaning of words such as dirt, sludge, swamp, goo, slush, shit and rain in Nazi discourse, arguing their connection with notions of what is frightening and impure, i.e., communists and femininity. When the persistent stench from under the pavement causes the mayor of Brumholdstein – a town that was formerly known as Durst, turned after the war into a postmodern development, cut off from history – to employ workers who discover a mass grave, the narrator comments on the situation in unequivocal terms: "For all anyone knows, all of Brumholdstein is sitting on one mass grave."[324] The mass grave revealed by rain, then a septic tank, stench, and finally the excavation of thousands of human remains of unknown origin, is the foundation of a new space, established in the name of the cleansing of German history of Nazism. Established, it will be recalled, in honor of Martin Heidegger (appearing in the novel as Brumhold). "Developed [postmodern – M.T.] forms" – wrote Wolfgang Welsch about architecture – "operate in an open whole. They no longer mourn the lost unity but build on a completely different foundation."[325] If we were to explain this foundation with the help of Theweleit's approach, we would have to see in it the struggle of masculinity (the mayor, the workers smashing the pavement with jackhammers, and finally the Hargenau brothers) with the cracking earth, coded as female.

> The exploding earth and rebellious metropolis owe their terror primarily to the fact that they embody the potential for – and may violently bring about – an eruption of his own interior. When this interior becomes too powerful, or when the larger, external body (the earth) opens up, or when the metropolis bursts its bounds of order, so that its interior reaches the man's body, the latter is destroyed. In violence and pain, the bodies

---

323 Thomas, *The White Hotel*, p. 10.
324 Abish, *How German Is It?* p. 139.
325 Wolfgang Welsch, *Nasza postmodernistyczna moderna*, trans. R. Kubicki, A. Zeidler-Janiszewska (Warszawa: Oficyna Naukowa, 1998), p. 180.

flow together; their boundaries are exploded: ripping drumhead, eyes wide open, detonating heart.[326]

The protagonists of Abish's novel, Helmut and Ulrich Hargenau, are sons of a Nazi and members of the denominated Brumholdstein community. None of them wants to remember the past. But that memory returns and affects the intimate relationships of these male characters with women who fall victim to male violence or fantasy based on the script already known from *The White Hotel*. Although Abish's and Thomas's fictions stem from different assumptions about the representation of the war, the meeting of these two authors in the common current of postmodernism, in which mud and swamp combine with a cesspool, a lake, and finally concrete, must lead to considerations based on Freudian metaphors of liquid states and end with a gender-focused critique of these images. The fascist ideology that both writers deconstruct identified Nordic masculinity with clarity, sublimity, purity, dryness, and above all with asexuality.[327] How then are we to understand graves filled with naked corpses, sometimes subjected as it were to secondary eroticization? Is this how Theleweit's commentator, Jonathan Littell, understood them, when in *The Damp and the Dry* he posted without comment two photos of the execution of women and children on the beach of Skede and Mizochu? In one of them (Skede), the image of corpses is blurred. In the other (Mizocz), we can even see the pubic hair of the women. However, we are separated from their sexuality by the clear boundary of the document. In postmodern representations, this kind of boundary does not exist. Yet does anyone who is looking feel that a boundary is missing?[328]

---

[326] Klaus Theweleit, *Male Fantasies. volume 1: Women Floods Bodies History*, trans. Stephen Conway in collaboration with Erica Carter and Chris Turner, foreword by Barbara Ehrenreich (Minneapolis: University of Minnesota Press, 1987), p. 242.

[327] Fascist ideology (in contrast to Christian ideology) separates human orgastic longing from the structure created by the authoritarian patriarchy and assigns it to various races: *"Nordic"* is equivalent to *bright, heavenly, exalted, pure, asexual*; *"Asiatic"* to *instinctual, demoniacal, ecstatic, sexual, orgastic*. Wilhelm Reich, *The Mass Psychology of Fascism*, trans. Theodore P. Wolfe (New York: Orgone Institute Press, 1946; 3rd ed.), p. 73; italics in the original.

[328] Cf. Dorota Głowacka, *Po tamtej stronie: świadectwo, afekt, wyobraźnia* (Warszawa: Instytut Badań Literackich PAN, 2016), pp. 160–193.

Chapter 6.
The Shadow of the Holocaust and the Hiroshima Mushroom: Paul Auster

In the 1980s, Paul Auster published four books of prose: *The Invention of Solitude* (1982), *The New York Trilogy* (1985–1986), *In the Country of Last Things* (1987), and *Moon Palace* (1989). But it wasn't until his 1992 novel *Leviathan* that he responded to fears of a worldwide nuclear conflict, which troubled the eighth decade of the century and which – according to Frank Kermode – were part the millenarian anxieties of the era.[329] Auster's response consisted first of all in the suggestion of a deeper connection between World War II, the post-war terrorist attacks that Walter Abish wrote about,[330] and fears of nuclear war, a connection based on a biological premise. Benjamin Sachs, the protagonist of *Leviathan*, was born on August 8, 1945, after the Enola Gay attack on Hiroshima and before Bockscar dropped the bomb on Nagasaki. In memory of both tragedies, he would call himself "America's first Hiroshima baby" and "the original bomb child."[331] As the builder of a home-made nuclear bomb, Sachs becomes primarily a victim of his own biomemory, understood as a reservoir of rituals at once instinctive and acquired. Is there not a similar mechanism in the case of a novel published five years earlier, which only loosely refers to Kermode's nuclear reflections? *In the Country of Last Things* is a narrative about all the fears that have plagued humanity for centuries: from the great famine, through a total epidemic, to anxieties over our loved ones. One can see in it a case of Barthes's *déjà lu* – a work composed of vague reminiscences that reading evokes like clear images, slipping from our mental grasp the moment our mind tries to interpret them. Auster treats history like a film script which is at once original and intertextual and in which Hiroshima and the Holocaust come to the fore. Their coexistence is reminiscent of Amy Elias's statement about the two world wars as having resulted in yet another war, the Cold War, and two narratives that required separate looks,

---

329 Frank Kermode, *The Sense of an Ending: Studies in the Theory of Fiction* (Oxford and New York: Oxford University Press, 2000), pp. 147–148.
330 See Abish, *How German Is It*.
331 Paul Auster, *Leviathan* (London and Boston: Faber and Faber, 1993), p. 23.

the Holocaust and Hiroshima.[332] But it is Ephraim Sicher's remark, recalled by Elias, that helps us to understand why in many stories both themes appear together: "The shadow of the Holocaust, together with the mushroom over Hiroshima, has thus fallen on our understanding of history, language, and literature. It informs the reading of previous texts and the writing of new texts in all the arts [...]."[333]

Before we turn to the representation of the Second World War in Auster's novel, let us look at Sicher's rhetoric and its implications for post-Holocaust literature. Both the expressions, "the shadow of the Holocaust" and "the mushroom over Hiroshima," are metonymies. Instead of the catastrophe with its history, meaning and repercussions, they refer to atmospheric visualizations of both events. Replacing the otherwise well-known story, Sicher's metonymic visualizations of catastrophes become historical specters, reminiscent of the specters of freedom that Sachs wants to destroy. These are not facts, but "facts within metaphors."[334] In the words of Jacques Derrida,

> Unlike the other wars, which have all been preceded by wars of more or less the same type in human memory (and gunpowder did not mark a radical break in this respect), nuclear war has no precedent. It has never occurred, itself; it is a non-event. The explosion of American bombs in 1945 ended a "classical," conventional war; it did not set off a nuclear war. The terrifying reality of the nuclear conflict can only be the signified referent, never the real referent (present or past) of a discourse or a text. At least today apparently. And that sets us to thinking about today, our day, the presence of this present in and through that fabulous textuality.[335]

Auster's fiction, especially *Leviathan* and *In the Country of Last Things*, to the extent it corresponds to Derrida's statement, draws on the nuclear-war imagi-

---

332 Amy Elias, *Sublime Desire. History and Post-1960s Fiction* (Baltimore and London: The Johns Hopkins University Press, 2001), p. 51: "What is shifting and is imaged as traumatized, generally speaking, is the post-Enlightenment, Anglo, androcentric consciousness of the West. More specifically, what the First World seems to be approaching in the aftermath of two world wars, the Cold War, and the real as well as metaphysical devastation of Hiroshima and the Holocaust is the need to address its own history as a psychic, social, and ideological problem."
333 Efraim Sicher, "The Holocaust in the Postmodernist Era," in Sicher, ed., *Breaking Crystal*, p. 304; see also Elias, *Sublime Desire*, p. 52.
334 Debra Shostak, "In the Country of Missing Persons: Paul Auster's Narratives of Trauma," *Studies in the Novel*, vol. 41, no. 1 (Spring 2009), p. 73.
335 Jacques Derrida, "No Apocalypse, Not Now (Full Speed Ahead, Seven Missiles, Seven Missives)," trans. Catherine Porter and Philip Lewis. *Diacritics* 14 (1984), No. 2 (Nuclear Criticism), p. 23. David Robson places Derrida's approach in the context of Northrop Frye's *Anatomy of Criticism* (1957) and Thomas Pynchon's *Gravity's Rainbow* (1973); David Robson, "Frye, Derrida, Pynchon, and the Apocalyptic Space of Postmodern Fiction," in *Postmodern Apocalypse. Theory and Cultural Practice at the End*, ed. Richard Dellamora (Philadelphia: University of Pennsylvania Press, 1995), pp. 61–78.

nary, becoming nothing more than a post-Holocaust fiction,[336] based on a pleasant, though insignificant, *déjà lu*. The specters of history, however, according to Debra Shostak's claim, belong not only to the rhetorical order, but also to the social order. They thus become a substance by means of which the social critique in which literature becomes entangled acquires historical power without becoming historical (or historically oriented). In the case of *In the Country of Last Things*, we can speak about a critique of both capitalism and consumer society. But critique here is based on the memory of the Holocaust and Hiroshima. This memory has no historical or ethical basis; it is fictitious or nonsensical and based on Kermode's assumption about the intrinsic absurdity of apocalypse.

> How can apocalypse or tragedy make sense, or more sense than any arbitrary nonsense that can be made to make sense? If *King Lear* is an image of the promised end, so is Buchenwald; and both stand under the accusation of being horrible, rootless fantasies, the one no more true or more false than the other, so that the best you can say is that *King Lear* does less harm.[337]

Despite the outrageous identification that Kermode carried out between fact and fiction (one wants to ask whether it is sufficiently justified by the assumption preceding the quoted passage[338]), the apocalypse becomes an area with no contradictions; an area of pure absurdity. The end is the end, Kermode argues, no matter whether it's been authored by Adolf Hitler or William Shakespeare or whether the characters are real people or fictional figures. The paradigm of the end is usually grounded in reality. Auster, Derrida and Kermode agree on this point.

Discussing Derrida's stance on postmodernism in the context of the 1980s, Wolfgang Welsch stated that "images of the apocalypse began to trouble us directly under the auspices of postmodernism."[339] This is not true. In the Epilogue to *The Sense of an Ending*, Kermode reminds us that the revival of apocalyptic thinking took place in the 1960s, thus was only partly related to postmodernism, and chiefly to the Cuban Bay of Pigs crisis, the assassination of President Kennedy, the Cold War, the escalation of the Vietnam War and the race riots in Watts; "[…] no one could ignore the imminence of events that could

---

336 See Shostak, "In the Country of Missing Persons," p. 70.
337 Kermode, *The Sense of an Ending*, s. 38.
338 The assumption is expressed in this statement: "If literary fictions *are* related to all others, then it must be said that they have some dangerous relations." Kermode, *The Sense of an Ending*, p. 37 (emphasis in the original).
339 Wolfgang Welsch, *Unsere postmoderne Moderne*; Polish translation *Nasza postmodernistyczna moderna*, trans. Roman Kubicki and Anna Zeidler-Janiszewska (Warszawa: Oficyna Naukowa, 1998), p. 201.

without too much exaggeration be characterized as apocalyptic."[340] Welsch points out that in Derrida's thinking two decades later there are no inspirations of this kind. Derrida's thinking differs from Kermode's chronological and coherent approach, with its focus on scenarios kept within the boundaries of the plot and laying special emphasis on the ending. As Welsch explains, "The Apocalypse is an empty message without a message. There is no Last Judgment, there is no truth."[341] He goes on to add a remark that seems particularly relevant to the understanding of Auster's *In the Country of Last Things*, "[…] there can be no apocalypse because it isn't present. The apocalypse is a hallucination of a fulfilled presence."[342]

The remarks of Kermode and Welsch contain several important premises for thinking about artistic representations of apocalypse. One suggestion is that these representations must be unrealistic; another – that St. John's *Book of Revelation* does not supply a satisfactory scenario for them. More important still is the idea that an apocalyptic scenario is inherently insufficient or at best one that increases the sense of the absence of the object. Every other apocalyptic scenario has this feature; Derrida writes about a nuclear war, and Kermode about the ending of *King Lear* and the "ending" of Buchenwald. The third premise, appearing chiefly in Derrida, concerns the questions of what art can achieve when faced with the impossibility of representing apocalypse. Welsch sees the following way out: artists must "try to play with the old stuff."[343] This is also the conviction on which Auster based the war imaginarium of his fiction. Elisabeth Wesseling has described the way the past exists in his novel as "history-in-reverse," relating its main themes to the stories of Isabella I of Castile and Ferdinand of Aragon and to Anne Blume from Kurt Schwitters' poem "An Anna Blume" from 1919.[344]

Playing with "the old stuff" in Auster's novel involves far-reaching transformations of the basic plot. A happy marriage of rulers has been replaced here by a beggary couple living in a toxic relationship, and instead of a heroine from a Dadaist love poem, Anna Blume is a diarist describing a dying world. Auster makes irony a factor that significantly modifies the original. Here is Linda Hutcheon's definition:

> […] parody is repetition, but repetition that includes difference […]; it is imitation with critical ironic distance, whose irony can cut both ways. Ironic versions of "trans-con-

---

340 Kermode, *The Sense of an Ending*, p. 181.
341 Welsch, *Nasza postmodernistyczna moderna*, p. 203.
342 Welsch, *Nasza postmodernistyczna moderna*, p. 203.
343 Welsch, *Nasza postmodernistyczna moderna*, p. 204.
344 Elisabeth Wesseling, "*In the Country of Last Things:* Paul Auster's parable of the apocalypse," *Neophilologus* 75 (1991), p. 497.

textualization" and inversion are its major formal operatives, and the range of pragmatic ethos is from scornful ridicule to reverential homage.[345]

Irony, on the other hand, is defined as a "marking of difference in meaning or [...] antiphrasis."[346] "Trans-contextualization," repetition, irony, and parody bring nothing but a sense of misery and emptiness to Auster's story. Grasping the relationship between the world as presented in *The Country of Last Things* and the sources of inspiration, the reader begins to realize that the basis of parody has undergone degradation, and that mockery is one of its most important elements. In Auster, mockery relates mostly to organized human collectives that resemble real-life unions, associations, factions, and corporations. One such group is the "sect" of the Runners, a constantly changing group of people for whom running is a form of self-destruction. The task of the Fecalists is very different; by collecting human feces to be burned, they provide renewable energy. In a country without no other resources, the human being and the human body are the only sources of energy. The city is guarded by the police, who, among other things, make sure no funerals are held. The National Library is the center of maintaining a special hierarchy as it brings together representatives of various religions, including Orthodox Jews who have recently lost their academic status.[347] Workers of the lowest order are object hunters, their role consisting in salvaging worn and old things. The work of junk and garbage collectors (called scavengers) is exploitative and leads to exhaustion and eventually death. Despite its absurdity, scavengers, like workers in the capitalist system, are subject to many restrictions, which include compulsory registration with an exploitative employer, acceptance of the minimum rate and unlimited working time, the need to have a wheelchair that must be bought separately, and which must be retrieved forcefully from thieves, etc. Since all forms of production have disappeared from the city, the production of utilities takes place through a system of some sort of recycling. From it, the profit is derived by the Resurrection Agents, the richest and most influential citizens, equal only to garbage collectors. The city is therefore the work (which may not be the best name to call it) of the management of secondary raw materials. To put it bluntly, it has been made from garbage and lives thanks to waste, human waste especially. This, as we have seen, also has an impact on the language of the novel created from ready-made texts or fixed phrases, which are "melted" to make up a separate, first-person memoir-type narrative. Frederic Jameson drew attention to the links between the politics of social dispersion and the non-satirical parody when he wrote,

---

345 Hutcheon, *A Theory of Parody*, p. 37.
346 "On the semantic level, irony can be defined as a marking of difference in meaning or, simply, as antiphrasis." Hutcheon, *A Theory of Parody*, p. 54.
347 The novel does not explain why this happened and what privileges this status brings.

If the ideas of a ruling class were once the dominant (or hegemonic) ideology of bourgeois society, the advanced capitalist countries today are now a field of stylistic and discursive heterogeneity without a norm. Faceless masters continue to inflect the economic strategies which constrain our existences, but they no longer need to impose their speech (or are henceforth unable to); and the postliteracy of the late capitalist world reflects not only the absence of any great collective project but also the unavailability of the older national language itself.[348]

The "land of the last things" in the grip of its invisible rulers does not speak with one voice. In fact, it does not speak at all. Its dead speech can only be heard thanks to Anne Blume's narrative, which, after Jameson, we can call a "linguistic mask."[349] Language which masticates words does not create parody, but pastiche, "speech in a dead language."[350] Writes Jameson: "But it is a neutral practice of such mimicry, without any of parody's ulterior motives, amputated of the satiric impulse, devoid of laughter and of any conviction that alongside the abnormal tongue you have momentarily borrowed, some healthy linguistic normality still exists. Pastiche is thus blank parody, a statue with blind eyeballs [...]."[351] Its food is history, but it is seen as "the random cannibalization of all the styles of the past"[352] and "the play of random stylistic allusion."[353] A random allusion of this kind may be the main character's confession to a group of Jews locked up in the national library that she is Jewish too. Neither the words, conveying a longing to belong to a community, nor the surprise that such a community has managed to survive – vaguely reminiscent of the Holocaust – play any significant role in Auster's post-Holocaust novel. They come and go like all other allusions. What are the consequences of this for the depiction of the Holocaust? First of all, it leads to the juxtaposition of the genocide of the Jewish people with other catastrophes, creating a series of associations which it is difficult to distinguish from one another. Wesseling calls the accompanying concept of history "the continual recycling of the selfsame material."[354] Auster's novel is also a case of reviving the theme of the Holocaust in the context of catastrophic and post-catastrophic moods of the epoch, and at the same time a reason to say a bit more about the meaning of *loci communes*.

---

348 Jameson, *Postmodernism*, p. 17.
349 Jameson, *Postmodernism*, p. 17.
350 Jameson, *Postmodernism*, p. 17.
351 Jameson, *Postmodernism*, p. 17.
352 Jameson, *Postmodernism*, p. 18.
353 Jameson, *Postmodernism*, p. 18.
354 Wesseling, "*In the Country of Last Things*," p. 499.

The Shadow of the Holocaust and the Hiroshima Mushroom 107

From a long list of topoi,[355] Auster has selected famine, rubble, crematoria, corpses, excrement, genocide and camps. In other words, he seems to have opted for some basic concepts without which it is difficult to imagine any narrative even vaguely referring to the Holocaust. However, he has also chosen to deprive his novel of one essential component, actors. It's not that there are no people in it. Those who are, in principle, exist outside the collective of perpetrators, victims and witnesses, becoming part of the invisible scenario described by Jameson. The palette of apocalyptic topoi serves Auster to depict a scenery of disaster and stir up a catastrophic mood to envelop it in. It does not lead to the construction of a linear story, in which the Holocaust would provide a culmination or an ending, a point made by both Elisabeth Wessling and Debra Shostak[356] in their discussion of the new apocalyptic paradigm pursued by Auster. Some topoi function in this apocalyptic and post-capitalist world according to different laws than in those governing Holocaust narratives. Crematoria are essentially power plants:

> Every morning, the city sends out trucks to collect the corpses. This is the chief function of the government, and more money is spent on it than anything else. All around the edges of the city are the crematoria – the so-called Transformation Centers – and day and night you can see the smoke rising up into the sky. [...] Throwing stones at death-truck workers is a common occupation among the homeless. [...] There is no coherent motive behind these attacks. They stem from anger, resentment, and boredom, and because the collection workers are the only city officials who ever make an appearance in the neighborhood, they are convenient targets.[357]

Genocide leads to cannibalism:

> For right then, in the tiny interval that elapsed before he shut the door again, I was able to see clearly in the other room, and there was no mistaking what I saw in there: three or four human bodies hanging naked from meat-hooks, and another man with a hatchet leaning over a table and lopping off the limbs of another corpse. There had been rumors circulating in the library that human slaughterhouses now existed but I hadn't believed them.[358]

And hunger, the leitmotif of all accounts of life in the Warsaw Ghetto and many post-war memoir narratives about it, gives the inhabitants of the city the possibility of a bizarre accommodation: "It is possible to become so good at not eating that eventually you can eat nothing at all. It is even worse for the ones who fight their hunger. [...] They think they are eating to stay alive, but in the end they are

---

355 On this topic see Sławomir Buryła, "Topika Holocaustu. Wstępne rozpoznanie," *World of Texts. Rocznik Słupski* 2012, no. 10, pp. 131–151. Cf also the thematic edition of *Narracje o Zagładzie* 2016/2.
356 Shostak, "In the Country of Missing Persons," p. 67.
357 Paul Auster, *In the Country of Last Things* (London and Boston: Faber and Faber, 1989), p. 17.
358 Auster, *In the Country*, p. 125.

the ones who are eaten."[359] Unlike the population of the ghetto, the inhabitants of the city can buy food at the markets. Unfortunately, the food is not fresh; it is more like leftovers and garbage, such as "oranges filled with sawdust"[360] or "bottles of piss pretending to be beer,"[361] and yet it is the most common cause of theft.

A separate repository of themes related to the Holocaust is created by apocalyptic stories about climate. Winters last half a year and are extremely harsh. For the rest of the year, strong winds blow, forcing people to spend time in confinement. Anna Blume blames the earth for weather changes. Nights are long, days too bright, and twilight does not arrive until it really must. In this way, Auster joins writers such as Andrzej Kuśniewicz, Paweł Huelle, Piotr Szewc or Tadeusz Konwicki, whose novels, published in 1986–1987, support the view of the Holocaust in terms of a global catastrophe, or, rather, of a catastrophe on a global scale in which the Holocaust partook. Climate also seems to be one of the main factors determining time in the novel. The words of the female protagonist – "I thought all the Jews were dead."[362] – make us assume that the Holocaust is a distant echo of the events taking place, their beginning and source. The time frame is marked by mysterious explosions, which may be terrorist attacks or a nuclear war. To construe their meaning, we might want to consider the period when *In the Country of Last Things* was written and published, the year 1987 associated with the earliest artistic responses to the Chornobyl disaster.[363] It too gave rise to a symbolic discourse, which is "both post-catastrophic and post-traumatic,"[364] the kind of discourse which Auster's fiction, especially *In the Country of the Last Things* and *Leviathan*, also represents. As Tamara Hundorova describes it, this discourse is determined not so much by its relation to the object as being "a circle of signs and meanings as well as symbols, associations, and motifs."[365] This insight gives us a set of general terms which allow us to read Auster's novel both as a response to nuclear fears and as a dystopia drawing on the post-Holocaust tradition of science fiction.[366]

If we accept the words of Anja Tippner that a post-catastrophic narrative is a story about life after a catastrophe, "on the rubble and ruins of a catastrophic

---

[359] Auster, *In the Country*, p. 3–4.
[360] Auster, *In the Country*, p. 5.
[361] Auster, *In the Country*, p. 5.
[362] Auster, *In the Country*, p. 95.
[363] Tamara Hundorova cites the example of Iurii Shcherbak's *Chernobyl: A Documentary Story* (1989). Cf. Tamara Hundorova, *The Post-Chornobyl Library: Ukrainian Postmodernism of the 1990s*, trans. Sergiy Yakovenko (Boston: Academic Studies Press, 2019), p. 7 ff.
[364] Hundorova, *The Post-Chornobyl Library*, p. 7.
[365] Hundorova, *The Post-Chornobyl Library*, pp. 8–9.
[366] See L.-H. Pascariu, "Entropy and Loss: Paul Auster's *In The Country of Last Things*," *Procedia – Social and Behavioral Sciences* 92 (2013), p. 679.

past,"[367] and the event that sets off the countdown of the "after" can only be the Holocaust, then nuclear narratives, as well as the Chernobyl discourse and science fiction dystopias fall within the purview of this definition. For Paul Auster's novel, this typology is of little importance. It is primarily a narrative about ghosts living in ruins, about the nightmare of the eternal life of the Holocaust, which after the death of the victims looks much worse than during their lifetime.

---

[367] Anja Tippner, "Postkatastroficzne relikty i relikwie: los obrazów po Holokauście," *Poznańskie Studia Polonistyczne. Seria Literacka* 25 (45), Poznań 2015, p. 239.

Chapter 7.
Vibrating Histories: Raymond Federman and Harry Mulisch

Among the novels published in the 1980s by Walter Abish, Paul Auster, Tadeusz Konwicki, Andrzej Kuśniewicz and Donald Michael Thomas, the plots of two are symbolic, expressing the period's idea of post-modernizing the Holocaust, Raymond Federman's *The Twofold Vibration* and Harry Mulisch's *Assault*, both published in 1982. More clearly delineated than elsewhere, four major themes occur in these two novels: childhood, oblivion, surprise and reckoning. While all four may be regarded as traditional, for various reasons they are also important in the context of Holocaust fiction. Among them, the last-named theme deserves special emphasis due to the fact that the narrative treatment of reckoning is related to changes in chronology and the age of the protagonist. Now the protagonist is a man in the 1980s for whom remembering the war poses a challenge. He is a child survivor who, if it were not for the loss of his whole family, might not remember the Holocaust at all. The climactic point in the narrative is at once a moment of awakening, a recovery of memory, a confrontation with childhood and a confirmation of adulthood. Federman and Mulisch represent their personal and painful experiences as a combination of timeless forces. Their narration is split into two voices: autobiographical and political; which implies that their "top" layer, understood as a consequence of the Holocaust and associated with the late 1960s, 1970s and 1980s,[368] gains priority over the "deep," the war-related layer, virtually becoming an autonomous theme. The twofold vibrations in these stories – to recall the title of Federman's novel – which are partly based on facts and partly on literary improvisation, present alternative Holocaust biographies, treating their versions of events as explanations of the condition of post-Holocaust society. Arguably, this alternative – about which I wrote earlier in connection with the fiction of the 1960s – only acquires its proper meaning in the context of the 1980s, and it is then that it becomes not only a complement, but also a completion of the literature of personal document.

---

368 Even later, in the case of *The Twofold Vibration*, due to some features of the novel which can be considered futuristic.

> [...] unfortunately the potential readers of this story may jump to the conclusion, false and hasty as it may be, that this story is autobiographical in the sense that it tells in a sort of camouflaged way the life of the author, namely me disguised as a nameless old man [...] but this is not true, I assure you [...]
> why pretend otherwise, and were this to be so then there would definitely be something wrong with the twofold vibration theory which sustains this extemporaneous story (TV 150)[369]

Holocaust narratives that feature double and most often even multiple vibrations are stories in which history and fiction intertwine. But to stop the process of defining them at this point would prune them ruthlessly and misrepresent their meaning; it would shorten the thought that needs developing. Therefore, I propose the following working version of the definition: *Vibrating stories about the Holocaust refer to it through the mechanism of erasure, which the subject treats ambivalently, as a desirable and unwanted activity, an activity which one controls or which is not performed consciously. The ambivalence of erasure frees the subject from the feeling of guilt and at the same time intensifies and deepens his or her guilt, becoming the cause of his or her instability and a kind of schizophrenia.* One feature of this type of Holocaust narrative needs special emphasis, their dependence on erasure:

> but if we deal with this matter of the camps at all, it will have to be clear that the central concern is not the extermination of the deportees, including the old guy's entire family, incidentally, father, mother, and sisters too, but the erasure of that extermination as a central event, and it is, I believe, the old man's ambivalence toward this erasure that charges his life emotionally and informs its risks, but perhaps I am anticipating too much (TV 13)

If novels from the 1970s, e.g., *Double or Nothing* and Anatol Ulman's *Cigi de Montbazon*, articulate the experience of erasure, they rarely describe its ambivalence. On the other hand, the experience of ambivalence is not accompanied in them by a return to past events aimed at reckoning and purification. The decade that followed brought about a profound change. Now the protagonist becomes Federman's "eternal gambler," someone who puts his fate in the hands of chance, someone who counts on losing rather than winning the lottery.

---

369 Raymond Federman, *The Twofold Vibration* (Bloomington: Indiana University Press & Brighton: Harvester Press Ltd., 1982); page numbers are given in parentheses in the main text following the abbreviation TV.

Childhood

Both writers present their childhood years from two different perspectives; one is that of a Dutchman (Mulisch), not involved in the Holocaust, and the other – a Jewish survivor (Federman). Also, the narratives devoted to them differ in length and amount of detail. While Mulisch's story abounds in detail and is thorough, Federman's is brief and told in leaps and bounds. *The Assault* tells the story of an ordinary Dutch family, waiting for the end of the war in the comfort of their own apartment. *The Twofold Vibration*, on the other hand, narrates *post factum* the life of a Parisian Jewish couple, a surrealist painter and his seamstress wife, their biography reduced to a handful of scenes. These basic differences notwithstanding, the two novels share a similar protagonist, a person who gets involved in the Holocaust – as the narrative progresses – to a far greater extent than he would like to do. *The Assault*'s Anton Steenwijk in his early boyhood is saved from a street shooting by sheer accident, and later must struggle with the burden of orphanhood and loneliness. *The Twofold Vibration*'s "old man" escapes a Nazi round-up thanks to his mother, who at the last minute manages to conceal him in a closet. Thus connected by the boy protagonist, both narratives address the themes of the cruelty of war and orphanhood. In both these lives, chance seems to be the ruling principle. The reader is finding it difficult to decide whether the protagonists deal differently with bereavement. Both are raised primarily by uncles and aunts, take up studies, become independent and finally, after many failed attempts at oblivion, decide to reconstruct the circumstances in which they lost their closest families. The choice of the mode of narration bestows distinctiveness on the two life stories, which are very much alike. Mulisch opts for a realistic, linear story and the novel's ending suggests an answer to the question about the meaning of the loss of the family and the Holocaust. Federman, from page one onwards, narrates both planes of events simultaneously. Unlike Mulisch, Federman does not reveal new facts to the reader but expands their alternative and fill out the "successive" narrative concerning the adult life of the old man.

Oblivion

This, at least to some extent, is the result of the understanding of history proposed by both writers: Mulisch refers to the War in Holand in terms of *silence*,[370] while Federman compares the Holocaust to an epic event and a Greek tragedy.

---

[370] "In the silence that was Holland then, six shots suddenly rang out" (A 16), Harry Mulisch, *The Assault*, trans. from the Dutch by Claire Nicolas White (New York: Pantheon Books,

Thus, through silence and speaking, terror before the storm and explosion, the two narratives articulate the subject's reactions to the tragedy of personal bereavement. Steenwijk must grow up to understand the fact that his brother and parents died not so much as a result of random shots fired after the murder of friend, a Dutch policeman who collaborated with the Nazis, but because of a Jewish family hidden nearby. Federman's narrative concerns a fundamental experience and an epic-scale event, i. e., the Holocaust understood as a narrative of total causative power,[371] thanks to which "light-weight" postmodernism becomes "weighted down" with reality (or rather an imitation of it). Answering Maciej Świerkocki's question posed in 1991 about the helplessness of the prose of the second half of the twentieth century when faced with the task of representing war, Federman explains the reality of his writing as follows:

> Earlier it was Hitler... Without him, I would probably be a poor Jewish tailor somewhere in Paris. To be sure, I am a famous writer. One draws the material for writing from reality. For example, nothing like this ever happened in John Barth's life... Maybe his wife divorced him, or he himself caused something traumatic to happen to him, but he never participated in a great historical unrest; he never went poor or hungry. I knew hunger, both in France and in America... I begged, I cheated, I stole, yes, I did all that to survive... I had to hide, too. The events of those years are still present in my work. The main part of my literary material comes from the years 1942–1952, from that decade. After that, my life began to resemble Barth's. I got married, I have children, my life is pleasant. Yet I can't write about this period. What bears artistic fruit happened to me a long time ago.[372]

According to Jerzy Kutnik, in *The Twofold Vibration* the Holocaust necessitates constant introspection in the process of creating fiction. This mechanism ensures that thoughts are on the move instead of being frozen in a moment of contemplation. It also explains how anyone can "glimpse" the meaning of their own past.[373] This "glimpsing" – also described as "leapfrogging" by some critics – is precisely what distinguishes Federman's mode of storytelling from Mulisch's,

---

1985). All quotations from this novel are marked by A followed by page number in parentheses.

371 "for the stupefying truth is that the Holocaust is the epic event of the 20th century never striking bottom in the resonance of its tragic fact, no question about that, even the most banal aspects of life in the camps, the most basic, the most innocent questions one asks about the daily routine of the deportees, such as did they brush their teeth, did they cut their nails, did they blow their noses in the camps, did they make love, did they ever smile, reach the level of Greek tragedy, or at least the level of the Theater of the Absurd, and therefore should not be left unanswered, especially now (TV 12).

372 "Przeżyć własną śmierć (rozmowa z Raymondem Federmanem)," in Maciej Świerkocki, *Postmodernizm: paradygmat nowej kultury* (Łódź: Wydawnictwo Uniwersytetu Łódzkiego, 1997), pp. 160–161.

373 Jerzy Kutnik, *The Novel as Performance. The Fiction of Ronald Sukenick and Raymond Federman* (Carbondale and Edwardsville: Southern Illinois University Press, 1986), p. 226.

The Assault being written in classic, realistic narrative prose, its truthfulness resulting from years of painstaking research. However, the fact that a writer chooses to reveal a past rather than letting it remain concealed causes his approach to be delusional, for it leads to a monstrous gesture of a renewed rejection of that past.

There is little evidence to back up the statement that the Holocaust is an important theme of *The Assault*. During the Germans' raid on the Steenwijks' house, suspicions are directed towards Benedict Spinoza's *Ethics*, lying on the table ("'That's what you people read here; Jew books.'" A 25) and the distressed mother ("The man aimed the flashlight, held by a soldier next to him, at her legs. '*Das genugt*, enough,' he said after a while. Not till much later when he was in college did Anton learn that the man thought he could tell by her walk whether she was Jewish." A 25). In the eyes of the narrator, the protagonist, Anton, freed by the Germans, looks "like a ragamuffin from the ghetto of Bialystok" (A 51). Only after years of silence and a protracted avoidance of the subject, during a conversation with a neighbor who witnessed the tragic event, does Anton learn about his personal connections with the Holocaust. Karin reveals that the body of a policeman killed in front of the Steenwijks' house, which Peter, their eldest son, tried to move to another place, was not supposed to be found outside one of the neighboring buildings, because a Jewish family was hiding there:

> "I had already taken a step towards toward their house, but then Father said, 'No, not there. They're hiding Jews.'"
> "Christ!" exclaimed Anton, slapping his forehead.
> "Yes, I had no idea, but father did, apparently. A young family with a small child had been hiding there since forty-three. I saw them for the first time on Liberation Day. Those people certainly would have been killed if Ploeg [the police officer who got shot dead – M.T.] had been found over there. They must have been watching us too, but they never knew what was really going on."
> The Aartses, whom nobody could stand because they kept to themselves, they had saved the lives of three Jews, and those Jews, with their presence, had saved their own. In spite of everything, Korteweg had been a good man! So this was why Ploeg's body had landed on the other side, at their own door, so that… Anton couldn't take any more. (A 183–184)

The Assault's wartime silence is broken by a sudden explosion. The tragedy of the Dutch family turns out to be no coincidence, but part of a social misunderstanding due to which some Jewish people survived the war "at the expense" of some Dutch people. Indeed, the word "expense" seems to be crucial for Mulisch's novel, because it confirms that the linearity of the narrative, like the aforementioned concept of the past, was merely an illusion. In fact, the confrontation of countless family details about Anton's post-war life with information about an anonymous Jewish family (which is given only once, although it could – as in Federman's case – appear on every page), makes us reflect on the significant role of perspective in Holocaust narratives. In the case of *The Twofold Vibration*, it is that of an orphaned Jewish child. In *The Assault*, a Dutch child bears the consequences of saving Jewish people, which involves losing his entire family. Mulisch describes the consequences by way of this puzzling reflection:

> Was everyone both guilty and not guilty? Was guilt innocent, and innocence guilty? The three Jews… Six million of them had been killed. Twelve times as many as there were people marching here. But by being in danger, those three people had unknowingly saved themselves and the lives of two others, and *instead of them, his own father and mother and Peter had died* […]. (A 184; my emphasis – M.T.)

What could be the reasons for arranging a series of absurd cases and circumstances into a narrative of reckoning? One of them is the fact that the plot is set off by the scene of Ploeg's murder in January 1945, when "almost all of Europe had been liberated and was once more rejoicing, eating, drinking, making love, and beginning to forget the War" (A 9). Another is the setting, which is the area of Haarlem near Amsterdam with a small housing estate, whose inhabitants are waiting in a familial atmosphere for the war to end. The third is the corpse of a policeman, boding misfortune to anyone outside whose house it will be found. However, the attempts to move the body, following the shooting with which *The Assault* opens, when we put them in the context of the ending, point to the (previously underestimated) role of determinism. Everything that happens in this novel has its consequences rather than – contrary to what Mulisch suggests – confirming the supreme role of chance. A sentence at the very beginning: "But every day Haarlem looked more and more like one of those spent gray clinkers that they used to take out of the stove, when there had still been coal to burn" (A 9), is complemented by a sentence at the end, describing a political demonstration in 1981, "With a quick gesture he tosses back his straight graying hair, dragging his feet a bit, as each step raised clouds of ashes, although there are no ashes in sight" (A 185).

Spinoza's *Ethics*, about which the German officers question Peter, seems to point to an essential conceptual foundation of the novel. Indeed, this tract may be regarded as the source of the undisturbed narrative silence of *The Assault*, expressed in the protagonist's recognition and acceptance of the necessity of fate, and then in the necessity to restrain desires and to calm down passions. "Insofar as the mind understands all things as necessary," – according to one of Spinoza's propositions – "it has a greater power over the affects, or is less acted on by them."³⁷⁴ Anton's oblivion may be interpreted as a form of Spinozian self-discipline, occasionally punctuated by brief conversations with extended family or neighbors. Anton does not want to know what happened in Haarlem in January 1945. Yet the memory returns when he is confronted with a memorial erected after the war which commemorates the name of his parents and the twenty-nine people held hostage by the Germans after Ploeg's death. However, at the moment of the final confrontation, when Anton begins to understand the connection between the murder of January 1945 and the Holocaust, his affirmation of determinism, taking the form of relativism ("Was everyone both guilty and not guilty? Was guilt innocent, and innocence guilty?"), is shaken. Cautious considerations of innocence and guilt give way to unequivocal accusations: my parents and brother died because of some Jews whose survival was pointless anyway because it defied algebra and logic… So why did they die?

Searches: museums and monuments

Memorials are an important object in both novels. Above all, however, both Federman and Mulisch want to describe the difference between how they are perceived, especially by the families of the victims depicted in the memorial, and their purpose, which reduces them to the function of commemorating Nazi crimes. In *The Assault*, a memorial erected shortly after the war depicts Dutch prisoners arrested by the Germans and murdered in Haarlem in January 1945. On the pedestal, there are also the names of the protagonist's parents and brother:

> The hedge, about a meter wide, was made of rhododendrons, whose leaves glistened in the magic light. It surrounded a low cement wall. On the square central base stood a grayish statue of a staring woman, hair hanging loose and arms reaching out. It was carved in a somber, symmetrically static, almost Egyptian style. Underneath was the date, with the words […] at the sides were the names of the dead in four rows. […] Anton's eyes were riveted on the names. They were recorded and preserved in a bronze alphabet […].
> Perhaps the provincial war monuments committee had debated whether their names really belonged here. Perhaps some of the officials had pointed out that the Steenwijks were, after all, not among the hostages, and were not really killed by a firing squad but simply murdered like animals. (A 73–74)

The monument which Federman writes about is located on the site of the former Konzentrationslager Dachau and consists of a "twisted" sculpture,

---

374 Benedict de Spinoza, *Ethics*, ed. and trans. Edwin Curley (London: Penguin, 1996), Part V, ii/282, p. 165.

we looked for a moment at the intricate piece of sculpture which was erected as a memorial, not bad, social realism with twisted human figures all meshed together and stretching for almost forty feet, we stood in front of it, [...] Miriam came closer to me, I am sick to my stomach, she said, Oh you'll be all right, I told her, you'll see, if I know the Germans it's presented just right. (TV 97)

In both cases, the memorial is located on the premises of a place commemorating a mass crime and has a symbolic character. Thus, its literal character does not hurt anyone's feelings, nor does it raise cultural or moral doubts accompanying human ashes and remains exhibited in camp museums.[375] The sculpture described by Federman, by Nandor Gilda, a former prisoner of the Dachau camp, fits into the paradigm of symbolic death. Ziębińska-Witek has written about it in relation to Tomasz Pietrasiewicz's exhibition-installation called "Elementarz" [Primer], which opened at the State Museum at Majdanek on 19 May 2003.[376] The dark brown bronze from which it was made brings it closer to an even more symbolic representation of the massacre described by Mulisch. The controversies addressed by both authors result from reflection on the documentation of the crime and its limitations. Not everyone – Mulisch and Federman seem to be saying in unison – is allowed to document and commemorate. Erecting memorials may be a shortcut to "absolving" criminals, especially those who are "guilty and innocent"; in no way does it reflect the pain, anger and many other ambivalent emotional states experienced by the victims' families.

Reflection on memorials and memorial sites is a narrative as yet absent in post-Holocaust fiction. It can be understood as a response to the growing role of camp museums and memorial sites around the world. In postmodern fiction, it is accompanied by a revisionist discourse, which raises the issues already mentioned: Who should be allowed to build museums at a site of genocide and how should such museums be built? How should German architectural ideas be evaluated? In his conclusions on the idea of the Holocaust and its representation, Federman comes close to Zygmunt Bauman's reflections in *Modernity and the Holocaust*. However, we must keep in mind that parallels between the two thinkers may be deceptive. Bauman writes about a smoothly running machine of bureaucracy, the weakness of social elites and an electronic battlefield,[377] thus

---

[375] For more on this subject, see Anna Ziębińska-Witek, "Estetyki reprezentacji śmierci w ekspozycjach historycznych," in *Obóz-muzeum. Trauma we współczesnym wystawiennictwie*, ed. Małgorzata Fabiszak and Marcin Owsiński (Kraków: Universitas 2013), pp. 32–36.

[376] As Ziębińska-Witek explains, this exhibition was dedicated to the children in the camp and consisted of, among other things, a wagon symbolizing the Holocaust and four wells embedded in the ground, referring to the three children who survived and one who died in the camp." Ziębińska-Witek, "Estetyki reprezentacji śmierci w ekspozycjach historycznych," pp. 41–42.

[377] See Zygmunt Bauman, *Modernity and the Holocaust* (Ithaca, NY: Cornell University Press, 2000), p. 216. "In 1966, more than twenty years after the gruesome discovery of the Nazi

sustaining an analogy between Nazi ideology and a factory system analogous to Fordism. Fascinated by postwar American society, Federman sees in the Fordist system an advantage over Nazism even in the realm of historical exhibition:

> [...] I once visited the Ford Company Museum in Dearborn, near Detroit, and it's presented just like this, large panels of photographs and documents which retrace the history of the Ford automobile [...]
> The only difference [...] is that at the end of your visit to the Ford Museum you enter a large well lit room and there, on a platform, you see the beautiful shiny latest model of a Ford, the new Thunderbird or LTD, the final product of all these years of innovation and hard work but here [in Dachau – M. T.], and I gestured to the space around us, the empty hall where we stood, here you find nothing, a void, an emptiness, a few words scribbled on the walls, this whole machine has led to this, to this vacuum, the whole Nazi machine has produced nothing, nothing but an absence, it was invented to fabricate death (TV 100–101)

Federman builds his critique of the commemoration of concentration camps by developing the common expression "death factory" as suggestive of the expectation that the place of production might fulfill some role, if not always a positive one. The idea of the perfection of German culture, expressed in the commemoration – regarded as paradoxical – of the crime scene by perpetrators[378] returns even later, during a further tour of Germany and the old man's stay in a hotel in Baden-Baden. As a response to his visit to Dachau, the old man first has sex with a random young woman, then goes to the casino and wastes all his savings, and finally makes a suicide attempt in his hotel room. After being rescued, he comments on this "bad luck" in the following words, "Goddammit, I can't even die in this fucking country, no, they won't let me die here" (TV 111).

"This fucking country" is, of course, Germany, Western Germany in the 1960s, to be precise. Neither Germany nor the Netherlands made the effort to discuss the Holocaust and its Nazi past until many years after the war, in the 1980s.[379] The theme of the "late effort" is taken up by Mulisch, who shows his protagonist in a

---

crime, a group of distinguished scholars designed the scientifically elegant and exemplary rational project of the *electronic battlefield* for the use of the generals of the Vietnam war" (p. 115; emphasis in the original).

378 By the logic of the plot, the old man must have visited the museum shortly after its opening. For him, his visit to Germany was above all a drastic confrontation with the place of death of his immediate family; he looks with mounting horror at the all-governing order.

379 Cf. *Historikerstreit. Spór o miejsce III Rzeszy w historii Niemiec*, ed. Jerzy Holzer, Londyn: Aneks 1990. Worthy of note is Anna Wolff-Powęska's statement: "However, it would be wrong to believe that there has been no discussion about the past in post-war Germany. The past has been the subject of an ongoing narrative. Victims have reported dramatic situations of survival. Witnesses have made attempts to understand and explain. Perpetrators, accused by their social environment, have been trying to prove their 'innocence.'" Anna Wolff-Powęska, *Pamięć: brzemię i uwolnienie. Niemcy wobec nazistowskiej przeszłości (1945–2010)* (Poznań: Zysk i S-ka, 2011), pp. 160–161.

situation of political isolation, as an individual unprepared to understand that the Holocaust could have taken place in his country, in his small native hometown of Haarlem. What Mulisch sets out to work through in *The Assault* is to make the reader aware of the operation of chance in the Holocaust, and in this way to draw our attention to the complicities and deficiencies of the system of bureaucracy in the extermination of the Jewish population, as studied by Bauman.[380] It is not Mulisch's purpose to convince his readers that anyone could be a Jew. He describes the case of some Dutch people who died at the least expected moment, at the end of the war, when no one expected Jews to be alive in the Netherlands, and in doing so he wants to draw our attention to the power with which the stereotype of their absence persisted in this country for many years and how willingly it was embraced. Citing historian Ido de Haan's 1998 study, Diane L. Wolf draws attention to the danger of equating Jewish and non-Jewish traumas:

> The discourses of trauma and victimhood applied to everyone alike – Jews, the children of Dutch Nazis, those who suffered from crime, and victims of incest. Thus, once again, the playing field was leveled, and everyone became a "survivor." De Haan pushes his analysis further by claiming that it is an "outright insult" to call the Occupation a national trauma because it implies that everyone – perpetrators and victims alike – suffered equally. He argues that we should directly name the Occupation for what it was: "The persecution of the Jews in the Netherlands as a crime of organized violence by German occupying forces in collaboration with Dutch officials and facilitated by Dutch institutions, rules, and morals."[381]

Both Federman and Mulisch also write about the "leveling" of traumas in their comments on the monuments in Dachau and Haarlem. Federman is horrified by the "entanglement" of the sculpture, while Mulisch's narrator is irritated by the commemoration of people "recorded and preserved in a bronze alphabet, the letters not even made of bronze [...]" (A 74). This may indicate that in the 1980s fictions we can find traces, if indistinct, of a different type of commemoration of crime scenes, one that reflects not only its planning, but also its randomness. We read about one such clue in *The Assault*, when Anton visits the monument for the second time: "The rhododendrons had grown into a massive wall covered with heavy clusters of blossoms, between which the stylized Egyptian statue of a woman had weathered" (A 160).

---

380 Zygmunt Bauman, *Modernity and the Holocaust*, p. 227 (section "The role of bureaucracy in the Holocaust"). The role of bureaucracy was also discussed very meticulously by Raul Hilberg, who subjected Nazi documents to thorough analyzes, from which the causative side of the Holocaust emerged. See Hilberg, *The Destruction of the European Jews*.
381 Diane Lauren Wolf, *Beyond Anne Frank: Hidden Children and Postwar Families in Holland* (Berkeley, Los Angeles, London: University of California Press, 2007), p. 110.

The idea of postmodernizing the Holocaust, mentioned at the beginning of this chapter, results from an alternative and unconventional understanding of history, which is the opposite of the "postconventional identity" that Jürgen Habermas wrote about in 1986.[382] It was supposed to result from the broken communication of young generations with the past. Mulisch and Federman record its continuity, making it visible, not in people born after the war, but in survivors. Their "scorching" is shown as rebellion against the peculiar trajectories of mourning celebrations, e. g., seeking understanding of what happened in conversations with perpetrators, reacting to various forms of commemoration of crimes, and finally passivity and emotional rigidity, including the difficulty of forming love relationships, raising children and entering into various social roles. The alternative has here the sense of an obligatory narrative, regarded as such not simply due to the low frequency of its occurrence (we may note in passings its absence from Polish literature), but also because of the liberation of the narrative from the documentary framework. The dream that the one can survive a catastrophe and free one's identity and one's sexuality from the memory of it, and that in this way one can also improve one's understanding of politics and history, is a dream dreamt not only by postmodernists. But only they seem to make it produce engaging literary representations.

---

382 Jürgen Habermas, "Eine Art Schadensabwicklung," "Sposób zacierania winy", trans. Małgorzata Łukasiewicz, in *Historikerstreit. Spór o miejsce III Rzeszy w historii Niemiec*, ed. Małgorzata Łukasiewicz (London: Aneks, 1990), pp. 81–89. "[…] inaugurating *Historikerstreit*, Habermas argued against German historians who lamented the loss of history (*Verlust der Geschichte*) but in fact attempted to instil national, if not nationalistic, myths. He associated memories with conventional forms of national identity, which should be subjected to public rational debate and, consequently, replaced with postconventional identity based on 'constitutional patriotism,' which justifies rational, universalistic principles of morality and democracy." Michał Łuczewski, Tomasz Maślanka and Paulina Bednarz-Łuczewska, "Bringing Habermas to Memory Studies," *Polish Sociological Review* 1/183 (2013), p. 336.

Chapter 8.
Allegories of the Holocaust: Marek Bieńczyk and Ewa Kuryluk

Allegory might seem to be a project radically different from the Holocaust discourse of memory. Images which are detached from reality are usually also radically removed from the essence of depictions of the Holocaust, that essence consisting in metonymic rather than allegorical testimony about facts and things. Testimony, as evidence of crimes, belongs to the language of memory, and should therefore be both individual and factual, rather than flashing with images from centuries ago. The postmodern novels by Ewa Kuryluk and Marek Bieńczyk, published in the 1990s, encourage us to rethink this issue and perhaps also to redefine the role of allegory in narratives about the Holocaust. The allegories deployed in *Century 21* and *Tworki* do not disturb the course of history, while creating narratives that defy the realist mode of representation. As Robert Scholes once argued in his treatment of allegory in general, narrative of this kind is primarily concerned with links between the fictive world and concepts, which leaves reality far behind.[383] Above all, allegory constitutes an alternative to the traditional literature of the personal document in the way it manifests knowledge about the world, thus fulfilling a similar function to postmodern narratives about the Holocaust, whose beginning, especially in Poland, coincided with the need for an alternative to historiographical discourse.[384]

Kuryluk's and Bieńczyk's novelistic allegories can also be regarded in terms of identity in that they concern people and their masks, which in a broad sense resemble or camouflage Jews hiding on the Aryan side. Examples of "identity

---

383 Robert Scholes, *The Fabulators* (New York: Oxford University Press, 1967), pp. 98–99.
384 I am thinking here primarily of Leopold Buczkowski's 1966 novel *Pierwsza świetność*, which can be regarded as the first postmodern Holocaust novel in Polish (all the usual objections raised by the numeral "first" notwithstanding). To make sense of the postmodern role of allegory, we should first of all recall Craig Owens's statement in the 1980 essays "The Allegorical Impulse: Toward a Theory of Postmodernism" (Part 2): "Postmodernism neither brackets nor suspends the referent but works instead to problematize the activity of reference." Craig Owens, *Beyond Recognition. Representation, Power, and Culture* (Berkeley, Los Angeles and London: University of California Press, 1992), p. 85.

allegories" can be found both in Bieńczyk's protagonists hiding in the Tworki hospital and in the story about Kuryluk's and her family's autobiographical incarnations hidden behind pseudonyms. In this chapter I want to look at both these projects and work out an appendix of sorts to the already existing commentaries to Kuryluk's and Bieńczyk's fictions by placing particular emphasis on the connection of allegory with the Holocaust and postmodernism.[385]

To begin with two short passages, this one comes from Kuryluk:

> And what's in store for the rest of us, Joseph? With my physique and white beard, I would make an excellent Wandering Jew. And you, I presume, can get two hot meals a day at the Sailors' Soup Kitchen. No, we won't commit collective suicide. Let's rather become engaged to Ms. Reality. I mean, you, the youngest, should buy her a bridal ring and pay compliments every day. (C21 250)[386]

The other scene is found in Bieńczyk:

> They are coming closer and closer; they are in a great apogee. The first on the right, Love, waves her free hand to the beat of some tune and takes a second to adjest the pastel skirt that has slipped out from under the belt. Her face lights up with a smile at the sight of another pair of eyes close by, blue and American, her hand fawning at the touch of another's hand. Next to it is the Lighthearted One, distinguished by her great height and the size of her shoes. She deliberately slows down, laughs at each of her several thoughts, and enjoys tomorrow's day and night. What does she care. That hand under her elbow, on the other hand, belongs to Hope. […] Bliss makes up this row, her hand entangled with Hope's, their ring fingers entwined. She squints her round eyes a bit against the pouring light, begins to hum a tune, and the legs of her pants puff up delightfully. (T 120)

Marek Zaleski, one of the few interpreters of the second passage, called this allegorical theatre a rococo *fête galante* and Petit Trianon.[387] Illuminating as this observation is, it confirms the unsealing between the worlds of fiction and concepts, diverting the reader's attention away from the subject matter of *Tworki*, which is related to the fate of Polish Jews in 1942, and directing it instead towards the conventions of love games from past centuries. I am finding myself compelled here to repeat Berel Lang's argumentation from his *Act and Idea in the Nazi Genocide*, where he argues the weakness of the figurative discourse on the Holocaust, which he describes in terms of that kind of unsealing: "the more

---

385 For my analysis of pseudonyms of the Holocaust in Ewa Kuryluk's work, see Marta Cuber, *Metonimie Zagłady. O polskiej prozie lat 1987–2012* (Katowice: Wydawnictwo Uniwersytetu Śląskiego 2013). The concept of allegory is not developed in that book.
386 Citations to these two novels are marked in the following way: C21 for Ewa Kuryluk, *Century 21* (Normal, IL, Dalkey Archive Press, 1992); T for Marek Bieńczyk, *Tworki* (Warszawa 1999), followed by page numer, in parentheses.
387 Marek Zaleski, *Echa Idylli w literaturze polskiej doby nowoczesności i późnej nowoczesności* (Kraków: Universitas, 2007).

specific and direct the historical address of such writing [imaginative writing about the Holocaust], the greater the constraints on its literary or poetic character. And conversely: the more consistently figurative or 'imaginative' it is, the greater the distance between it and the claims of historical reference or authenticity."[388] Lang's further considerations aim to show that this distance is undesirable, and it is usually the rhetorical (figurative) layer of the text that is responsible for its deployment.

> In historical discourse, the references asserted preclude or at least determine generalization; by contrast, the alternative possibilities of poetry are constantly present (even after they are rejected). In figurative discourse, together with the distance between the figure and its referent, there is set in motion a process of inference and generalization which becomes itself part of the text.[389]

I suggest that, even though Lang is not discussing *Century 21* or *Tworki*, his reflections provide us with a springboard for thinking about the role of allegory in Holocaust-related narratives. We find in them the thought-provoking idea of intentionality that Lang attributes to the creators of figurative discourses. An author has to decide on a specific rhetorical figure and make that figure stand out in his or her literary work, towering over the text. Although Lang does not illustrate his point with examples (he laconically mentions metaphor), one can imagine a work in which allegory would exemplify his line of argumentation. And I submit that it is allegory, much more than the content of genocide narratives, that occupies the reader's attention as she wonders about the accuracy of the figures used and perhaps tries to find some regularity in the way they are woven together. Lang, therefore, is far from being an ally of this trope; nor would he be one, if such a hypothetical situation occurred. In his opinion allegory, like other figures of speech, fosters literary generalization, creating a distance between itself and its referent, which, as Marek Zaleski's commentary exemplifies, does not necessarily lead to Nazi genocide, but might go off at a tangent.

However, Lang does not address what seems particularly useful in understanding the role of allegory in twentieth-century prose, including its postmodern variety. This type of reflection appears in Scholes's 1967 book *The Fabulators* and it significantly expands the range of meaning attributed to figures of speech. Allegory in the sense developed by Scholes is one of the three main ways, along with romance and satire, of departing from the model of the realist

---

388 Berel Lang, *Act and Idea in the Nazi Genocide* (Chicago and London: University of Chicago Press, 1990), p. 140.
389 Lang, *Act and Idea in the Nazi Genocide*, p. 144.

novel. As an example of allegory, Scholes takes up Iris Murdoch's *The Unicorn*.[390] Paul de Man also recalls this unrealistic and sometimes even anti-realistic character of allegory, writing that "[…] more than ordinary modes of fiction, allegory is at the furthest possible remove from historiography."[391] As we will see later in this chapter, de Man's objections are not always taken into account in literature.

In a brief allegoresis preparatory to his analysis of *The Unicorn*, Scholes uses the allegorical toolbox to tell the story of novelistic allegory. To this end, he creates a meta-allegory that becomes a story about people gifted with a talent for storytelling from the country of the Novel and their relationships with their neighbors from the countries of Philosophy and History. The mutual relations and influences of these countries resemble the history of the modern novel in Europe. First, allegory prevails, then the realistic novel takes the lead, and in the second half of the twentieth century there appears – to put it in the simplest of terms – a third type of prose, one that combines the experiences of the predecessors, which Scholes calls "a new kind of Allegory," composed of all ideas, some old, some innovative.[392] The essence of this new allegorical novel is made up of two interpenetrating layers, allegory and plot. A new allegory can therefore be read out of love for the plot, but at the same time there is the problem of the ideas written into the plot, "For in the work of an allegorical fabulator, fiction and ideation are always intertwined."[393]

Iris Murdoch's novel fulfills this premise in a special way. It is a story of surprises and discoveries experienced by the reader and the protagonist, Marian Tylor, who is employed as a governess at Gaze Castle, the country house owned by the Crean-Smiths, a wealthy couple now separated. Although the author tells in detail the story of the owner of the house, Hannah, these particulars do not serve to build either a realist, a moral or a psychological plot. Hannah's intriguing passivity,[394] combined with legends of her aggression, causes the reader to look beyond the plot, as it were, for answers to the question about Mrs. Crean-Smith's

---

390 Robert Scholes, *The Fabulators* (New York and Oxford: Oxford University Press, 1967), 106ff; see also Leszek Kolek's review, "'The Fabulators', Robert Scholes, New York 1967, Oxford University Press 1967, pp. X, 2 nlb., 180," *Pamiętnik Literacki*, 65/1 (1974), p. 352.
391 Paul de Man, *Aesthetic Ideology* (Minneapolis, MN, and London: University of Minnesota Press, 1996), p. 51.
392 Scholes, *The Fabulators*, p. 99.
393 Scholes, *The Fabulators*, p. 105.
394 Hannah resembles a symbolic figure described by Maria Podraza-Kwiatkowska as a symbolic variant characterized by somnambulism, unreality, reverie, staring into the distance, absence, pallor and mystery. The description of Hannah as slender, pale, red-haired, and permanently confined is strongly reminiscent of this type. It also evokes associations with Arnold Böcklin's 1885 painting "The Silence of the Forest" discussed by Podraza-Kwiatkowska. Cf. Maria Podraza-Kwiatkowska, *Symbolizm i symbolika w poezji Młodej Polski* (Kraków: Wydawnictwo Literackie, 1994), p. 112.

identity. For her impact on the community, locked in a mansion between swamps, heather and the sea, and its mimetic romantic relationships disproves the assumption that Hannah herself could be the source of her strength, which affects the realism of the narrator's representation of this heroine: "'She is our image of the significance of suffering. But we must also see her as real. And that will make us suffer too.' [...]. 'The unicorn is also the image of Christ. But we have to do too with an ordinary guilty person.'"[395] The instructions given to us by the protagonists of *The Unicorn*, to treat Hannah with deadly seriousness, befitting the realism of her guilt and crimes, at once carry the suggestion that this crime contains an idea that partly contradicts the plot and is related to the innocence of suffering combined with punishment for murder. In addition to the tight bond between the countries Novel and Philosophy, as Scholes would put it, Murdoch proposes another solution. Reaching back to Plato's *Phaedrus*, she develops a new, albeit singular and highly individual understanding of allegory: "'You remember at the end Socrates tells Phaedrus that words can't be removed from place to place and retain their meaning. Truth is communicated from a particular speaker to a particular speaker.'"[396]

The definition of allegory outlined in *The Unicorn* can therefore be reduced to the idea of moving words from place to place, as a result of which they lose their original meaning and gain others (such as the eponymous unicorn's denoting not only innocence, but also freedom), specified in the preliminary conditions of communication. In the case of Murdoch's novels, relativism and morality are among those conditions, which in less favorable circumstances (or uncontrolled by the author's will) can change into their opposite. This is precisely what Murdoch warns us against in creating the figure of Hannah, a character iridescent like a pre-Raphaelite symbol, one who is a few things rolled into one: a fair angel, a criminal, a devoted friend and an absolutely passive pawn in the histrionics enacted by the inhabitants of Gaze Castle. "The equation of the modern allegory" – according to Scholes – "does not say that Hannah's suffering is significant because it is a type of Christ's. It says that Hannah's suffering and Christ's are equally significant, and the significance depends on what we believe about it."[397]

---

395 Iris Murdoch, *The Unicorn* (London: Vintage Books, 2000), p. 98. Scholes also draws attention to the double dimension of *The Unicorn:* "*The Unicorn* is, on its esthetic level, a fabulator's manifesto, in which the book itself is seen as fulfilling the purifying function of the traditional scapegoat, by providing the ritual purgation for those initiated into its mysteries." Scholes, *The Fabulators*, p. 117. That that sense, Murdoch's novel, like her heroine, can be regarded as a scapegoat.
396 Murdoch, *The Unicorn*, p. 100.
397 Scholes, *The Fabulators*, p. 124.

This type of allegory, however, is relatively distant from Lang's critique and the assumptions of the two novelists whose works I am discussing in this chapter. In contrast to the crumbling narratives of Bieńczyk and Kuryluk, Murdoch gave her existential allegory a coherent plot structure, that of a thriller or a crime novel. If we were to treat Scholes's insight about the adherence of fiction and ideas as a prerequisite for creating a multi-level novel as the basis for our reflections on allegory, then the novels by the Polish postmodernists, and especially *Century 21*, could only be described as extremely incoherent. However, before we pass our judgement, worth noting is a fundamental difference between the ideas represented by the three authors. Murdoch reflects on empathy, suffering and its radiation, guilt and truth in a discourse devoid of historical contours, suspended in a timelessness, which enables her fictional inquiries to attain a level of generality and allows us to call *The Unicorn* both a contemporary legend about Christ and a moral and psychological novel with gothic motifs. *The idée fixe* in *Tworki* and *Century 21* is the Holocaust. These two authors put more energy into excluding or withdrawing the Event from the narrative than in relativizing It. As a consequence, the Event, under the allegories of words, remains in its tragic sublimity invariably silent and ruthless. The way in which Bieńczyk and Kuryluk understand allegory resembles its definition in Jerzy Ziomek's *Retoryka opisowa* [*Descriptive Rhetoric*]. "Allegory [...] should have one presumed hidden meaning, but one for this time, for this situation, and in this context."[398] Examples from *Tworki*, where Goethe, Bismarck, Rubens and Dürer are names of psychiatric patients (T 31), or from *Century 21*, in which Pompeii is an allegory of the Holocaust (W21 187ff), and the name Carol Kar, which is a modification of Anna Karenina, is a mask to conceal Ewa Kuryluk (who in turn hides many other contemporary figures and their problems under the names of Goethe, Propretius, Host, Berenice or Djuna Barnes) – they seem to confirm this rule.[399]

The allegorical novels of the 1990s differ from Murdoch's in one more important aspect. In addition to the less balanced relationship between ideas and plot, they are characterized by greater freedom in "moving words from place to place" than in *The Unicorn*. Kuryluk explains this in a self-referential confession: "There was nothing she [Carol] couldn't combine." (C21 211). Bieńczyk ex-

---

[398] Jerzy Ziomek, *Retoryka opisowa* (Wrocław: Ossolineum, 2000), pp. 235–236.
[399] The allegory of twentieth-century power, introducing slavery, is Pharaoh Euergetes. Anna Karenina resembles the heroine of Leo Tolstoy's novel, the writer himself, Greta Garbo, a Mexican hair salon and a neighbor of Eva Kuryluk. Bel Bonafiduci, a professor at Princeton University, is a character with the features of Henryk Kowalski, born in 1941 in Kielce, who also resembles to some extent Miriam Kohany's first husband (i.e., Maria Kuryluk's, Ewa's mother), Teddy Gleich. Moses Maimonides, on the other hand, resembles Stefan Themerson and Ewa Kuryluk. Cf. Ewa Kuryluk, *Manhattan i Mała Wenecja. Rozmawia Agnieszka Drotkiewicz* (Warszawa: Wydawnictwo Zeszytów Literackich, 2016), pp. 15, 24, 76.

presses a similar idea when he explains his poignant attitude to allegory in his essay *Melancholia. O tych, co nigdy nie odnajdą straty* [*Melancholia. About Those Who Will Never Recover Their Loss*].[400] Here he discusses the relationship between allegory and melancholy and ends up suggesting that allegory is a figure of melancholic and postmodern writing at the same time. Bieńczyk reminds us after Walter Benjamin that "[…] allegories are to thought what ruins are to objects,"[401] thus naming the authority in the field of rhetoric. In *Origin of the German Trauerspiel*, Benjamin defines allegory as the ruin of images in relation to the phenomenon of "natural history [*Natur-Geschichte*],"[402] claiming that "The allegorical physiognomy of natural history, which is brought onstage in the trauerspiel, is actually present as ruin. In the ruin, history has passed perceptibly into the setting. And so configured, history finds expression not as process of an eternal life but as process of incessant decline.[403] In a sense, this is a polemical approach to de Man's position, which separates allegory from the representation of history.[404] Benjamin analyzes historical allegories as the source and evidence of the disintegration of history in literature. Thus, corresponding to Benjamin's vision of the "angel of history,"[405] there are allegories with the memory of forms in a state of decay, which, however, does not interfere with the representation. "With decay, and with it alone, historical occurrence shrinks and withdraws into the setting."[406]

Bieńczyk's commentary in a chapter of his book on melancholy ("Alegoria na drodze melancholika," which could be rendered as "a melancholy person encounters allegory"[407]) seems to be an obvious and natural source of ideas for *Tworki*, a novel published a year after that essay on melancholy. Although it does not represent the Holocaust, due the overall character of Bieńczyk's theory of melancholy, reminiscent of a natural cataclysm or a monstrous catastrophe, the Holocaust is part of the novel's entire theatre. In fact, the novel's time span covers the time after the Holocaust, as remembered by the narrator sitting outside the

---

400 Marek Bieńczyk, *Melancholia. O tych, co nigdy nie odnajdą straty* (Warszawa: Świat Książki, 2012).
401 Bieńczyk, *Melancholia*, p. 87.
402 Walter Benjamin, *Origin of the German Trauerspiel*, trans. Howard Eiland (Cambridge, Mass. and London: Harvard University Press, 2019), p. 188.
403 Benjamin, *Origin of the German Trauerspiel*, p. 188.
404 Even though, in fact, we cannot be talking here about any debate as such for, as Adam Lipszyc argues, "de Man intensively draws on Benjamin." Cf. Adam Lipszyc, *Sprawiedliwość na końcu języka. Czytanie Waltera Benjamina* (Kraków: Universitas, 2012), p. 203.
405 "It is in his 'Theses on the Philosophy of History,' an extended meditation on the claims of the past on us, that Benjamin describes his now oft-cited 'angel of history': 'Where we perceive a chain of events, he sees one single catastrophe which keeps piling wreckage upon wreckage and hurls it in front of his feet.'" Bellamy, *Affective Genealogies*, p. 71.
406 Benjamin, *Origin of the German Trauerspiel*, p. 190.
407 Bieńczyk, *Melancholia*, pp. 86–94.

hospital on a bench. Allegory acts as the basic trope in this depiction of the characters' fate. It may be accompanied and assisted by comparisons, periphrases and metaphors,[408] but it is allegory itself that plays the honorable role of the main literary device in Bieńczyk's tale of a group of Jews hidden in a hospital near Warsaw.

Ewa Kuryluk also creates an allegorical theatre of the Holocaust by assembling her novel from various fragments of stories overheard or written earlier. The repetition of the forms of the past that makes up *Century 21* resembles an endless conversation. Its complexity, resulting from the lack of an addressee of the monologues and the changing of speakers, also has an allegorical dimension, with a possible source in painting. The metamorphoses of the characters are reminiscent of Kuryluk's paintings, in which, as she puts it, "I also take on various forms, as in painting of the past, when in one self-portrait I was a black Ik, in another a blonde tennis player with a ball in the form of a guy, and on the third, entitled *Erros Center*, a sex bomb with a huge butt."[409] It is a practice, as Kuryluk confesses in an interview with Agnieszka Drotkiewicz, mediated in the fascination with the seventeenth-century painting of Artemisia Gentileschi, and especially in her *Allegoria della pittura*, an allegory of painting and self-portrait, which is "one of the first examples of the coincidence of person and subject in European art."[410] The characters appearing in *Century 21* under assumed names, like the patients of the hospital in Tworki, also resemble Benjamin's allegories. Their belonging to history, as it will later turn out, crumbles at the touch of a hand as quickly as a moth-ridden piece of fabric. "The allegorical intention invariably refers to some ancient loss, to that inevitable, ever-present character of the becoming of human history as ruin; [...]. Loss-infected historical events do not give man the opportunity to retrieve the lost meaning."[411] No wonder, then, that in *Century 21* the only obvious thing that remains seems to be historical chaos. The combination of historical fiction (the stories of Berenice, the Host and Propertius) with contemporary narratives must lead to the conclusion that Kuryluk is not after realistic representation. Rather, she is after allegory in the sense defined by Scholes; yet her purpose is completely different. But are we here

---

408 My defense of allegory and its primacy in *Tworki* over other rhetorical figures is in opposition to other scholars, e. g., Katarzyna Chmielewska and Arkadiusz Morawiec, who tend to ascribe leading role to other tropes. Cf. Katarzyna Chmielewska, "Klęska powieści? Wybrane strategie pisania o Szoa," in *Stosowność i forma. Jak opowiadać o Zagładzie?* ed. Katarzyna Chmielewska, Michał Głowiński, Katarzyna Makaruk, Alina Molisak, and Tomasz Żukowski (Kraków: Universitas, 2005), pp. 258–264; Arkadiusz Morawiec, *Literatura w lagrze, lager w literaturze*, pp. 357–358.
409 Kuryluk, *Manhattan i Mała Wenecja*, p. 55.
410 Kuryluk, *Manhattan i Mała Wenecja*, p. 144.
411 Bieńczyk, *Melancholia*, p. 93.

already in the realm of anti-realism as a feature which some critics attribute to *Tworki?*[412]

Before examining allegory in its unrealistic dimension, let us look at a specific instance of its use, reminiscent of its traditional meaning as identified with an enigma (a riddle).[413] In both novels, the authors use the trick of giving their characters the names of historical people associated with art. In *Century 21*, we have one instance of this, a collection of names behind which Kuryluk as it were hides herself, her relatives and her friends, these identity allegories constituting a toolbox of autobiographical fiction and even novels of the *roman à clef* type. For example, a protagonist quotes a conversation with Carol Kar in which she introduces herself as the daughter of the director of Państwowe Wydawnictwo Naukowe (Polish Scientific Publishers PWN): "In the *Great Polish Encyclopedia* my dad edited, it went under *Bohemian bonhomie*, or how to approach a lady not on a white horse but on a skate board" (C21 259). Ann Kar and Karl Eglizer also seem to fulfil a similar function, namely that of literary incarnations of the autobiographical narrator and her relatives. The two are talking about the Holocaust survivor *mameła*, "Your *mamerle!* A victim who keeps excavating her old Pompeii in order to make a new one out of our lives. A survivor who perceives the entire earth as her very own graveyard, and brushes aside other claims to suffering" (C21 187). As already mentioned, the American and European artistic community as described by Kuryluk consists not only of the invariants of the names of legendary artists; it primarily consists of icons of ancient, romantic and modernist culture: Moses Maimonides, Johann Wolfgang Goethe, Malcolm Lowry, Italo Svevo. But these are incomplete, ruined, and defective icons, which speak the language of trivial associations, slavishly attached to verbal sounds treated as if some serious, intrinsic meaning was preserved in them. As in this passage:

> Around one o'clock black marketeers hula-hooped around huge hips, sighing and sweating. After two the founders of forbidden sects, Judaism, Christianity, and Islam, sucked at Persephone's fragile tits, while naked Psyches buzzed around their pricks. Finally around 4:00 a.m. all of us, including myself and another scribe, shrank to the size of newborn Tannhausers and slipped for an hour into the cave, tepid and pulsating, of Madonna Laura, our most familiar lady. Imagine! (C21 169)

The impermanence of these allegories and the image of chaotic history of modernity they create are evidenced above all by the theatre in which the protagonists play their roles: the almost spectacular love affairs and betrayals, civilization diseases, parties, and drunkenness. Yet, against the background of the kaleidoscopic adventures of Karenina, Vronsky, Berenice and the thinkers and

---

412 Chmielewska, "Klęska powieści?" p. 261.
413 Ziomek, *Retoryka opisowa*, p. 234.

writers, another theatrical spectacle is taking place, that of the shadows of the Holocaust. These shadows wear elaborate disguises which make them nearly unrecognizable and nearly impossible to remove. Their meaning consists in concealing the secrets of the biography of the author of *Century 21*. We need to note one more important feature of the novel's allegories: the thin thread that connects the biographies of past artists and the biographies of their contemporary incarnations. Anna Karenina travels around Spain in the mid-1840s, reflecting on Vronsky's mid-life crisis. Goethe, who is struggling with the same problem, is an inveterate womanizer, his conquests including Fellini's mistresses. Maimonides corresponds with Hamlet about Eli Weasel and mentions his father's business transactions with Bruno Schulz, while Djuna Barnes suffers from AIDS.

The image of Love, Light-heartedness, Hope and Bliss in the passage quoted from Bieńczyk's novel at the outset of this chapter points to the lack of connection between content and representation within the same type of allegory. He builds these impersonations of feelings theoretically, in a manner reminiscent of the allegorical pictures, "moral emblems," in Cesare Ripa's *Iconologia*. One of the most important elements of these constructions were so-called attributes, i.e. "additional signs, objects with which the main character – a personification – is sometimes equipped. Thus, for example, scales held by a blindfolded female figure which personifies Justice; an hourglass in the hand of a half-naked old man – Time, etc. All these are attributes that make the allegory readable, complement and turn the iconic sign called the scheme into a pleromat."[414] Skirt-adjusting Love, Light-heartedness sporting big shoes, Hope with no makeup on her face, Bliss pulling her companions to the left – not only do these images fail to resemble those in Ripa's work, but above all they have no attributes that bestow a special meaning on the images. Shoes, cuffs, a belt and a skirt belong, not to a world of ideas, but to the novel's reality and serve no purpose other than unmasking the characters. We can avail ourselves here of Gregory L. Ulmer's explanation:

> But there is an all-important difference between montage-allegory and the object as emblem in baroque and romantic allegory. In the latter, adhering to the model of the hieroglyph in which the particular object of nature or daily life is taken over as a conventional sign for an idea, the object is used "not to convey its natural characteristics, but those which we have ourselves lent it." In collage, on the other hand, the allegorical significance is literal, derives from the natural characteristics themselves.[415]

---

414 Andrzej Borowski, "Cesare Ripa czyli muzeum wyobraźni", in Cesare Ripa, *Ikonologia*, trans. Ireneusz Kania (Kraków: Universitas, 2004), p. vi.

415 Gregory L. Ulmer, "The Object of Post-Criticism," in *Postmodern Culture*, ed. Hal Foster (London: Pluto Press, 1985), p. 97; the inset quotation is from Benjamin's *Origin of the German Trauerspiel*.

Allegories of the Holocaust 133

False, crumbling allegories are also used by Bieńczyk to describe psychiatric patients, who are given, as in Kuryluk's book, the names of legendary artists. A special role among them is played by Antiplato, a philosopher-poet, who comments on the fictional events as though he were a one-man Greek choir: "existence has become an unfixed and uninspired sentence, twisted and borrowed. A response without a calling, an echo of an echo, which never stops leaking" (T 49). Significant is above all the birthday gift for Sonia, which the poet arranges into an enigma: "The one who barks is not the first; the one who barks back is not the second. In this wood there is no wilderness. This is the wood of the wood. The one who is chasing is running away. The deer is shooting while the boar is counting the bullets. The hunt is on, but the game is nowhere in sight and will not show" (T 92). Antiplato's story is a graphic representation of the situation of the Tworki inmates who, like hunted game, are taking shelter from other animals hunting them. It is also a literary illustration of Małgorzata Melchior's words:

> In the animal world, the art of imitation and self-masking – mimicry – is a common survival strategy. Taking the form or appearance of something else, blending into the environment are the ways endangered species use to "deceive predators and avoid death." This comparison may seem inappropriate, but the situation of Jews on the Aryan side, chased and hunted down, did turn them into "game." At least that's how it felt to them. In order to survive, they had to "change their skin," become someone else, so as not be known for Jews.[416]

Antiplato's hunting allegory, however, is not as perspicuous as the critic's explanation might suggest. It creates the impression of being poorly thought-out and based on a confusing image, a picture that has been dislodged from its frame. However, this is to strengthen the effect of its horror and draw the reader's attention to the absurd situation in which the Jewish people hidden in Tworki found themselves. "The hunt is on, but the game is missing and nowhere to be found."

In the language of Bieńczyk, which also includes alexandrines, as described by Benjamin in *Origin of the German Trauerspiel*, the world, like Benjamin's alexandrine, is based on the antithesis of the classical shape of the façade and the "phonetic wildness on the inside."[417] The allegory is the work of that wild gallop of words and of the allegorical gaze which, like melancholy, divides, empties of meaning and dissociates.[418] "In the anagrams, onomatopoeic locutions, and

---

416 Małgorzata Melchior, *Zagłada a tożsamość. Polscy Żydzi ocaleni na "aryjskich papierach". Analiza doświadczenia biograficznego* (Warszawa: Instytut Filozofii i Socjologii PAN, 2004), p. 206.
417 Benjamin, *Origin of the German Trauerspiel*, p. 222.
418 "If the object becomes allegorical under the gaze of melancholy, and if melancholy causes the life to flow out of it and it remains behind as something dead, though secured in eternity,

many other sorts of linguistic devices, word, syllable, and sound, proudly flaunt themselves – emancipated from every traditional nexus of meaning – as a thing that can be exploited allegorically."[419] If the object becomes allegorical under the gaze of melancholy, and if melancholy causes life to flow out of it and it remains behind as something dead, though secured in eternity, then this is how it lies before the allegorist, delivered over to him for good or ill grace.

According to Benjamin, "dissociative principle of allegorical perception"[420] leads to linguistic alienation and causes words to resemble beautiful ruins in their meaning and form. However, these are not ruins through which the nothingness of language comes into appearance, but beautiful ruins, equal to "the gods, rivers, virtues, and other similar natural forms shimmering into the allegorical."[421] "We address each other in diminutives, acronyms, alliterations, and rhymes imitative of the Song of Solomon." (C21 207) say the protagonists of *Century 21*, paraphrasing *Origin of the German Trauerspiel* and creating in their conversations historical allegories of the Holocaust. Here is one example:

> In Salzburg Trakl doesn't accompany the countess on her visit to the marquise. The chateau is a ruin, rose petals reside on the ground. He doesn't desire to settle in a quiet place. Incest is his crime. The name of his sister is Margaret, Sextus reminds himself. Treblinka is born out of her broken eye. Women stand naked in line, menstruate, throw up. Read Trakl and remember: the wolf is out everywhere, undoing humanity the moment you choose not to care. Holocausts come and go. (C21 73)

And here is another:

> By the way: how are they dressed? What about toys? Is Rachel carrying in her arms a Barbie doll? Is Aron robbed of his beloved Mauss by a Moravian pervert? If yes, the brute's name must be Shveyk, and it's best to suggest that he rapes the Auschwitz animal – survivor in a clover field. (C21 178)

Not a single story emerges from the allegorical narratives of Bieńczyk and Kuryluk which can be repeated in its entirety. Rather, these are dumps of anecdotes, flashy, as we can see especially in *Century 21*, and bombastic *homages* on the theme of the Holocaust, subordinated to the principle of narration, which is to talk about the past in order, not to organize and confirm it, but to show the past in flashes of "moments of danger."[422] At this point a fundamental difference

---

then just so does it lie before the allegorist, delivered over to him for good or ill grace." Benjamin, *Origin of the German Trauerspiel*, pp. 195–196.
419 Benjamin, *Origin of the German Trauerspiel*, p. 224.
420 Benjamin, *Origin of the German Trauerspiel*, p. 225.
421 Benjamin, *Origin of the German Trauerspiel*, p. 225.
422 "To articulate the past historically does not mean to recognise it 'the way it really was' (Ranke). It means to seize hold of a memory as it flashes up at a moment of danger." Walter Benjamin, *Illuminations*. qtd in Graeme Gilloch, *Walter Benjamin: Critical Constellations* (Cambridge, Oxford, Malden: Polity, 2002), p. 225.

emerges between the unrealistic allegory of Murdoch and the historical allegories of the two Polish authors. The world of *The Unicorn* is shaped by a single, mathematically conceived narrative. Meanwhile, the antitheses of the language of *Tworki* and *Century 21* reflect the hypocrisy of the world, which, as Bieńczyk wrote in his commentary to Antoni Malczewski's *Maria*,[423] exists on the border between the original meaning of words and the semantic shift, and therefore in the area designated in this chapter by Plato's reflection.

Murdoch's references to Plato in *The Unicorn* are ambiguous. Although her characters seem to be talking about the *Phaedrus*, the *Cratylus* is in fact the dialogue on language and the consequences of shifting meanings. Difficulties with identifying the source of the quotation do not have to result from Murdoch's mistake, but from the differences between the English and the Polish translations.[424] A passage closest to the statement about shifting meanings is found in the *Cratylus* – not the *Phaedrus* – and reads as follows: "For if he [the name giver] did begin in error, he may have forced the remainder into agreement with the original error and with himself; there would be nothing strange in this, any more than in geometrical diagrams, which have often a slight and invisible flaw in the first part of the process, and are consistently mistaken in the long deductions which follow."[425] In her comment on Plato, Murdoch speaks about truth as the essence of changing meanings, thus burdening the reality with moral consequences (for some of the characters, Hannah is a personification of Christ, while for others – a criminal). Benjamin does not attach this kind of moral interpretation to allegory. Nor is it present in Bieńczyk's and Kuryluk's postmodern narratives about the Holocaust.[426] Their depictions of a reality made up of rearranged words are overseen, as it were, by a sentence from Benjamin's *Origin of the German Trauerspiel* which states that "Any person, any object, any relation can signify any other whatever."[427] Language's possibilities of estab-

---

423 Marek Bieńczyk, "Estetyka melancholii," in *Trzynaście arcydzieł romantycznych*, ed. Elżbieta Kiślak and Marek Gumkowski (Warszawa Wydawnictwo: Wydawnictwo Instytutu Badań Literackich, 1996), p. 14.
424 Scholes does not clarify this either. He points out the links between Murdoch's novel and the "the Greek concept of Até" emerging from the conversation between Effingham and Max." Scholes, *The Fabulators*, p. 125.
425 Plato, *The Cratylus*, trans. Benjamin Jowett. https://www.gutenberg.org/cache/epub/1616/pg1616-images.html.
426 For the separate issue of links between *Tworki* and the *Phaedrus*, see Aleksandra Ubertowska's *Świadectwo – trauma – głos. Literackie reprezentacje Holokaustu* (Kraków: Universitas 2007), p. 289.
427 Benjamin, *Origin of the German Trauerspiel*, p. 184. Also Jacques Derrida draws upon Benjamin's theory in "Shibboleth: For Paul Celan," where he proposes the following definition of allegory: "Let us call this – by way of allegory – an *allegory*, the bearing [*portée*] of a word for the other, to the other or from the other. The allegory follows the revolution or *vicissitude* of the hours, from evening to morning, the *times in their turns, in vicem vice*

lishing the truth are therefore of secondary importance; its natural state is that of movement and the changes it brings about.

The thus-emerging difference between the novel analyzed by Scholes, which is completely devoid of historical references, and the historical allegories of postmodernism, brings into view another particular issue, namely, the identity of those whom the allegory at once represents and conceals. This raises a dramatic question concerning the allegorical modality (as understood by Benjamin) of the predicament of hiding as related to the Jewish population. It is appropriate immediately to note that identity allegories – as in the case of the family of Carol Kar, Sonia, or Marcel – are exclusively textual and literary, and do not concern the extra-literary reality. Therefore, the question about the allegorization of hiding on the Aryan side is not directed against the idea of conveying the terror of reality by means of a figure of speech, but is asked in order to consider the possibility of extending the content of the allegory by a rather unexpected dimension.

Read alongside each other, *Tworki* and *Century 21* form a story about hiding Jews in and through the text, either during the war (Bieńczyk) and after the war (Kuryluk). Their common theme is thus a hidden Jewish identity. Regardless of the allegorical dimension of concealment, each narrates a story about Jews without Jews.[428] Lack of meta-reflection, especially in *Tworki*, makes it especially clear that one of the problems in these fictions is the fate of Jewish citizens on "Aryan papers." Above all, however, interesting is way in which the text responds to this challenge. In Małgorzata Melchior's *Zagłada a tożsamość* we read:

> The "assumed" and as it were "external" identity of a person – in the case of persons with Aryan papers – could only have the character of an instrumental identity. It was, after all, a means with which to minimize the threat and keep alive the hope of avoiding extermination.[429]

At the same time, the way in which the *Tworki* protagonists are described does not allow us to distinguish those different identities: "external" from "internal" and "real" from "assumed." Olek has "so much [...] sapphire in his eyes as a woman needs the sea" (T 44); "and messing up this thick blond hair will get you more than one of those red nails broken" (T 44). Marcel, on the other hand, is almost the twin brother of Jurek, who is not a Jew, but a Pole: "Just as Jurek chose the School of Economics before the war, he supported the Polonia football club, he also preferred western movies to Dr. Wilczur..." (T 53). Only Sonia has a

---

versa." Jacques Derrida, "Shibboleth: For Paul Celan," trans. Joshua Wilner and Thomas Dutoit, in Jacques Derrida, *Sovereignties in Questions: The Poetics of Paul Celan*, ed. Thomas Dutoit and Outi Pasanen (New York: Fordham University Press, 2005), p. 58.
428 Morawiec, *Literatura w lagrze, lager w literaturze*, p. 356.
429 Melchior, *Zagłada a tożsamość*, p. 294.

swarthy face and dark eyes, and her manner of speaking has a "cute" syntax, but no one would think of calling her Jewish...

"Aryan" Jews recalled their instrumental identity by using theatrical metaphors, including those of "character impersonation," "masking," and "role-playing."[430] If we were to add allegory to this set of devices, we would have to say that it was meant to remain inscrutable, constituting, for the person employing it, a certain scheme whose purpose was the closest feasible impersonation of a stereotypical Pole. That is why in the procession of "disguises" created by the inhabitants of Tworki, those whose concealment is the most profound seem not to be wearing any masks at all. Ewa Kuryluk creates a similar situation by placing her mother, brother and herself – all Holocaust survivors – among several dozen non-Jews. Kuryluk uses the allegory of identity to blur or talk over, as it were, the difficulty in stating simultaneously two truths: one about the stigma of salvation and the other about its inheritance by children. The situation becomes clear in *Frascati*, an autobiography published as many as seventeen years after *Century 21*: "'Carol in your novel is Charles's daughter?' 'And yours, Mom.' 'And Peter too?' 'Yes.' 'I like the way Karol keeps pupating [...] – from Karenina to Berenice [...] – from a Jewish woman who wants to hide, to a Jewish woman who wants to reveal herself because she thinks salvation is sinful.'"[431]

"For allegory, anything can mean something different, although no thing means what it means and none merges symbolically with what it signifies," wrote Adam Lipszyc about the fragmented and antinomian space of allegory.[432] In the most general sense, the allegories of Bieńczyk and Kuryluk show a total dispersion of meaning created by the Holocaust, which is expressed in the longing for contact with transcendence, but also, as Lipszyc explains, with the name.[433] This is why the name of Sonia from *Tworki* eventually becomes a signature, and why all other names can be considered falsified or replaced. That is also why the protagonists of *Century 21* constantly change or exchange names, falsifying not only their content, but above all their own identity. After all, there are much fewer of those protagonists than we initially assume. The presence of figurative language in narratives about the Holocaust, according to Lawrence L. Langer is inevitable, even though it diverts attention from the "abnormality of the routine."[434] It would explain the final and paradoxical

---

[430] Melchior, *Zagłada a tożsamość*, p. 260.
[431] Ewa Kuryluk, *Frascati* (Kraków: Wydawnictwo Literackie, 2009), p. 136.
[432] Lipszyc, *Sprawiedliwość na końcu języka*, p. 207.
[433] Lipszyc, *Sprawiedliwość na końcu języka*, p. 213.
[434] Lawrence L. Langer, *Holocaust Testimonies: The Ruins of Memory* (New Have and London: Yale University Press, 1991), p. 22. "What might seem like fantasy to us became a sign of 'ordinary' reality for him [a Holocaust victim], so he could make the adjustment enabling him to accept this 'abnormality' as part of his normal daily routine."

character of the allegories discussed here: the shattered and stray meaning returns to itself, even when it has been nearly obliterated. And so in these novels everything is called the Holocaust.

Chapter 9.
"They found their way home... through the rivers, through the air": Anne Michaels

In the literature on the subject, the terms "bog people" and "bog bodies" refer to mummified bodies from the Iron Age found in peat bogs in northern Europe (Denmark, Jutland). In the years 2004–2005, they were shown at the exhibition "The Mysterious Bog People,"[435] which aroused a lot of controversy, especially in Canada, and gave rise to a discussion about the exhibition of human remains and the ethical ramifications of this type of activity.[436] Anne Michaels's 1996 novel *Fugitive Pieces* opens with a monologue by the main character, a Holocaust survivor Jakob Beer, who calls himself a "bog-boy"[437] (FP 5) and compares himself to the "Tollund Man, Grauballe Man" and to "the boy they uprooted in the middle of Franz Josef Street" (FP 5). These comparisons and metaphors are not part of that discussion. Preceding it, they are part of a richly documented reflection on the dead body, undertaken by Michaels in the context of the Holocaust and other natural disasters in reference to the mystery of "peat-bog corpses,"[438] already mentioned by D. M. Thomas in his 1981 novel *The White Hotel*. The fact that it is literature, and not art or museology, that initiates discussion on how reflection on the dead body can be broadened to include the Holocaust and the commemoration of its victims is of fundamental importance here. This fact allows us to see in Michaels's novel a "report" written in symbols on the state of science and the possibilities that science has at its disposal of transforming existing customs. This reflection should be combined with the conviction that the fictions of Michaels and Thomas, which scholars classify as postmodern, in fact indicate a decline of postmodernism and the impending

---

435 https://www.livescience.com/3902-mysterious-bog-people.html (accessed 27.07.2023).
436 Stuart McLean, "Bodies from the Bog: Metamorphosis, Non-human Agency and the Making of 'Collective' Memory," *Trames* 2008, 12(62/57), 3, pp. 299–308.
437 Anne Michaels *Fugitive Pieces* (London and Oxford: Bloomsbury, 1997). All quotations are marked FP followed by page number in parentheses.
438 "He [Freud] turned the conversation to some 'peat-bog corpses' that apparently have been found in northern Germany. They are said to be the bodies of prehistoric men, mummified by the effect of the humic acid in the bog water" (WH 10).

changes resulting from the critique of narrativism and the category of the weak subject.

The theme of Michaels's novel – as pointed out by critics – are various kinds of memory combined with reflection on Canada's multiculturalism.[439] The main narrative strand of the novel deals with the Holocaust and the memoirs of two Jewish émigré artists, which are narrated in separate sections of the plot. The first part belongs to Beer, found by a Greek archaeologist in Biskupin during the war. The other tells the story of his friend, whose parents survived the nightmare of the Holocaust in Poland. Both protagonists have experienced the troubling memory of loss and death, and the lack of an effective or satisfactory way to mourn. The critical reception of the novel has been dominated by memory and post-dependency studies. Some critics have discussed competing memories[440] and science (especially geography and geology) as a memorial metaphor.[441] Others have treated the bodies from the swamps as a textological trope, serving to construct a unique framework for post-memory:

> Bog bodies are preserved and transformed by means of chemical processes which "represent their gradual re-absorption by the natural world to which [they] have been consigned" (McLean, 300). However, their recovery into modernity transforms them again into cultural texts demanding interpretation (McLean, 307). Therefore, cultural memory is not only a "faculty exercised by individuated human subjects", but "a continuously unfolding process involving shifting and heterogeneously composed collectives", which might include "human beings, technologies…history, architecture, chemical reactions, animals, plants, micro-organisms, landscape, geology and climate" (McLean, 306).[442]

In the perspective of new animism, this kind of reading may not suffice. According to the proposals of Nurit Bird-David, Tim Ingold and Ewa Domańska, in the objects of Michaels's reflections – the dead bodies, the limestone rocks and things collected by the protagonists of *Fugitive Pieces*, and above all in their rituals dedicated to the spirits of the dead – we should rather see an actual and meaningful proposal for post-Christian practices of cultivating the memory of the Holocaust in the twentieth and twenty-first centuries. Only then will this poetic, occasionally extremely dense, and non-linear novel also prove to be of

---

439 Brygida Gasztold, "A Narrative Inquiry into Canadian Multiculturalism: *Fugitive Pieces* by Anne Michaels," *TransCanadiana* 6/2013: pp. 207–225.
440 Julie Spergel, *Canada's "Second History": The Fiction of Jewish Canadian Women Writers* (Hamburg: Kovac Verlag 2009).
441 Molly E. Rauch, "Geologies of Silence." *The Nation* April 7, 1997, pp. 35–38.
442 Catherine Coussens, "'Secrets of the Earth': Geology and Memory in Anne Michaels's *Fugitive Pieces*," *Annals of the University of Craiova*, Series: Philology, English, Year XI (2010), No.2: 73–87. Inset quotations are from Stuart McLean's essay "Bodies from the Bog: Metamorphosis, Non-Human Agency and the Making of 'Collective Memory,'" *Trames* 12.62/57 (2008): 299–308.

practical use by helping us to better understand the direction in which the transforming power of posthumanities needs to be oriented.

The "bog bodies" are in fact the only dead bodies described by Michaels. Much more important, it would seem, are the corpses of Beer's Jewish parents, those of Greek Jews locked in the ghetto on the island of Zakynthos, and those of many other victims of the Holocaust. However, those leave no trace in the narrative. According to Domańska:

> Isn't it worth considering that Nature's powers of preservation and conservation may be better than those of culture? Archeological and geological research assures us that what really endures, not for hundreds but thousands of years, is preserved underground, in buried in layers of the earth or in the oceans. To be sure, it will undergo the processes of erosion, corrosion, chemical changes, humification and mineralization, but it will survive in one form or another.[443]

Thomas, talking about "peat-bog corpses" in the context of an anecdote devoted to the conflict between Sigmund Freud and the secretive and antisocial Carl Gustav Jung, the author of a memoir about the discoveries of archaeologists, leaves this fact without comment (the text of the novel shows that it should be connected with the massacre at Babi Yar, but Thomas does not explain how this connection is supposed to be understood). Michaels, on the other hand, places the find among other archaeological-geological topics (primarily such as the fascination of Athos Rousos, a geologist from Zakynthos, with limestone rocks). Therefore, it would seem that Domańska's belief in Nature's powers of preservation as superior to culture's applies to *Fugitive Pieces*. Indeed, it reflects the researcher's views on how to handle the remains of Holocaust victims or bodies that have never been found.

The metaphysics Rousos offers to his protégé is expressed in the following way:

> Athos confirmed that there was an invisible world, just as real as what's evident. Full-grown forests still and silent, whole cities, under a sky of mud. The realm of the peat men, preserved as sanctuary. The place where all those who have uttered the bony password and entered the earth wait to emerge. From underground and underwater, from iron boxes and behind brick walls, from trunks and packing crates... (FP 49)

Rousos's animistic beliefs about the interrelations of dead bodies, spirits, rocks, things, and people, however, have a scientific foundation. One could even say that they perfectly respond to the challenge made in *Necros* that indigenous and traditional types of knowledge should interpenetrate each other.[444] In addition to

---

[443] Ewa Domańska, *Nekros. Wprowadzenie do ontologii martwego ciała* (Warszawa: Wydawnictwo Naukowe PWN, 2017), p. 188.
[444] Domańska, *Nekros*, p. 54.

being a lover of poetry and magic, the archaeologist from Zakynthos, "'Athos is like his beloved limestone. The sea will dissolve him into caves, dig holes into him, but he lasts and lasts'" (FP 78). It was Athos who, while still a child, became fascinated with peat people, first the fossils from Lyme Regis, then the limestone figure of Venus of Willendorf.[445] Limestone, according to Stuart McLean, precipitates from the body immersed in peat, preventing bacteria from breaking it down, softening the bones and turning the skin into a coating of sorts.[446] The subject of Athos's doctoral thesis, however, became limestone rocks ("the karst fields of Yugoslavia"; FP 32), the transformation of limestone into marble, and in particular its significance as a "crushed reef of memory" and "organic history squeezed into massive mountain tombs" (FP 32). From the point of view of Holocaust studies, Athos's most important interest in limestone is his search for the Auschwitz sub-camp known as Arbeitslager Golleschau. As part of the activities of this unit, there was a limestone quarry, founded in July 1942, and a cementing quarry located on the premises of the former Goleszów cement plant, belonging to Ost-deutsche Baustoffwerke GmbH – Golleschauer Portland Zemment AG. The hardest work was done by Jews employed in the quarries. They blew up the rocks with dynamite and loaded chunks of rock onto the wagons by hand. "On average, everyone had to load about 6 tons of stone onto the steam train wagons during one shift."[447]

The above-quoted book by regional historian Paweł Staniczek, in which he analyses residual sources, was published in 2015. Writing her novel in the 1990s, Michaels could not have been familiar with Staniczek's work. Therefore, we should regard her description of the work of laborers moving limestone rocks – as well as her reflections on the "Bog People" – as transcending its time and, in its scientific and magical intuition, creating a new paradigm of knowledge, produced primarily through artistic activity and art.

One of these intuitions is the already mentioned relational ontology, which considers all subjects with dead bodies at the forefront as part of a long chain of beings carrying the memory of the past. It is formed by the dead, rocks, stones, magnetized minerals, air currents, river silt, and ash eskers. This mixing of various living objects builds a world without borders, a world in which the spirit does not forget the body, the skin remembers the world, the human pulse is not oblivious to magnetic lines, and the murderer blends with the victim. As we can

---

445 To which is attached the following telling anecdote about someone Athos knew: "This man, who'd been at the top of our prehistory class, actually presented the 'Willendorf Venus' to Himmler as proof that 'Hottentots' had been conquered by ancient Aryans! He falsified digs to prove that Greek civilization started in . . . neolithic Germany! Just so the Reich could feel justified in copying our temples for their glorious capital" (FP 104).
446 McLean, "Bodies from the Bog," p. 302.
447 Paweł Staniczek, *Arbeitslager Golleschau – dzieje podobozu* (Goleszów 2015), pp. 23–24.

see, especially in the last example, the animistic concept of community, which Ingold describes, among other things, as mycelium, radically departs from such fundamental oppositions as the perpetrator and the victim. This departure leads, not to distortion or falsification of history, but has the intention of helping in the effective passage of mourning and liberation from grief caused by excessive attachment to the (already mentioned) post-Christian concepts. Particularly important in this context seem to be the indigenous rituals performed by the community of the island of Zakynthos in order to bid farewell to the spirits of the departed. Athos and Jakob take up those rituals just before leaving for Canada ("We must have a ceremony. For your parents, for the Jews of Crete, for all who have no one to recall their names." FP 75). These mourning rites include, above all, throwing chamomile and poppies on the waves, pouring fresh water on the sea, eating *koliva* (bread and honey; FP 75), singing and *anakoufisi* (waiting for spirits' message to be brought by birds; FP 76). In this way, the living want to "reward" the spirits for their tiring journey, to give them water and food, and make their unburied bones rest on the sea bed, to break into atoms and become part of life again. An even more intense dialogue with ghosts is conducted by Jakob himself, who during the war, just after escaping from the hiding place in Biskupin and the killing of his parents, feels their spirits penetrating his body. This is because the dead have not been buried, and heavy stones have not lain on their graves. Now the protagonist is trying, by breathing hard, to chase those ghosts away. However, he fails to do so with the apparition of his sister, Bella, who stays with him until his death, penetrating the bodies of his subsequent wives and partners.

The insular customs described in the novel are not only those of European Jews, but also of the indigenous people of Canada from Manitoulin, whose ghosts Beer's future wife met when she was a child. In the story of the first settlers and their artefacts, exhibited in one of the ethnographic museums, Michaels draws attention to the ineffectiveness of fighting ghosts by curing the things and places that used to belong to them. The rituals of gift and water offering are meant to ensure their gentle departure and thus to restore them to the life of the earth. It is worth adding that one of Athos's teachings addressed to Jakob concerns the preparation of one's burial, which is to provide the body with the memory of the earth.

In the second part of the book, the problem of contact with the spirits of the dead is presented primarily as a friend of the deceased Beer puts his house in order, looking for notes of the former poet and preparing them for publication. The experience of contact with the things of the dead turns out to be the experience of life:

> It's a strange relationship we have with objects that belonged to the dead; in the knit of atoms, their touch is left behind. Every room emanated absence yet was drenched with your presence. When I uncovered the couch, I found a blanket still dripping from one end of it, and the indentations of your bodies – invisible weight – still in the cushions. (FP 265)

Michaels compares these observations to the families "frozen into stone," petrified during the eruption of Vesuvius, and earlier, to homunculi, the frozen victims of polar explorers. Her entire novel is as it were permeated by the search for an effective method to survive the catastrophe in a form made permanent by nature, the type of survival attained by the bog bodies, Indian butterflies dried up like leaves, moths that come to resemble the bark of trees. To the question about the color of flesh transformed to spirit (FP 7), however, the author responds by suggesting that abandoning belief in the mortality of the body results in entering, or even sneaking, into someone else's life. Michaels's animistic vision of the Holocaust, based on both indigenous knowledge, Jewish mythology (such as the belief in dybbuks and in the Zohar lore[448]) or knowledge of natural processes, and, above all, natural sciences, causes her to accept the possibility that not all victims of the Holocaust are irretrievably dead. Some of them have survived and continue their existence as living organisms:

> After burying the books and dishes, the silverware and the photos, the Jews of the Zakynthos ghetto vanish.
> They slip into the hills, where they wait like coral; half flesh, half stone. They wait in caves, in the sheds and animal stalls of the farms of Christian friends. (FP 40)

One has to ask, what is the point of such an open denial of the facts (that the Holocaust did not claim all the victims, and that some of them survived in the lives of others) and their replacement with figures and metaphors?[449] The new animism is one of the currents of thought rejecting unrealistic rhetoric. The use of imagery proposed by Michaels aims to separate the experience of mourning itself from its natural, yet ineffective, appropriating religious contexts, in-

---

448 "The Zohar says, 'All visible things will be born again invisible'" (FP 48).
449 One of the key places in *Fugitive Pieces*, where the role of metaphor as a way of expressing thoughts indirectly while maintaining the metaphorical way of articulating them is questioned, is a reflection on the similarity of rock grottoes as ghost graves to mass graves in which the Nazis buried or burned Jews. According to Michaels, these Jewish graves, which later resembled blisters (p. 121), simply signify communication between different subjects. A different interpretation is possible and, after Domańska, we can assume that the language of the earth refers to the forms of nature's marking places of mass murder, among which the most common are lush vegetation and, especially, the occurrence of specific plants (e.g., mugwort and nettle in temperate climates). These issues are addressed in Mikołaj Smykowski's PhD, *Ekologie Zagłady. Krytyczne studium z antropologii krajobrazu poobozowego na przykładzie Byłego Obozu Zagłady w Chełmnie nad Nerem*. Wydział Historyczny, Uniwersytet im. Adama Mickiewicza w Poznaniu, 2019.

cluding the secular one. In memory studies, as represented by Coussenes, this strategy serves primarily to develop a concept of collective memory the aim of which is to connect the experiences of the living and the dead and to create a kind of line or switch between them. However, the category of memory turns out to be unproductive and lacking in dynamic. Moreover, due to its narrow, non-performative meaning, it does not cover the mourning practices described above, and completely ignores everything that can come from them. However, the problem that lingers is that of one's right to lack of burial, as repeatedly emphasized in Jewish literature on the Holocaust, from Irit Amiel, through Renata Jabłońska, to Maria Orwid, and also addressed by Domańska in *Nekros*. The postulate that human remains do not have to be buried in the ground or that they should not be exhumed Domańska interprets in terms of resistance to authority. "Absent remains are in such a situation a symbol of escape from it, of rebellion by disappearance, and a sign that perhaps nature is better at protecting what the culture greedily seeks to appropriate and control."[450] In this situation, the key experience turns out to be Michaels's decision to set the action of her novel far from Europe, first on a Greek island, reminiscent of Arcadia and somewhat untouched by war, and later in Canada, where people's memories of natural disasters include above all the destruction caused by Hurricane Hazel, which in 1954 devastated the southeastern part of Canada, as well as Toronto. Thanks to this choice of setting, in which there are no dead Jewish bodies, but where the memory of them remains, mourning the departed – which in countries like Poland or Germany has a political dimension – becomes a process that admits of revision when examined from a distance. Michaels proposes to make the earth a place to live again and not to nurture thinking about death, catastrophe or the end of things. For this reason, in accordance with Ingold's philosophy, she makes water and air the surface on which new life is taking shape: "Though they were taken blind, though their sense were confused by stench and prayer and screams, by terror and memories, these passengers [Jews transported in cattle trains – M.T.] found their way home. Through the rivers, through the air" (FP 52).

In this context, ashes travelling up the chimneys of crematoria or down rivers thus turn out to be "persons-other-than-people," where one can hear not so much the absurdity as the desperation of attempts to preserve the remains of the victims in one form or another, as well as the desire to give them dignity by emphasizing that the body can take on various organic forms. It seems, therefore, that the most important thing here is a constant physical presence.

---

450 Domańska *Nekros*, pp. 123–124.

As Tokarska-Bakir has argued,

> If we agree with the fact that the Holocaust was a transformative event, an event which, as Jacek Małczyński writes, [...] "moved the earth and compromised all the tools used to measure the earthquake," in posthumanities one can see the rebirth of the "experience of the Holocaust" – "the experience that does not exist." Speaking (indexically?) on the other side of the gas chamber wall, this phenomenon, at its own pace and in its own right, is recalibrated. It disperses into the mineral-geological-vegetable-animalistic world, and in the process confuses epistemological [...] and ethical tropes. As in the Jewish midrash, truth grows out of the earth. The Holocaust, on the other hand, would still remain itself: an erratic boulder, dragged through a posthumanist glacier, indifferent to its charms and spells.[451]

The most puzzling image in this passage is the erratic boulder of the Holocaust. Contrary to appearances, it is not dead, but like the pebble in Ingold's essay, it affects the environment. Tokarska-Bakir tries to convey the bond between the glacier and the boulder in terms of magic ("charms and spells"). Meanwhile, it seems that it is precisely the abandonment of the divisions into real and spiritual or magical and real, and especially the abandonment of metaphor as a merely rhetorical concept, that allows us better to understand some of the insights of post-anthropocentric and post-secular humanities. In literature, of course, they had their examples much earlier. For example, Czesław Miłosz's 1945 poem "Dedication" depicts an animistic, Slavic custom in its final stanza:

> They used to pour millet on graves or poppy seeds
> To feed the dead who would come disguised as birds.
> I put this book here for you, who once lived
> So that you should visit us no more.[452]

Milosz's poem is an exorcism and expulsion of spirits (among them Jewish ones). *Fugitive Pieces*, on the other hand, is about making bearable life lived among various beings, including those who died as victims of the Holocaust. Considering the dead present in contemporary culture in this way, and above all making them alive again, allows us to look anew at the media through which they return, including horrors, comics, and thrillers.[453] Perhaps they should no longer be analyzed in the context of post-memory or hauntology, but precisely in the perspective of new consciousness and spirituality, including new animism. Di-

---

451 Joanna Tokarska-Bakir, "Jeffrey Jerome Cohen: od olbrzymów – przez antropologie potworności – do postantropologii kamieni," in *Migracyjna pamięć, wspólnota, tożsamość*, ed. Ryszard Nycz, Tomasz Sapota, Roma Sendyka (Warszawa: Instytut Badań Literackich PAN, 2016), p. 357.
452 Czesław Miłosz, "Dedication," in Czesław Miłosz, *The Collected Poems 1931–1987* (New York: The Ecco Press, 1988), p. 79.
453 For instance in Igor Ostachowicz's novel *Noc żywych Żydów*, Krzysztof Zajasa's *Oszpicyn* and in Ewa Andrzejewska's prose "O Mieście i Jakubie."

gested by pop culture, animism returns in the form of various beliefs, not all of them intelligible, creating alternative modes of our relations with the world of non-humans.

Chapter 10.
The Babel Library of the Holocaust: Nicole Krauss

My leading text in this chapter will be Jorge Luis Borges's "The Library of Babel," published in *Fictions* in 1941. This oft-quoted story is not referred to in any study of Holocaust literature or of the Holocaust itself I am familiar with. I will use Borges's story as an instruction manual trying to find in it, not only foundational insights into postmodern fiction, but into postmodern *Holocaust* fiction, as a phenomenon that manifested its full force in the first decade of this century.[454]

As an example of this "eruption" I will discuss Nicole Krauss's novel *The History of Love* (2005), inspired by the idea of the Borgesian library and its interpretations by John Barth, Umberto Eco, and Anna Burzyńska. In addition to these challenging inspirations, which gravitate towards the metaphor of the library of Babel, another, opaque game is afoot here, one between the fictions of Borges, the author of "The Book of Sand" (1975), and Krauss's novel. We can observe it on many levels, including that of chronology. The key event for *The History of Love* – the rescue of the main character and the narrator of the story – took place in July 1941 in Słonim, where German troops entered to carry out a pogrom of over a thousand Jews. At that time, Borges lived far from Europe, although, working as a librarian in Almagro in Buenos Aires, he was much closer to the Old Continent than it may have seemed. Krauss has created a vivid picture of the blind Argentinian writer, describing his neighborhood and the location of one of the copies of *The History of Love* in a nearby second-hand bookstore. In this way, she suggests that Borges could have read her novel and significantly influenced its poetics. On this probability, that Borges may have read a love story related to the Holocaust, I in part rely in my interpretation in this chapter. I

---

[454] Besides Krauss, two postmodernist Holocaust novels were then also published by Jonathan Safran Foer, *Everything Is Illuminated* (2002; Polish translation by Michał Kłobukowski, *Wszystko jest iluminacją*, Warszawa 2003) and *Extremely Loud, Incredibly Close* (2005; Polish translation by Zbigniew Batko, *Strasznie głośno, niesamowicie blisko*, Warszawa 2007). Among Polish novels were *Zimno* by Piotr Czakański (Katowice 2006), *Byłam sekretarką Rumkowskiego. Dzienniki Etki Daum* by Elżbieta Cherezińska (Poznań 2008) and *Fabryka muchołapek* by Andrzej Bart (Warszawa 2008).

propose to treat this premise, unrealistic as it is, as an inspiring (and above all intriguing) assumption for further consideration.

The narrator of "The Library of Babel" offers a vision of its totality in the face of catastrophe: "[…] I suspect that the human species – the unique species – is about to be extinguished, but the Library will endure: illuminated, solitary, infinite, perfectly motionless, equipped with precious volumes, useless, incorruptible, secret."[455] He also recalls that he spent his early youth searching for particular books and catalogues. Only a book discovered several hundred years earlier, most likely written in Yiddish (this hypothesis was later abandoned in favor of others), was to contain "examples of variation with unlimited repetition,"[456] which laid the foundations for the most important law of all book collections and all rooms intended for their storage: "the Library is total."[457]

Totality, multiplicity, infinity and the perspective of a melancholic loser are features of the Library that characterize postmodern Holocaust fiction. The governing assumption here seems to be the existence of an unlimited number of languages available to a writer, capable of revealing and at the same time blurring and concealing history. This assumption in turn is related to the existence of an infinite archive of memories of the Holocaust (its materialization, close to the idea of surviving the catastrophe, being the Ringelblum Archive[458]). Both assumptions make up the vision of an ideal text about the Holocaust, the text of Babel, with space for every testimony in any shape or form. An infinite number of human experiences makes necessary a totality of literary responses.

It seems, however, that this vision of the Library of Babel testimonies has its limitations. John Barth was the first to point them out in relation to Borges's fiction in his 1967 essay *The Literature of Exhaustion*. Barth writes in it about the Library of Babel as a metaphor for the end of all novelistic narratives, arguing that an infinite number of elements corresponds to a finite number of combinations:

> The infinite library of one of his most popular stories is an image particularly pertinent to the literature of exhaustion: The "Library of Babel" houses every possible combination of alphabetical characters and spaces, and thus every possible book and statement, including your and my refutations and vindications, the history of the actual future, the history of every possible future, and, though he doesn't mention it, the encyclopedia not only of Tlön but of every imaginable other world […].[459]

---

455 Jorge Luis Borges, "The Library of Babel," in Jorge Luis Borges, *Labyrinths* (London and New York: Penguin, 2000), p. 85.
456 Borges, "The Library of Babel," p. 81.
457 Borges, "The Library of Babel," p. 81.
458 This became the leading motif of another postmodernist novel, Yann Martel's *Beatrice and Virgil* (2010).
459 John Barth, "The Literature of Exhaustion," in John Barth, *The Friday Book. Essays and Other Nonfiction* (New York: G. P. Putnam's Sons, 1984), p. 75. Originally published in *Atlantic*, 220/2 (August 1967): 29–34.1984).

A juxtaposition of Barth's remarks with Holocaust literature (as a category broader than fiction) may serve as a historical testimony as well as a metaliterary commentary. In addition to the characteristic features, such as the aforementioned self-commentaries or the imbalance of the status of literary fiction, postmodern Holocaust literature is also a reflection on "the difficulty, perhaps the unnecessity, of writing original works of literature."[460] However, a detail violates the consistency of the thus emerging model. Another American postmodern author, Raymond Federman, whose mother saved him from the Nazis by hiding him in a closet, speaks about the difference between the two life-experiences in a passage already quoted in an earlier chapter:

> One draws the material for writing from reality. For example, nothing like this ever happened in John Barth's life... Maybe his wife divorced him, or he himself caused something traumatic to happen to him, but he never participated in a great historical unrest; he never went poor or hungry. I knew hunger, both in France and in America... I begged, I cheated, I stole, yes, I did all that to survive... I had to hide, too. The events of those years are still present in my work. The main part of my literary material comes from the years 1942–1952, from that decade. After that, my life began to resemble Barth's. I got married, I have children, my life is pleasant. Yet I can't write about this period. What bears artistic fruit happened to me a long time ago.[461]

The element named here is the Event – the only one, unique, nightmarish, not eligible to universalization. And yet Federman, a survivor, does speak about it in his Holocaust fiction, which is increasingly detached from this source, the combinations leading to countless transformations of the Event being infinite (in 2005, when *The History of Love* came out, it is already pure fiction). We can therefore assume that the Library of Babel has a Yiddish Book in its collection, a book that represents faith in uniqueness and singularity. But the memory of the Book has become a variant of the old memory, the memory of the Old, Lost Book. Following up on the idea that "every copy is unique, irreplaceable, but (since the Library is total) there are always several hundred thousand imperfect facsimiles: works which differ only in a letter or a comma,"[462] Borges envisages one perfect book, hidden "[o]n some shelf in some hexagon [...] there must exist a book which is the formula and perfect compendium of *all the rest* [...]."[463] The Library of Babel exists because of these contradictory beliefs: the containment of multiplicity in unity and unity in multiplicity, longing for the original and awareness of the supremacy of an infinite number of copies. And although these beliefs are

---

460 Barth, "The Literature of Exhaustion," p. 69.
461 "Przeżyć własną śmierć (rozmowa z Raymondem Federmanem)," in Maciej Świerkocki, *Postmodernizm: paradygmat nowej kultury* (Łódź: Wydawnictwo Uniwersytetu Łódzkiego, 1997), pp. 160–161.
462 Borges, *Library of Babel*, p. 83.
463 Borges, *Library of Babel*, p. 83; emphasis in the original.

ages old and even anachronistic, analyzing them in the context of the Holocaust Library of Babel can yield interesting results.

One is the confrontation of Barth's idealistic view with Federman's poignantly realistic position (not directly related to my considerations in this chapter). In "The Literature of Exhaustion," Barth uses the figure of Theseus in the Cretan labyrinth to describe the predicament of wandering in the library. In this figure we recognize a chosen one, the enlightened, liberal democrat. Unlike the ignorant populace who "will *always* lose their way and their soul,"[464] he can always find his way around and out. In the interview with Maciej Świerkocki, Federman exposes Barth's postmodern Parnassian idealism by pointing out that the Event, when it has become the essence of one's life, does not result in plots that end in simple and happy solutions. Like Borges's labyrinths, the Event requires complex, cobbled together and wrinkled scenarios ("I begged. I cheated. I stole. Yes, I did all that to survive."); scenarios, let us add, whose protagonists, as in many of Federman's novels, are common people.

Another result is described in the final sentence of "The Literature of Exhaustion"; it is the victory of the mythical hero. Compared to him, Borges does not have to write all the books he has invented. It is enough for him to walk through the labyrinth of their possibilities, "acknowledge them, and with the aid of very special gifts [...] go straight through the maze to the accomplishment of his work."[465] The resulting aristocratic work of the victor will shine like the highest shelves of the Library of Babel in defiance of the ignorant populace. The only problem is these common people – to return to the historical context – are the actual survivors of the Holocaust and they are the people who, perversely, by the irony of fate, have been chosen. They are a people of thousands of testimonies, books, big and small, and their copies, which survived, or emerged from, the catastrophe.

Assuming that Barth and Federman drew opposite conclusions from "The Library of Babel," where we read that "the human species [...] is about to be extinguished,"[466] one can also posit the existence of two, rather than one, models of the post-modernization of the Holocaust. One of them is the fiction of playfulness, celebration of the victory of structure over the matter of life as well as numerous mythological transformations of language and alienating actions of the avant-garde, leading to the denial of the values of the class to which the artist (such as Barth) belongs.[467] This model is distanced from the Event. The Library of

---

464 Barth, "The Literature of Exhaustion," p. 75; emphasis added.
465 Barth, "The Literature of Exhaustion," p. 54.
466 Borges, "The Library of Babel," p. 85.
467 Roland Barthes wrote about the distorting and meaning-bending role of myth and about the avant-garde and about hypocritical artists fighting against bourgeoisie in the name of so-called higher values. See Roland Barthes, *Mythologies*, trans. Annette Lavers (New York: The

Babel functions as ethical entertainment, a mental acrobatic feat, ultimately something false.[468] Let's listen to what Barth has to say:

> The insufferability of the fiction, once this correspondence is recognized, makes its double point: that language may be a compound code, and that the discovery of an enormous complexity beneath a simple surface may well be more dismaying than delightful. E. g.: the maze of termite-tunnels in your joist, the intricate cancer in her perfect breast, the psychopathology of everyday life, *the Auschwitz in an anthill casually DDT'd by a child*, the rage of atoms in a drop of ink – in short, *anything* examined curiously enough.[469]

An example of the other model, one close to Federman's position, is the experimental novel, aimed, sometimes randomly, at describing the Event, at once revealing and covering the Holocaust.

Wolfgang Koeppen's *Jakob Littners Aufzeichnungen aus einem Erdloch*[470] and Elżbieta Cherezińska's *Byłam sekretarką Rumkowskiego. Dzienniki Etki Daum* illustrate the literature based on the first model. Both are loose fantasies on a loss or purloined testimony, now edited by the contemporary author, who acts as a ghostwriter.[471] The other model, apart from Krauss's fiction, is found primarily in the novels published in the first decade of the new century, including Andrzej Bart's *Fabryka muchołapek*, Piotr Czakański's *Zimno*, and Jonathan Safran Foer' *Extremely Loud & Incredibly Close*.

Before the Library of Babel became the starting point for reflections on the narrative of the Holocaust, in two researchers, Umberto Eco and Anna Burzyńska, it evoked considerations different from those presented here, from a realistic reflection on book lending to a theoretical one on the pluralistic and multitextual character of postmodern culture.

In his talk about the concept of the library given on March 10, 1981, on the occasion of the twenty-fifth anniversary of the Municipal Library of Milan and in the part devoted Borges's story, Eco made this noteworthy comment: "So if the library is, as Borges would have it, a model of the universe, we are trying to make it a universe to the measure of man. I wish to remind you that a library tailored to

---

Noonday Press, 1991), pp. 120 and 138–139 (essays "The signification" and "The bourgeoisie as a joint-stock company").

468 Barth was telling Świerkocki about the entertainment dimension of such postmodernism, praising Federman precisely for what, for the author of *Double or Nothing*, constituted a serious cognitive problem – a "light" description of the Holocaust. "Ocalić powieść (rozmowa z Johnem Barthem)," in Maciej Świerkocki, *Postmodernism*, p. 147.
469 John Barth, "Seven Additional Author's Notes (1969)," in John Barth, *Lost in the Funhouse. Fiction for print, tape, live voice* (New York: Anchor Books, 1988), p. 204; emphasis added.
470 Ruth Franklin, *A Thousand Darknesses: Lies and Truth in Holocaust Fiction* (New York and Oxford: Oxford University Press, 2011), pp. 163–182.
471 I write at some length about this in my book *Czyja dzisiaj jest Zagłada? Retoryka – ideologia – popkultura* (Warszawa: Wydawnictwo IBL PAN, 2018).

man is also a merry library, where one can have coffee with cream [...] Are we going to transform utopian vision into reality?"[472] In this otherwise very pragmatic essay, Eco also mentions another, seemingly even more mundane, role of libraries, that of making it possible to conceal and discover manuscripts.[473] Reading Eco's comments in the context of his fiction, we become aware of their significance for the postmodern discourse on the Holocaust as essentially related to covering up and revealing the Event, regardless of the paradoxical nature of this kind of statement.

Burzyńska wrote about the library of Babel as a symbol of postmodern discourse in the 2000s, asking what the transition from the Tower of Babel to the Library of Babel would involve.[474] By that time, the biblical edifice had so commonly been brought up in the context of debates on postmodernism that Burzyńska called it a stereotype and a label, phrases like "the modern Tower of Babel" or the "Babel of the twentieth century" being used as generalized representations of postmodernism.[475] The occurrence of this trope in a slightly different version, the Library of Babel, was a novelty. "The difference between the Tower of Babel and the Library of Babel," Burzyńska wrote, "is obvious. For Borges, the Library of Babel is no longer simply about multilingualism, but also about multitextuality. That is, it suggests the textualization not only of the world, but also of the universe, *always already* existing and always *already written*."[476]

According to the assumptions of both Eco and Burzyńska, the postmodern Library of Babel means both the real world of lending library (Eco) and the world of text, and even the entire textual postmodern culture (Burzyńska), the latter expressing cognitive optimism and a conviction about the salutary properties of difference. Products of thus-understood culture are not works that demonstrate the exhaustion of its paradigm(s); they are "texts from texts." Burzyńska describes such works as "defiantly intertextual" and names as examples the novels of Barth, Pynchon, Barthelme, Federman and Berger.[477] Krauss's *The History of Love* also belongs to this group, the difference being, however, that this novel is

---

472 Umberto Eco, *O bibliotece* [*De Bibliotheca*], trans. from the Italian by Adam Szymanowski (Wrocław: Ossolineum, 1990), p. 33.
473 Eco, *O bibliotece*, p. 11. This historical role of the library is also the theme of *The Name of the Rose* (1980).
474 Anna Burzyńska, "Postmoderna: pomiędzy Wieżą Babel a Biblioteką Babel," w: *Postmodernizm. Teksty polskich autorów*, ed. Anna Maria Potocka (Kraków: Bunkier Sztuki, 2003), pp. 53–78.
475 Burzyńska, "Postmoderna," p. 55.
476 Burzyńska, "Postmoderna," p. 68 (emphasis in the original). Worth quoting here is Maciej Świerckocki's statement: "[...] the frame of reference for postmodernism is the entire literary output, literature's whole 'excess' [Pl. *nadmiar*], the world's entire 'library,' as Borges would have put it, himself one of the most widely appreciated postmodernists among contemporary authors." Maciej Świerckocki, p. 70.
477 Burzyńska, "Postmoderna," p. 69.

about death, and reads almost like a postscript to this sentence from "The Library of Babel": "Perhaps my old age and fearfulness deceive me, but I suspect that the human species – the unique species – is about to be extinguished, but the Library will endure [...]."[478]

In terms of structure, Krauss's novel is dominated by multiplicity. The narrative is literally made up of several parallel stories: that of Leo Gursky, a writer and an immigrant, born in Słonim (Slonim) at the beginning of the 20th century; that of his Belarusian friend, Zvi Litvinoff, also an immigrant; that of Isaac Moritz, Gursky's son; that of a novelist, Alma Singer, the daughter of a casual reader of *The History of Love*; and that of Bird, her mentally sick brother. Reading most of the novel is taking place in a state of ignorance. Although the reader assumes that the stories told will at some point meet to make up one whole – after all, they all concern the eponymous book – we do not know when or how, and which are the essential threads. Let's first look at the story of the Holocaust. It is told by Gursky, who as a teenager survived the pogrom in Słonim, during which he lost his mother, two sisters, two brothers and his closest friends. His friend, Litvinoff, and Alma survived in mysterious circumstances and independently of each other left for Chile and the United States, respectively.

Shortly after Alma's departure and before the Słonim massacre, Gursky began writing *The History of Love*. He sent the first eleven chapters overseas.

> In the summer of 1941, the *Einsatzgruppen* drove deeper east, killing hundreds of thousands of Jews. On a bright, hot day in July, they entered Slonim. At that hour, the boy happened to be lying on his back in the woods thinking about the girl. You could say that it was his love for her that saved him. In the years that followed, the boy became a man who became invisible. In this way, he escaped death. (HL 12)[479]

Only after many years, having met the longed-for Alma in the person of a strange girl, did he reveal the details of his rescue:

> Once I was hiding in a potato cellar when the SS came. The entrance was hidden by a thin layer of hay. The footsteps approached, I could hear them speaking as if they were inside my ears. There were two of them. One said, *My wife is sleeping with another man*, and the other said, *How do you know?* and the first said, *I don't, I only suspect it*, to which the second said, *Why do you suspect it?* while my heart went into cardiac arrest, *It's just a feeling*, the first said and I imagined the bullet that would enter my brain [...]. (HL 238; italics in the original)

In an atmosphere of terrifying fear, hiding, holding his breath, and eavesdropping, Gursky states: "Because of that wife who got tired of waiting for her soldier, I lived. [...] I like to imagine [...] how by accident she saved me with that

---

478 Borges, "The Library of Babel," p. 85.
479 Nicole Krauss, *The History of Love* (London and New York: Penguin Books, 2005). The quotations are marked HL followed by page number in parentheses.

thoughtless act of grace, and she never knew, and how that, too, is part of the history of love" (HL 240).

Krauss's dedication appended to her novel reads, "For My Grandparents, who taught me the opposite of disappearing and For Jonathan, my life." On the same page we also find four black-and-white photographs of her grandparents. This dedication and some elements of the plot (all the ancestors of the characters come from Poland and are Jews) point to an autobiographical character of the novel.

Historians have given us a much crueler story of the Slonim pogrom, which allows us to assume that the American author has significantly softened her representation of the past. Raul Hilberg, describing the liquidation of the ghetto a year later, did not mince words:

> During an operation in Slonim many houses were set afire, until the entire ghetto was a mass of flames. Some Jews who still survived in cellars and underground passages chocked to death or were crushed under collapsing buildings. [...]
> The mode of the shooting depended a great deal on the killers' sobriety. Most of them were drunk most of the time – only the "idealists" refrained from the use of alcohol. The Jews submitted without resistance and without protest. "It was amazing," a German witness relates, "how the Jews stepped into the graves, with only mutual condolences in order to strengthen their spirits and in order to ease the work of the execution commandos." When the shooting took place in front of the ditch, the victims sometimes froze in terror. Just in front of them, Jews who had been shot were lying motionless. A few bodies were still twitching, blood running from their necks. The frozen Jews were shot as they stepped back from the edge of the grave, and other Jews quickly dragged them in.[480]

In Krauss's novel, there are no macabre scenes like these, even though Gursky and Litvinoff certainly knew about them (as well as Bird and Alma, who are reading Hilberg's book). Instead, a library appears, like a sealed wound, and its appearance is both literal, in the sense of books in the characters' lives, and metaphorical, that of a multilayered, postmodern novel.

At this point, we need to say a bit more about libraries in the novel. Mainly Gursky uses the city library and thanks to his interest in books various quotations find their way into *The History of Love*, from Leo Tolstoy's *Anna Karenina*, James Joyce's *Ulysses*, and from his son Isaac's stories. Gursky is also looking for his book in that library and is trying to find out who impersonated him as the author *The History of Love*. He learns that the manuscript, which he gave to a friend for safekeeping before leaving Poland, was published by Litvinoff as his book.

Alma Singer's mother also uses libraries. She studies Spanish and Hebrew at Oxford in order to be able to read *The History of Love* given to her by her future

---

[480] Hilberg, *The Destruction of the European Jews*, p. 249.

The Babel Library of the Holocaust

husband. At the Bodleian Library, "[s]he ordered up so many books that whenever the clerk who worked at the desk saw her coming, he tried to hide" (HL 40). After the death of her beloved husband, she goes through a period of depression and spends her days translating or reading, neglecting her children and herself. "The wall of dictionaries between my mother and the world gets taller every year," Alma confesses (HL 46; heading of section 19.). One day, Mrs. Singer receives, from a mysterious sender, a request to translate a book once given to her. From that moment on, she translates that book piece by piece and keeps sending the passages across the ocean the same way its author, Gursky, once did.

The metaphorical library Krauss writes about, an image of something completely different from a book rental or a private book collection, emerges from death. One could even say that death has created it. The characters read countless books, quote from them, and rewrite them, keep notebooks and diaries. Indeed, they even steal the very novel Krauss herself wrote. The reason is mourning. Gursky mourns the family he lost in Slonim, and later the loss of his son and his would-be wife. Alma and the Bird mourn their father. Alma's mother mourns her husband. Rosa mourns Litvinoff. To reading books, which leads to social isolation, loneliness, and sometimes to savagery as a reaction to bereavement, Krauss refers in terms of "disappearing," the word which in the dedicatory note is used in reference to her grandparents as those who taught her "the opposite of disappearing." But Gursky's entire life becomes a disappearing act, from going to America to conversations with his son, to whom he never confessed that he was his father.

The complicated life stories of people who have been scorched, who are overwhelmed by or chase books, and who are marked by disappearance helps us better to understand the project of Krauss's "defiantly intertextual" novel. Essentially, this is a case of the Derridean *hypomnesis*, an incomplete or lost memory,[481] which, when confronted with the fullness of books, libraries, and ideas, draws attention to mourning after the Holocaust and, in this bizarre and sometimes excessively experimental way, shows its power as literature.

"Fictions," according to Arkadiusz Żychliński – "[...] intensify the time of the possible experience of an alien (that is, previously unknown) experience."[482] The library, I would argue, familiarizes us with the experience of death as ours and at once not yet ours. Alma's mother names her son Emanuel "after the Jewish historian Emanuel Ringelblum, who buried milk cans with testimony in the Warsaw Ghetto [...]" (HL 35). Alma, apparently unintentionally, keeps collecting

---

481 Tadeusz Rachwał and Tadeusz Sławek, *Maszyna do pisania. O dekonstruktywistycznej teorii literatury Jacquesa Derridy* (Warszawa: "Rój," 1992), p. 168.
482 Arkadiusz Żychliński, *Laboratorium antropofikcji. Dociekania filologiczne* (Poznań: Wydawnictwo Naukowe Uniwersytetu im. Adama Mickiewicza; Warszawa: Instytut Badań Literackich PAN, 2014), pp. 296–297.

her father's belongings (including books) under her bed hoping to be able to make sense of his untimely and irreversible passing. Krauss uses other people's stories to break through to the experience of the Holocaust that her family experienced and to record it with the help of the figure of the Library of Babel. This makes her writing representative of third-generation Holocaust literature, based on indirect contact with the Event, which, though absent, is being made present through countless books, typescripts, and manuscripts. At times it is difficult to draw a line between them and decide which are testimonies and which are copies, plagiarisms or parodies.

Regarded in the context of Holocaust literature, the Library of Babel, rather than a grim joke, is a sophisticated method of making contact with the past, reminiscent of a collage or irreducible multiplicity, referring to the unconscious rather than to empty symbols.[433] Mediated in this peculiar way, enclosed by other texts, commentaries to texts, numerous types of narration, etc., this kind of testimony – a multi-layered, rhizomatous novel, based on numerous quotations – may be an alternative not only to documents of the Holocaust. It was conceived as an alternative to the vigorously developing trend of post-memory literature of the 1990s and 2000s. As Krauss's book shows, ten years ago, a great literary potential lay, not in that trend, but in discredited, pantextual fiction.

---

483 Gilles Deleuze and Félix Guattari, *A Thousand Plateaus. Capitalism and Schizophrenia*, trans. Brian Massumi (Minneapolis and London: University of Minnesota Press, 2005), p. 35.

Chapter 11.
Postmodern Narcissism and Its Functions: Andrzej Bart

Working assumptions

Andrzej Bart's novel *Fabryka muchołapek*, published in 2008, has turned out to be, next to Marek Bieńczyk's *Tworki*, the most important representative of Polish postmodern Holocaust-related literary works. It has also become something of a model narrative for this type of literature and a magnet of sorts due to the way it has attracted the attention of critics, eager to denounce the ills of postmodern narcissism, its shallow representations of the past, the eager deployment of nostalgia, the trivialization of history, as well as the replication of the staple figure of the self-absorbed author. This figure assumes the role of someone who holds a mirror up to society, but has no idea how to improve the thus reflected image. In *The Culture of Narcissism* (1979, rev. ed. 1991), Christopher Lasch argues:

> A society that has made "nostalgia" a marketable commodity on the cultural exchange quickly repudiates the suggestion that life in the past was in any important way better than life today. Having trivialized the past by equating it with outmoded styles of consumption, discarded fashions and attitudes, people today resent anyone who draws on the past in serious discussions of contemporary conditions or attempts to use the past as a standard by which to judge the present. Current critical dogma equates every such reference to the past as itself an expression of nostalgia.[484]

As a result of this nostalgic equation, Jean-François Lyotard wrote in 1986, the eclectic entertainment narrative is created, where the past is treated in terms of financial investment. "Such realism accommodates all tendencies, just as capital accommodates all 'needs,' providing that the tendencies and needs have pur-

---

[484] Christopher Lasch, *The Culture of Narcissism: American Life in An Age of Diminishing Expectations* (New York and London: W. W. Norton, 1979/1991), p. xvii (Preface).

chasing power."[485] The influence of postmodernism on art is often determined by money, understood more or less symbolically.

Bart's novel may be regarded as an expression of the narcissistic self-consciousness of postmodernism; yet it is also its critique. Bart expresses this through the story of the phantom court trial of Chaim Mordechaj Rumkowski, the president of the Litzmannstadt Ghetto, where many well-known dead people appear as witnesses, including Janusz Korczak, Hannah Arendt and Dawid Sierakowiak. However, I am interested not in this story, but in the narrative conducted alongside it, whose protagonist is the author of a report on the court proceedings. His is called Andrzej, and he is Bart's *porte parole*. By drawing attention to this theme in *Fabryka muchołapek*, as yet underrepresented in the novel's critical reception, I want to show that the search for contact with a representation of the Holocaust does not necessarily lead to the past, its reconstruction or a reflection on history. Sometimes it involves constructing a narcissistic fantasy by the contemporary subject, which turns elements of the Holocaust scenario into libidinal objects that help him understand himself. To organize my assumptions, I will once more avail myself of Hayden White's essay "Postmodernism and History,"[486] where the scholar discusses the attitude of postmodernists to history in three points, relevant to my analysis of Bart's novel. Postmodernist attempts to come to terms with history, especially with the history of the Holocaust, involve (1) treating it as a narrative that keeps stubbornly returning, as well as being confusing and burdensome. For postmodernists, (2) "historical past" is a pure abstraction; they do not conceal the arbitrariness of their approach to historical knowledge and detect in historical research the bias of academic politics and dogmatism. (3) The past interests postmodernists mainly in its present aspect, as a phantasm and "the return of the repressed." Therefore, White notes, "This formulation of the postmodernist notions of the past and history is framed in vaguely Freudian terms in the interest of highlighting their intended therapeutic function (as against the merely didactic function of traditional, professional historiography). This formulation also allows one to account for what the critics of postmodernism take to be its fallacies, errors, and outright delusions."[487]

In this chapter, I examine how a psychoanalytic reading of the metatextual layer of Bart's novel could change its previously established meaning, and whether the reviewers, in their focus on the theme of the Holocaust, have not omitted other, equally interesting though perhaps more troublesome, meanings

---

485 "Realism" in Jean-Francois Lyotard, "Answering the Question: What Is Postmodernism?" translated by Regis Durand, in Jean-Francois Lyotard, *The Postmodern Condition: A Report on Knowledge* (Minneapolis; University of Minnesota Press, 1984), pp. 71–82.
486 White, "Postmodernism and History." Cf. White "Postmodernizm i historia," pp. 35–41.
487 White, "Postmodernism and History." Cf. White, "Postmodernizm i historia", pp. 36–37.

of the work. To this end, I juxtapose the contemporary narrative that accompanies the historical one[488] with Lacan's concepts of narcissistic fantasy and narcissism, looking in Bart's novel for structural features of narcissistic narrative as discussed by Linda Hutcheon. This leads me to believe that the supreme significance of *Fabryka muchołapek* could only crystallize several years after the novel's publication, when it began to be seen as an example of postmodern fiction. To understand the parodic potential and social functions of Bart's novel, I will compare it with *Radegast*, a 2008 film directed by Borys Lankosz, for which Bart wrote the script.

I set off with an examination of the cover of *Fabryka muchołapek,* with its perverse version of a narcissistic *mise-en-abyme*. I conclude by seeing narcissism as a way to deal with a recurring and uncomfortable past that Bart considers in both individual and supra-individual dimensions. Looking at *Fabryka muchołapek* as a story that belongs to the culture of narcissism and postmodernism allows us now to read it differently than critics did ten years ago. Then it was read as a novel about the "trial of Rumkowski,"[489] and this protagonist – if we leave out the self-absorbed writer-narrator – was called "the king of the Jews," "a renegade, an accomplice of persecutors and at the same time a self-proclaimed messiah full of good intentions."[490] Treating narcissism as a psychoanalytic concept, developed theoretically first by Sigmund Freud and then Jacques Lacan, it is impossible to defend this interpretation. I argue that the narrative dynamic of *Fabryka muchołapek* corresponds to secondary narcissism, understood as "the loving capture of the subject in his image. It has value as a point of reference that forms the Self – the object of narcissism – only if it is inscribed as meaningful in the chain of meanings in which the mother's desire is expressed."[491]

What does this mean in the context of Bart's novel? First of all, this approach involves transferring its events from the Second World War to the present and in constructing a parallel narrative, historical and contemporary, one that corresponds to two psychoanalytic mechanisms, introjection and projection. In neither of the two narratives does Rumkowski play a dominant role. Besides the

---

488 According to Perry R. Anderson, as recalled by Frederic Jameson, World War II and the Holocaust are also the theme of historical fiction, or of the historical romance, as indicated by the great number of popular stories with those themes on the global publishing market. Fredric Jameson, *The Antinomies of Realism* (London and New York: Verso 2013), p. 259.
489 Sławomir Buryła, *Wokół Zagłady. Szkice o literaturze Holokaustu* (Kraków: Universitas, 2016), p. 99.
490 Dariusz Nowacki, "Pociąg do Hollywood. O prozie Andrzeja Barta," in *Skład osobowy. Szkice o prozaikach współczesnych*, part 2, ed. Agnieszka Nęcka, Dariusz Nowacki, Jolanta Pasterska (Katowice: Wydawnictwo Uniwersytetu Śląskiego, 2016), p. 43.
491 Pierre Dessuant, *Narcyzm. Przegląd koncepcji psychoanalitycznych* [*Le narcissisme*], trans. Zuzanna Stadnicka-Dmitriew (Gdańsk: Gdańskie Wydawnictwo Psychologiczne, 2007), p. 116.

writer called Andrzej and in some respects similar in biographical terms to Bart (they share a wife named Beata, work on a script like that of the actual film *Radegast*, and have a career as filmmakers), two female figures play an important role, Regina and Dora. Why does the Self, which merges with the specter of Rumkowski, revolve around these two objects? And why does the narrator, who clearly likes the figure of the President of the Ghetto – as the novel makes clear – focus the story on the figures of both these women? Is he trying to get closer to the symbolic mother (an entity that does not exist in the novel in the traditional sense of a literary character)? Would he prefer to make sense of this introjection in its relation to the Holocaust? Who is Rumkowski in this context? In the considerations that follow, I put forth several hypotheses, some of which are meant as excursions rather than traditional interpretive arguments. Through them, I want to suggest that a group of four actants (Rumkowski, Regina, their son, and Dora), consisting of foster parents, an adopted son and a lover, makes up a field of vague yet intriguing identifications.

Photographs, screens, interfaces

The issue of narcissism is suggested by the cover of *Fabryka muchołapek*, which brings to mind the images on playing cards.[492] Yet instead of the image of a man composed as if of two asymmetrical corpora, we see a double photograph of the author. The top of the picture shows a black figure of Bart looking at equally dark outlines of a building. On his left, there are indistinct plants. Everything blends with a tea-yellowish background. The basis of the photo is the lower part of the cover. It shows Bart looking at the buildings of an old, abandoned factory made of red brick with a yellow hue. To the right, behind the factory, we see some bushes. In front of it is a puddle that reflects the image which makes up the upper part of the cover.

In *Radegast*, one of the Jewish survivors, when sharing memories about the Łódź ghetto, spreads before the camera some photos of his friends and then places them in a machine that looks like a microfilm reader. With its help, he casts the images on the screen of a small TV. The camera shows the interference during this screening, which obscures the photo images. We also see the images on the TV screen reflected in the survivor's photochromic glass lenses in the glasses he is wearing. The whole operation brings in again the tea color; we see it on the plates of photos placed on the reader, on photos reflected in the glasses and on the

---

[492] Nowacki, "Pociąg do Hollywood. O prozie Andrzeja Barta,"; Paulina Małochleb, "Murarz buduje, a ja majaczę," *FA-art* nr 1–2; Paulina Małochleb, "Iluzja i mistyfikacja. O powieściach Andrzeja Barta," *Śląskie Studia Polonistyczne* 2012, nr 1/2 (2).

image of the man bustling around the house reflected on the surface of the convex TV screen (or the glasses).

Sarah Kember has argued that before the advent of new technologies, photography reflected the ordering and taming of the world.[493] Digital "manipulation" of images, as used, for instance, by the protagonist of *Radegast*, has disrupted this convention. Lankosz presents in detail the entire process of handling an analog photo image, from scanning to the fragmented pixels flowing across the TV image and the accompanying change in the color of the photograph. His portrayal of this process employs the language of postmodernism. Distant as this language may be from the parascientific procedures and perfectionism of traditional photography,[494] it does illustrate the role of new media in creating narratives about the Holocaust, which under their influence not only reveals, develops and shapes, but is also subject to various modes of archiving.

Similar reflections are prompted by the 2000 documentary film *Hiob* [Job] by Andrzej Bart in the joint capacity of director and author of the screenplay. While in *Radegast* only single scenes refer to postmodernism (and do so mostly in the compositional sense), here the whole picture seems postmodern. Its protagonist, Marek Rudnicki, a graphic designer, tells a Holocaust survival story and does so in two ways. One is a classic documentary narrative; we see him in his Paris apartment, sitting or walking. The other version uses mediated narration, with Rudnicki as the protagonist of a "film within a film," where he plays himself. We watch his face (a "talking head") places as it were inside a TV set found in the artist's apartment. The aim of this multi-perspective and multidirectional narrative is "to expand the public sphere by the use of various strategies of thinking about the past, in which there is no fruitless conflict between predetermined positions, but is recognized a need to negotiably constitute new groups and interests."[495]

One of such "interests" may be an attempt to see the Holocaust as a source of petrified images, ones which are too easy to use and manipulate, as is evidenced by the editing technology used by Bart and similar to Jean-Luc Godard's films, especially to *Notre musique* (*Our Music*, 2004). In *Hiob*, such images are supplied by photographs of sacred sculptures, photographs from the Warsaw Ghetto and

---

493 Sarah Kember, "'The shadow of the object': photography and realism," in Sarah Kember, *Virtual Anxiety: Photography, New Technologies and Subjectivity* (Manchester and New York: Manchester University Press, 1998), pp. 17–36. "[…] photography was considered to be the means of representing this reassuring world in which everything appeared to stay in its time, space and place" (p. 21).
494 Cf. William J. Mitchell, *The Reconfigured Eye: Visual Truth in the Post-Photographic Era* (Cambridge, Mass.: The MIT Press, 1994), p. 8.
495 Tomasz Łysak, *Od kroniki do filmu posttraumatycznego. Filmy dokumentalne o Zagładzie* (Warszawa: Instytut Badań Literackich PAN, 2016), p. 293.

of contemporary European cities. Another reason for the post-modernization of history is Bart's belief in a non-dogmatic and distanced attitude towards the traditional understanding of facts that postmodernists assume when discussing the past. In the words of White,

> Postmodernists [...] tend to believe that nobody owns history, that anyone has a right to study it for purposes both theoretical and practical, that the past of history and the past of memory are quite different things, and that finding out what happened in the past is less important than finding out "what it felt like" for the patients as well as the agents of past events. This is why postmodernists favor the genre of the "testimony," use of experimental, even surrealistic literary devices and mythological plots, strive for cinema-like "special effects," and use poetic tropes and figures rather than concepts, and a mixture of documentary with "fictional" techniques for the presentation (*Darstelllung*) of a past more indeterminate than clear in outline, more grotesque than heroic in its stature, more malleable than fixed in its form.[496]

Meanwhile, the old man from Lankosz's *Radegast*, in the representations of documents from the Holocaust, is primarily looking for dead friends. Images from the past "settle" and are reflected in his glasses And this is how we see him in this shot, wrapped as it were in a panorama of images. The confrontation becomes more dynamic when, in one of the photos, he recognizes himself when young. All reflections, repetitions, processed copies and wandering images suggest yet another founding narrative for the 1980s postmodernism, Jean Baudrillard's precession of simulacra. When one reads chosen passages as a commentary on the *Radegast* scenes just discussed, the words of the French sociologist sound extremely relevant:

> It is no longer a question of imitation, nor duplication, nor even parody. It is a question of substituting the signs of the real for the real, that is to say of an operation of deterring every real process via its operational double, a programmatic, metastable, perfectly descriptive machine that offers all the signs of the real and short-circuits all its vicissitudes.[497]

The double, introjective-projective dimension of *Fabryka muchołapek* corresponds both to its structure, the two parallel stories, and to the claims of psychoanalysis that support the assumptions I am proposing here. The screen – that of the camera, of the television and camcorder, sometimes only symbolically suggested or even completely invisible – highlights this problem. It is an object-symbol, emphasizing the multi-layered narcissism of Bart's message. As Andrzej Gwóźdź has argued:

---

496 White, "Postmodernism and History." Cf. White, "Postmodernizm i historia", p. 37.
497 Jean Baudrillard, "The Precession of Simulacra," in Jean Baudrillard, *Simulacra and Simulation*, trans. Sheila Faria Glaser (Ann Arbor: The University of Michigan Press, 1994), p. 2.

> The screen is present as the effect of a double movement: projective (the penetrating reflector) and introjective (the consciousness as a recording surface) [...]. This corresponds to the psychoanalytic concept of identification; on the one hand, I myself as a subject liberate the image and am a duplicate of the projector; on the other hand, I deposit it and I am a duplicate of the screen, and in both cases I invariably remain the camera, and the objects return to my mental screen, as it were, in the act of returning the illuminated objects to my brain through the cinema screen.[498]

The journey of reflections and representations, as described by Bart, Baudrillard and Gwóźdź, has the features of narcissistic identification:

> Narcissistic identification – the word identification, without differentiation, is unusable – that of the second narcissism, is identification with the other which, under normal circumstances, enables man to locate precisely his imaginary and libidinal relation to the world in general. That is what enables him to see in its place and to structure, as a function of this place and of his world, his being. [...] The subject sees his being in a reflection in relation to the other, that is to say in relation to the *Ichideal*.[499]

Analysis of the cover of Bart's novel and of the film with his screenplay shows that this journey, which Lacan calls "metabolism of images,"[500] takes place on a level that is unobvious and tends to be overlooked by critics. Moreover, that it can lead one into areas that are both bizarre and problematic, and we cannot be sure if this path is worth taking. One thing, however, seems to be certain: the *castling* of reflections of the nature of narcissistic identification enables and necessitates, in the context of Bart's work from the late 2000s, a reflection on the presence of the subject (and presence in general). This becomes evident when one applies to it a carbon copy of *Las Meninas* and interpretations of this picture.

Mise-en-abyme

Narcissistic artifacts, considered at the level of structure, have their mysterious reference, which I mention only hypothetically. One is a canvas painting in 1656 by Diego Velázquez, and the Portuguese title, *Las Meninas*, translates as "ladies-in-waiting." It depicts "an artist painting a picture in the presence of a court group, in a large hall with several windows, decorated with numerous paintings

---

[498] Andrzej Gwóźdź, "Mała ekranologia," in *Wiek ekranów. Przestrzenie kultury widzenia*, ed. Andrzej Gwóźdź and Piotr Zawojski (Kraków: Rabid, 2002), p. 21.
[499] Jacques Lacan, "The two narcissisms," in: Jacques Lacan, *The Seminar of Jacques Lacan, Book I: Freud's Papers on Technique, 1953–1954*, trans. John Forrester (Cambridge: Cambridge University Press, 1988), pp. 125–126.
[500] Jacques Lacan, *On the Names-of-the-Father*, trans. Brice Fink (Cambridge and Malden, MA: Polity Press, 2013.), p. 10.

and a mirror."[501] Here, I am interested, not in the painting itself, but in the fact that it has become a commonly cited example of *mise-en-abyme*, a phenomenon that, following Linda Hutcheon, is defined as textual (mirror-like) auto-referentiality and self-reflectivity,[502] and is sometimes combined with parody (which, also following Hutcheon, leads to wrong generalizations). It seems obvious that the photos and screens discussed above are examples of *mise-en-abyme*. The actual challenge consists in understanding their role in Bart's novel. Michel Foucault's commentary on Velázquez's painting, in which he shows that mirror reflection is "the frailest duplication of representation" may help in this.[503] If we were to refer this commentary to *Fabryka muchołapek*, we should first of all consider why the reflections of the writer's figure on the cover of the novel are obscured. Next, we'd need to rethink the role of the theatrical court trial over Rumkowski and try to think of reasons for the criticism's fixation on it. I believe that Bart's representation can be regarded as a veil for the theatre that takes place on the psychoanalytic plane and consists in the journey of the Self between libidinal objects, freed from the past and presented as specters of the Holocaust. However, as Foucault's discussion of *Las Meninas* assures us, it is a rather troublesome journey, one in which different experiences, positions and glances merge into one, leaving the "pure representation of [some] essential absence."[504] In the case of *Fabryka muchołapek*, the absence has been defined in various ways: from disappointment with the poorly presented figure of Rumkowski to a misunderstanding of the very essence of postmodern literature. This absence means, first of all, the non-obvious presence of the writer (or his absence). But it also points to a significant defect of Rumkowski as the main character: his passivity (in terms of him being an actant) and muteness (in terms of his being a participant in the narrative, who in the face of many accusations and opinions about himself not only fails to take a stand, but mostly remains silent). Bart leaves empty these usually clearly defined places in the narrative, instead offering the reader the freedom to... read. According to Hutcheon's theory, categories such as "producer" and "receiver" mean abandoning living, individual subjects and creating something that can be called their trace, a "site" of the subject.[505] Encountering the reflection of the author in the text (Andrzej the writer) or the silent Rumkowski, the reader actually does see a lot of free space. In fact, the reader observes a distinct theater of shadows unfolding before her eyes, despite

---

501 Andrzej Witko, "Wprowadzenie," in *Tajemnica "Las Meninas". Anthologia tekstów*, selected and edited by Andrzej Witko (Kraków: Wydawnictwo AA, 2006), p. 10.
502 Hutcheon, *A Theory of Parody*, pp. 20, 31.
503 Michel Foucault, *The Order of Things. An Archeology of the Human Sciences* (New York: Pantheon Books, 1970), p. 308 (chapter "Man and his Doubles").
504 Foucault, *The Order of Things*, p. 308.
505 Hutcheon, *A Theory of Parody*, p. 85.

the fact that other events attract her attention more intensely. Wrote Foucault, "In Classical thought, the personage for whom the representation exists, and who represents himself within it, recognizing himself therein as an image or reflection, he who ties together all the interlacing threads of the 'representation in the form of a picture or table' – he is never to be found in that table himself."[506]

Let's now look at the brief history of the critical response to this "absence," which shows how the surrogate themes, ones describing the surface of the novel, have dominated its reception.

Misunderstandings

Regardless of the doubts expressed by some critics, *Fabryka muchołapek* is a breakthrough in Bart's work. The evidence comes primarily from the numerous reviews and discussions of this novel, then from awards and nominations, thirdly from translations into foreign languages, and, fourthly, from its significance for the development of the Holocaust discourse in Poland and abroad. Even though Bart's novel was not received as enthusiastically as *Tworki*, to which it was sometimes compared in slightly depreciating tones,[507] this fact has not fundamentally diminished its significance. An analysis of the studies devoted to it shows that the occasion of criticizing *Fabryka* exposed the weakness of literary studies as incapable of dealing with the issue of the post-modernization of the Holocaust.[508] Marlena Sęczek, author of the entry about Bart published in the online dictionary *Polscy pisarze i badacze literatury przełomu XX i XXI wieku* [*Polish Writers and Literary Scholars of the Turn of the Twenty-First Century*] has recorded 15 reviews and 5 articles in the Polish press about *Fabryka muchołapek*, as well as 8 reviews and 1 article about *Rewers*.[509] Nowacki, at the end of his essay, taking the Polish-language press as the criterion of his research, lists 11 reviews and 2 articles about *Fabryka muchołapek* and 5 reviews and 2 articles about *Rewers*. In addition to this, *Fabryka muchołapek* is also the subject of two uncited essays, one by Danuta Szajnert and another by Emilia Słonimska.

Critical commentaries can be grouped according to three criteria: aesthetic (represented by all those who appreciated *Fabryka muchołapek* for its entertainment value, seeing in it a brilliantly written popular novel), discursive (important for critics who value the sensational possibilities of prose and its impact on the Holocaust discourse of the years 2008–2018) and cognitive (appreciated by

---

506 Foucault, *The Order of Things*, p. 308.
507 Nowacki, "Pociąg do Hollywood," p. 42.
508 Nowacki, "Pociąg do Hollywood," p. 42–44.
509 http://www.ppibl.ibl.waw.pl/mediawiki/index.php?title=Andrzej_BART (accessed 01.09. 2023).

historians of Holocaust literature and historians of the Holocaust itself, who, given the importance of *Fabryka muchołapek* for knowledge about the Holocaust, and especially for the knowledge and evaluation of Rumkowski's activities, questioned the value of the novel). It should be added that numerous critical opinions, including intuitive ones, have revealed another important feature of the novel, i. e., its susceptibility to the influence of current Polish fiction constructed around the themes of post-memory, pop-cultural, intertextual, topographic, affective or animal studies in culture. This does not mean, of course, that the text of *Fabryka muchołapek* can respond to every theoretical challenge. However, it testifies to the novel's rich intertextual references[510] and temporal levels. The knots created by these references, the reader and the author seem so complicated that it is necessary to use different interpretive tools in the process of disentangling them.

Let's take a closer look at the reception. Proponents of the thesis about the entertaining, popularizing and light tone of Bart's novel have emphasized its role in the debate about Rumkowski, as well as the controversy that has arisen over the years around this figure. They have also emphasized the tone of tenderness, not characteristic of Bart's style,[511] and that of naïve kindheartedness.[512] Researchers representing post-memory and post-traumatic studies on the Holocaust assessed *Fabryka muchołapek* in a completely different way. On this occasion, a bold, if not entirely lucid opinion has been voiced, suggesting that "the excellence of *Fabryka muchołapek* consists in the fact that it is not another 'Holocaust lipstick,' a type of story that we see constantly being published, because there is demand for it."[513] That the novel offers a deeply thought-out approach to the Holocaust seems to consist in the fact that it is "a project that consistently brings out, through its strongly manifested metafictional layer, the end of traditional narratives and the ethical character of Holocaust literature."[514] Such opinions have not been voiced by literary historians concerned with the Holocaust, including Jacek Leociak, Michał Głowiński, Sławomir Buryła, Justyna Kowalska-Leder and Monika Polit. The author of *Czarne sezony* bluntly called Bart's novel a "dud,"

---

510 Danuta Szajnert, "Przestrzeń doświadczona, przestrzeń wytworzona – literackie topografie Litzmannstadt Getto (rekonesans). Część druga," *Białostockie Studia Literaturoznawcze* 6 (2015), pp. 7–25.
511 Nowacki, "Pociąg do Hollywood," p. 42.
512 Sławomir Buryła, "Bez wyroku," *Więź* 2009, p. 13.
513 Małochleb, "Murarz buduje, a ja majaczę," p. 51.
514 Krystyna Pietrych, "(Post)pamięć Holocaustu – (meta)tekst a etyka. *Fabryka muchołapek* Andrzeja Barta a *Byłam sekretarką Rumkowskiego* Elżbiety Cherezińskiej" in *Inna literatura? Dwudziestolecie 1989–2009*, vol. 1, ed. Zbigniew Andres and Janusz Pasterski (Rzeszów: Wydawnictwo Uniwersytetu Rzeszowskiego, 2010), p. 214.

adding that "his [Bart's] talent is irrelevant to the presentation of facts."[515] The tone of Kowalska-Leder's assessment of the novel may seem to sound milder, but the actual judgement is equally harsh:

> the reader is familiar with the views of Janusz Korczak, Hannah Arendt or Dawid Sierakowiak. To be sure, we do admire Andrzej Bart's knowledge and the artistry of his prose, but this novel will not teach us anything we do not already know; nor will we be emotionally confronted with anything that's new. The problem lies in the fact that Bart refuses to tackle what from the reader's point of view is the essential and at once the most difficult challenge, how to make sense of Chaim Rumkowski's conduct, and thereby to answer at least some of the questions that have arisen concerning this man.[516]

At this point, it is worth recalling a passage in Buryła's review, attributing excessive naiveté to Bart: "Full of warmth, kindness, understanding and gentle humor is the representation of simple Jews in *Fabryka muchołapek*. There is compassion in such passages for ordinary people for whom the Holocaust had in store a cruel fate."[517] *Fabryka muchołapek* has also been described as a postmodern novel. With perhaps one exception,[518] those were intuitive descriptions, based on hunches and associations, rather than specific theoretical concepts. Two comments are characteristic in this respect. One comes from an article by Bartosz Dąbrowski and sounds ennobling: "Bart, finding a different poetics than in the case of Bieńczyk and Szewec for talking about the Holocaust, institutes post-memorial issues in the area previously reserved for the style of postmodern writing (Nye, Pynchon, Grossman)."[519] The other, from the discussion of Agnieszka Izdebska and Danuta Szajnert, is much less favorable and reduces the concept of a postmodern novel about history, adopted by the author of *Rewers*, to a pocket-size dictionary and nutshell-type knowledge.[520] Worth recalling is Nowacki's opinion from 1993 about *Rien ne va plus*, which, unfortunately, has remained relevant: "Reviewers who spoke immediately after the publication of Bart's book [...] wanted to see in it a postmodern novel. This is mere labeling, for

---

515 Michał Głowiński, Marta Tomczok, Paweł Wolski, "'Pisanie jest ze swej natury niemoralne'. O narracji i Zagładzie z Michałem Głowińskim rozmawiają Marta Tomczok i Paweł Wolski," *Narracje o Zagładzie* 1 (2015), p. 150.
516 Justyna Kowalska-Leder, "Andrzej Bart, *Fabryka muchołapek*, Wydawnictwo W.A.B., Warszawa 2010" [review], *Zagłada Żydów. Studia i Materiały* 6 (2010), p. 322.
517 Buryła, "Bez wyroku," p. 13.
518 Małochleb, "Murarz buduje, a ja majaczę," p. 33.
519 Bartosz Dąbrowski, "Postpamięć, zależność, trauma," in *Kultura po przejściach, osoby z przeszłością: polski dyskurs postzależnościowy – konteksty i perspektywy badawcze*, ed. Ryszard Nycz (Kraków: Universitas, 2011), p. 263.
520 Agnieszka Izdebska and Danuta Szajnert, "The Holocaust – Postmemory – Postmodern Novel: *The Flytrap Factory* by Andrzej Bart, *Tworki* by Marek Bieńczyk and *Skaza* by Magdalena Tulli," in *The Holocaust in the Central European Literatures and Cultures since 1989 / Der Holocaust in den mitteleuropäischen Literaturen und Kulturen seit 1989*, ed. Reinhard Ibler (Stuttgart: ibidem Press, 2014), p. 143.

I find no justification in these opinions."[521] Critics have written more about examples of postmodern fiction than about theories of the postmodern. First of all, intertextual references show that when writing his book about Rumkowski Bart drew on William Shakespeare's *Coriolanus*, Mikhail Bulgakov's *The Master and Margarita*, Franz Kafka's *The Trial* and *The Castle*, Philip K. Dick's *The Man in the High Castle*, as well as Sándor Márai's diary and Gershom Scholem's *Żydzi i Niemcy. Eseje. Listy. Rozmowa* (the writer mentions the last-named two works in the afterword).[522] There are also aesthetic features regarded as essential to postmodernism. Critics have detected traces of irony, pastiche, and parody in *Fabryka muchołapek*.

Suggesting at the outset that *Fabryka muchołapek* can be seen as a model example of a type of approach to the Holocaust, I pointed out the major strategies of its reception. On the one hand, critics have looked with interest at the rise of postmodernism, capable of taking up dramatic, relevant and topical themes; on the other, they have tended to reduce it to the simple matter of style. In my opinion, the groundbreaking nature of Bart's novel can be captured in these three aspects: (1) the concept of postmodernism, which is interesting and close to Hutcheon's theories (2); making some scenes in *Radegast* a source of a parody of *Fabryka muchołapek* and thus stitching together two works, telling different stories about the Holocaust, into one; (3) finally, making the novel a field for the writer's narcissistic fantasy. These aspects put together cause *Fabryka muchołapek* to be a much more difficult test for a felicitous fictional approach to the Holocaust than *Tworki*, with its melancholic vision of emptiness left by the departed Jews. Except that it was a test of the structural rather than linguistic capabilities of the text, and also bearing in mind that the author who undertook it has a different reputation than Marek Bieńczyk, already known at that time as a historian of Polish Romanticism and the author of *Terminal*. Meanwhile, to many critics, Bart has remained something of a jester. As Nowacki has put it: "[…] in Bart's writing, people have tended to see little more than fun, a series of antics; all in all – so much innocent frolic."[523]

---

521 Nowacki, "Czy Bart lektury wart?" *FA-art* 11 (1993) nr 1 (11), p. 80.
522 This reference is to the Polish edition of Scholem's collection of essays *On Jews and Judaism in Crisis: Selected Essays*, which differs from the English.
523 Nowacki, "Czy Bart lektury wart?" p. 79.

Narcissistic narratives

At the end of her *Narcissistic Narrative* (1980), Hutcheon writes: "[...] Narcissus may die by the mirroring pool; but the fact remains that, in another sense, he also lives on, still self-regarding, *received* into the next world with open arms."[524] This enigmatic statement refers to the meaning of concepts such as narcissistic narratives and parody, which Hutcheon has described based on her understanding of postmodernism as literature that guarantees literary longevity and even a second life. Modernism, especially in architecture, admittedly values artistic forms which are cut off from tradition. This reveals postmodernism's renovating feature, as a trend, in a broader sense, that links art back to the past and restores dialogue between the past and the present. Hutcheon has analyzed diegetic narratives about the past, i.e., stories which explicitly address their reader, in which the fictional world has to be put together in the act of reading and which do not allow us to forget that literature is an artifact. She has concluded that, for example, the novels by John Barth (e.g., *The Floating Opera*) or John Fowles (*The French Lieutenant's Woman*) are self-reflexive.[525] She describes this "mirror" property of prose as hidden narcissism, which consists of diegetic and linguistic models, represented by detective, fantasy, erotic, and humorous types of fiction. *Fabryka muchołapek* is a narcissistic narrative of the diegetic and linguistic type, and for two reasons. First, one of the themes of the novel is the process of creating a literary work ("On December 31, 2007, also sleepy, I am finishing *Fabryka muchołapek*."[526]). Second, Bart combines the storytelling and the story told (we are reading the story about what happens before our eyes and, at the same time, about the creation of a novel recounting that). And Bart treats history as a text, rather than a collection of facts.[527] Thus, the narcissism of *Fabryka muchołapek* permeates both its structure and ideology; moreover, it gets allegorized and thematized (as is the case in most self-reflexive fictions).[528]

Considering that Hutcheon reflected on the relationship of narcissistic narrative to history only in studies of metanovels and parodies (working with a set selection of examples), let us turn to her 1986 review article on the historiographical metanovel, parody and the intertextuality of history. There seem to be numerous popular novels whose claim to historical credibility is rendered

---

524 Linda Hutcheon, *Narcissistic Narrative. The Metafictional Paradox* (New York and London: Methuen, 1984), p. 162.
525 Hutcheon, *Narcissistic Narrative*, p. 28.
526 Andrzej Bart, *Fabryka muchołapek* (Warszawa: W. A. B., 2008), p. 275.
527 "Postmodernism and History." Cf. White, "Postmodernizm i historia," p. 38.
528 Hutcheon, *Narcissistic Narrative*, p. 22–23.

problematic by their metafictional self-reflexivity (and intertextuality).[529] *Fabryka mucholapek* is also a novel about *writing a novel*, and as such was inspired by numerous other novels, films and scientific works. Moreover, its historical layer raises doubts, as expressed in the opinions of critics we have looked at. Since these doubts are incoherent and lead to questioning the meaning of the entire novel, it is worth trying to see in them a hybrid and complex structure, which Hutcheon refers to as parody. We need to bear in mind, however, that Hutcheon does not mean any simple imitation of a group of texts, but a "power to renew," with social and political consequences.[530]

To examine the parodic potential of *Fabryka mucholapek*, we need to limit the field of its intertextual interactions to one, albeit the most important, context, that of *Radegast*. The film's action takes place on several planes. Lucille Eichenrgreen, author of a 2000 book entitled *Rumkowski and the Orphans of Lodz*, which rehashes false accusations of sexual harassment of former pupils of a prewar orphanage by the President, visits contemporary Łódź. This eighty-something-year-old lady, who came from a wealthy Hamburg family, visits the several places she remembers from her stay in Poland during the war. These memories are of poverty and backwardness as the main features of the 1941 Łódź, the images including the railway station overrun with vegetation, dirty staircases in tenement houses located within the ghetto, lack of running water or a sewage system. Her contemporary impressions are much the same: "Nothing has changed. It's still the same. The stairs are still as dirty as they were in the ghetto."[531] The revulsion of Eichengreen's impressions, intensified by the dramatic memory of separation from her younger sister transported by the Germans to an extermination camp, is softened and toned down by the narrator (played by Bronisław Wrocławski), who reads out passages from Rumkowski's speeches and recounts the stories of some Jewish people from the West. We see him wandering around the same yards in a dustcoat like one of the phantoms that appear from time to time in the film, and we listen to him spin fantastic stories about people he never met. For example, about Franz Kafka's sisters and what his life in the Łódź ghetto might have been like. These two basic narratives (for the voices of Eichengreen and the narrator are the main ones, speaking more than any other character in the film) are accompanied by several others, including the recollections of Stella Tchaikovsky, Roman Freund, Erwin Singer and Nachman Zonabend. There are also photos and documents from the ghetto, which show not only the drama, but also the everyday life of the people living in it. There are also

---

529 Cf. Linda Hutcheon, "Subject In/Of/To History and His Story," *Diacritics* 16 (1) (Spring 1986), pp. 78–91.
530 "Parody today is endowed with the power to renew." Hutcheon, *A Theory of Parody*, p. 115.
531 Borys Lankosz, *Radegast* (2008): 44:56.

pictures from several contemporary cities, including Berlin, Prague and Łódź. Among the several symbols used in the film are: a red balloon carried by the wind on the platform of the Berlin U-Bahn; a cattle car at Radegast station; the figure of the narrator framed by the Star of David in the Rzuchowski Forest; Eichengreen walking alone on the paved sidewalk; anti-Semitic graffiti on walls of buildings; the sound of a camera shutter combined with images of material remains of the Jews of Łódź... The images do not convey an unambiguous message, to say the least. On the one hand, Eichengreen and Czajkowska emphasize the differences between the poverty of Bałuty[532] and the wealth of the West. On the other hand, one is reminded of scenes in which the deported rich were trading their belongings for a chance of survival and class inequalities were getting evened out at a terrifying pace. The author of *Rumkowski and the Orphans* recalls that it did not take her long to realize that it would be easier for her to survive when she became Polish, if at the cost of compromising good manners and sophisticated taste.

Apparently, then, Bart and Lankosz made "a film about Jews from Western Europe crammed into the ghetto in Łódź."[533] Yet, by allowing them to express critical opinions about the backwardness of Łódź during the war and today, they did not present an unambiguous narrative that would only arouse pity in the viewer. The occasionally grotesque and symbolic images and scenes in *Radegast* describe – in various degrees of ambiguity – the category of victim and survivor, situating them against the background of such problems as class divisions, place of birth, resourcefulness and social capital. The film begins with scenes at the train station in Berlin and an outrageous, ironic – considering what happens later in the film – Yiddish song from the Łódź ghetto, "Es geyt a yeke": "Yeke is coming, carrying his portfolio, looking for fat or margarine. He won't buy anything here, but he will get a visa to the Marysin cemetery...."[534] Later we learn that the noun "yeke" was used to describe visitors from the Czech Republic, Austria and Germany, and that it refers to vests that emphasized the wearer's difference from the local population. The main theme of the film then is the situation of the Jewish population from Western Europe, who in 1941 suddenly found themselves in poverty-stricken Łódź. Bart must have known that by asking Eichengreen for comment, he would get a story bordering on contempt and haughtiness. Be it as it may, he did not repeat it in *Fabryka muchołapek*, although he maintained the perspective of a female storyteller.

A difficulty in identifying the parodic aspects of *Fabryka muchołapek* has to do with the chronology of the two relevant texts, the novel and the film script. We do not know which of them was created first and whether one of them overtook,

---

532 An area of Łódź; the housing estate Radogoszcz (formerly Radegast) is part of it.
533 Bart, *Fabryka muchołapek*, pp. 34–35.
534 Lankosz, *Radegast*, 1:01–1:13.

as it were, the other, since both were presented to the public (published/shown) in the same year and could have been born in the artist's mind at the same time. We may assume that the transfer between the two narratives occurred both ways, although some considerations indicate that the novel was a continuation of the film, supplementing the issues which it, the film, treated in a manner that was too conventional or subordinated to the narratives of witnesses and testimonies. Here are some of the common features. Stella Czajkowska, a pianist now living in Sweden ("… and suddenly here comes the aristocracy of the Western Jews, who up to that point had basically lived in freedom."[535]), recalls an episode with sweets (Rumkowski made her and other girls chase sellers of candy). Both the film and the novel also talk about Franz Kafka and his sisters. In *Radegast*, we can even see the ruined interiors of the tenement houses where they lived. However, the fantasy of the ghetto-confined author who could have died in the Kulmhof camp take up much more space in the novel and reaches a point which some critics have thought to have been in violation of good taste.

"This song is written for money"?[536]

The novel addresses the theme of the "great meeting of two worlds"[537] only to a small extent (for example, Bart cites excerpts from Gershom Scholem's collection of essays *Żydzi i Niemcy*; already mentioned). We learn that Andrzej, identified as a writer, is trying get an "important German manufacturer"[538] interested in making "a film about Jews from Western Europe squeezed into the ghetto in Łódź,"[539] and "on the spot"[540] invents a "ghetto joke" (otherwise presented in the film as nothing but the truth) that "In the Łódź ghetto we can have more Nobel Prize winners on one square meter than the rest of the world."[541] But that's where the matter ends. It should be remembered, however, that the features of *narcissistic* fiction are hidden in the novel behind numerous devices and conventions. Let us take a closer look at what lies behind the motif of searching for a producer for a film perplexingly like *Radegast*. One thing is a major obstacle, and that's lack of money. One day the writer is visited by a gentleman who seems to be a devil, maybe even Mephistopheles himself. The devil finds him exhausted, malaise-

---

535 Lankosz, *Radegast*, 30:34–30:35.
536 The lyrics of Republika's song "Mamona" do not appear in *Fabryka muchołapek*. For me the song has been an additional source of inspiration.
537 Lankosz, *Radegast*, 30:18.
538 Bart, *Fabryka muchołapek*, p. 34.
539 Bart, *Fabryka muchołapek*, p. 34–35.
540 Bart, *Fabryka muchołapek*, p. 35.
541 Bart, *Fabryka muchołapek*, p. 35.

stricken, and hungover. Rather than offering him a contract, he tells him to pen an account of the court proceedings in the Rumkowski case and pays on the spot: "In these trying times I bring money to your doorstep, like some kind of courier."[542] This "Faustian" scene is a one-off episode in the novel. The devil does not return to collect the work thus commissioned and is not trying to find out whether and how it was done. Although he promises Andrzej a bonus in the form of an unforgettable adventure (which may have to do with Dora, reminiscent Małgorzata), he never settles the bill. The author of *Fabryka muchołapek*, being a "novel within a novel," the content of which is an account of the trial, thus appears as a mercenary writer, a hack and a hired ghostwriter, and therefore a character not much different from the actual author (or rather the authoress) of another widely read book about the Łódź ghetto published in 2008, *Byłam sekretarką Rumkowskiego. Dzienniki Etki Daum [I Was Rumkowski's Secretary. Diaries of Etka Daum]* by Elżbieta Cherezińska. The fact that the fictional account, *Fabryka muchołapek*, was written for money is crucial to the psychoanalytic interpretation of the novel. The writer takes more liberties with documents than the film; he fantasizes freely and even admits to making false statements. In a word, this makes *Fabryka muchołapek* (the published novel) a piece of postmodern narcissistic fiction, corresponding to White's assumptions about the postmodern understanding of history.

In my opinion, the most interesting deviation from the agreement made by the hero with the devil is the handing of the narrative over to Regina. We should return at this point to the question posed at the outset, concerning the way in which the novel's I (which is closest to Andrzej) moves between two female objects. If we assume that the contemporary plane of the narrative, that which recounts the pact with the devil, is a fantasy, then Regina and Dora may be regarded as libidinal projections. This would be the Lacanian interpretation of this situation,

> The essence of the image is to be invested by the libido. What we call libidinal investment is what makes an object become desirable, that is to say how it becomes confused with this more or less structured image which, in diverse ways, we carry with us.[543]

The novel's I desires the place occupied by both women in their relation to Rumkowski; one is his wife, the other is his former secretary. Although Bart does not identify his female protagonist with Dora Fuchs and changes her biography, the name itself allows us to suspect that the writer's intentions are far from obvious. To begin with, the narrator often shows the Rumkowski trial from

---

542 Bart, *Fabryka muchołapek*, p. 16.
543 Lacan, "Ego-ideal and ideal ego," in Lacan, *The Seminar of Jacques Lacan*, Book I: *Freud's Papers on Technique, 1953–1954*, p. 141.

Regina's perspective. Why would he do so, if the novel is concerned neither with her marriage nor the personal life of the President? Second, the narrative focuses on the figure of Dora, whose role – we suspect – is to distract the writer, Andrzej, from working on the book and script, and thus to detach him from reality. It is worth considering what both these women represent in psychoanalytic terms. Aren't they perhaps fantasies of the narrator or projections of his affects and fears, ways in which he is trying to get closer to or away from Rumkowski? Perhaps that's why we can read *Fabryka muchołapek* as a dream of a narcissistic rapture of the Self, which, according to Lacan, resembles falling in love. The novel's I, wanting to establish contact with himself, which is possible only in establishing a symbolic relationship with the figure of Rumkowski, looks for substitute contacts with women who are close to Rumkowski in the world of history or fiction. A larger context for this involves Rumkowski's relationship with children, especially with Marek, his adopted son.[544] However, the novel's I takes advantage of the possibilities offered by the medium of the novel and fixes this rapture in a love script related to motherhood. Lacan recalls the scene from Goethe's *The Sorrows of Young Werther* in which Charlotte caresses a child. It is the moment when Werther falls in love with her.

> Remember the first time Werther sees Lotte, as she is cuddling a child. It's an entirely satisfying image for the *Anlehnungstypus* on the anaclitic plane. It is the way the object coincides with Goethe's hero's fundamental image that triggers off his fatal attachment. [...]
> That's what love is. It's one's own ego that one loves in love, one's own ego made real on the imaginary level.[545]

A Lacanian love scene takes place right at the beginning of the novel. It is set in a living room and told in a grotesque convention of the safe and soporific atmosphere that prevailed in the train moving at night. We see a long, green couch around which stretches a space "rather like a warm and safe house, and the monotonous clatter of wheels sound like the crackling of a fire on the mantelpiece."[546] On the first page of the novel, therefore, we get a hint that its source lies in a mental fantasy. The meaning of this fantasy is not hidden anywhere. It can be seen already in the first scene, in which a handsome old man checks whether his beautiful wife and beautiful child are asleep, and then quietly sneaks out of the room. And from that moment on, although we see him again at the trial, he seems to be absent, mute, devoid of power. He can only make silent gestures: "Chaim stood up suddenly, turned towards the hall and bowed. A few people started

---

544 As a matter of fact, the Rumkowscy had no children.
545 Lacan, "Ego-ideal and ideal ego," p. 142.
546 Bart, *Fabryka muchołapek*, p. 5.

clapping."[547] In Bart's novel, we can see the narrative about the search for a (symbolic?) father. It is him that the novel's I wants to meet. However, access to his father-Rumkowski is prevented by his own muteness. During the trial, the king (in Freud, the symbol of the father)[548] is silent. That is why the I enters into relationships with surrogate objects (like Dora, who puts on Sonia Rykiel's dress, which heightens her sexuality to an unbearable degree) to finally find itself in another.

> In fact, the virtual subject, reflection of the mythical eye, that is to say the other which we are, is there where we first saw our *ego* – outside us, in the human form. This form is outside of us, not in so far as it is so constructed as to "captate" sexual behaviour, but in so far as it is fundamentally linked to the primitive impotence of the human being. The human being only sees his form materialised, whole, the mirage of himself, outside of himself.[549]

By applying Lacan's remarks on narcissism to *Fabryka muchołapek* we are able to see that the bond between the virtual narrator and Rumkowski is much more complicated than the plot seems to let on. It is a bond that, in Lacanian terms, unites us with the other, the other who "we are." Separated from the narrative and called the writer Andrew, the "I" betrays a weakly and grotesquely motivated interest in the President (a pact with the devil); too weak and too grotesque to allow us to believe in the sincerity and reality of his intentions. The fantastical motivation of this interest causes us to ask for a real motive that makes the narrator indulge in historical reminiscences and in the illusion that he would like to reconstruct a Holocaust-related story. This mirage of his own making and the "primitive impotence of the human being," which the writer Andrzej wants to see "outside himself," seem to concern Rumkowski, who during the process loses his characteristic energy and strength, and in a puzzling way becomes frozen inside. Is it not true, then, that it is precisely this impotence that creates a plane of mutual understanding between the writer Andrzej and Rumkowski and a field of possible identification?

> After reading the horoscope from the weekly "La Bataille," which appeared on September 3 almost a hundred years ago, I called myself a mediocrity in the diary, and then something even worse at the bottom of the page [...]. But I read on: those born under the sign of Virgo are not endowed financially; they have no access to gold, and are out their element in gambling or stock market speculation, supervisory bodies, or financial operations [...]. In my subskin life, a life that may be more real, I can be brave, resourceful and, like others, ready to gratify someone else's whims for a penny.[550]

---

547 Bart, *Fabryka muchołapek*, p. 95.
548 Cf. Sigmund Freud, *The Interpretation of Dreams* (1913), translated by Abraham Arden Brill; https://en.wikisource.org/wiki/The_Interpretation_of_Dreams.
549 Lacan, "Ego-ideal and ideal ego," p. 140; italics in the original.
550 Bart, *Fabryka muchołapek*, p. 64.

Complaining about his own impotence and fantasizing about Rumkowski's weakness, combined with fantasizing about the strength of the women around him, makes this field of identification a narcissistic narrative in yet another sense. In the comment, "Bart's book is for me an example of narcissistic kitsch,"[551] Jacek Leociak pins down the problem faced by Holocaust researchers who find themselves forced to evaluate a novel that pretends to be Holocaust-related as a way to approach and convey the experiences of a contemporary subject. The "narcissistic kitsch" found in *Fabryka muchołapek*, as a category that negatively evaluates narcissistic fiction, seems to require some tuning. The narcissism of Bart's novel consists not only in the unbearable exposition of the authorial and narrative self or in the use of certain compositional devices. When we look at it, bearing in mind Lacan's remarks about substitute objects and the exteriorization of I, one can assume that the writer Andrzej reports the trial not for money or out of fear of the devil, but for himself. For the sake of integrating one's own I, he replaces real objects by elements of fantasy and memory, which allows him to restore contact with reality after the reparations are over. We see this happen in the passages in which Bart bestows on the imagination the capacity of questioning reality. It will be recalled that the novel ends on December 31, 2007 ("sleepy, I'm finishing *Fabryka muchołapek*"[552]). The writer receives this diagnosis: "Feeling the resistance of the real world, the patient turns his energy towards the world of imagination."[553] And yet he finishes the work dreaming of a Czech pen from the war (or rather gets annoyed at the thought of wanting to put a dot over the "I" with it; but that would have far-reaching effects; it would be too much like committing onself). The pen was manufactured by "Pramen&Sohn" before the father and the son – most likely Czech Jews – came to Teresín. "I feel great. Time to forget about the phantoms."[554] The sentence, one of the last in the novel, gives the impression of Bart's desire to assure his readers that the narrative of the Holocaust has had the aim of… helping the narrator to get well.

To define the functions of narcissistic postmodernism in *Fabryka muchołapek*, let us collect earlier remarks. The freedom with which the author treats history is so great, and the authorial comments which suggest that he relates history primarily to himself are so frequent, that considering *Fabryka muchołapek* in the context of the culture of narcissism seems to result from the structure of the novel. Important as this approach is, it is also obvious (1). Hayden White has encouraged the use of psychoanalytic tools in describing the relationship between postmodernism and history. The examination of narcissistic post-

---

551 Jacek Leociak, "O nadużyciach w badaniach nad doświadczeniem Zagłady" [On the Abuses in Research of the Holocaust Experience], *Zagłada Żydów. Studia i Materiały* 6 (2010), p. 14.
552 Bart, *Fabryka muchołapek*, p. 275.
553 Bart, *Fabryka muchołapek*, p. 275.
554 Bart, *Fabryka muchołapek*, p. 275.

modernism in this context, referring to the imaginary history of the Łódź ghetto, can therefore be treated as an extension of this encouragement, requiring appropriate additions and corrections (2). In this case, it seems interesting not only to specify what type of postmodern novel *Fabryka muchołapek* can be regarded as, but also to see how it softens history and reconciles us with the past "that won't go away."[555] First of all, Bart's goal is to reveal the weaknesses in our understanding of the Holocaust (which he also exposes in *Radegast*). Second, Bart tends to believe that history and its phantasms are most often driven by narcissism, "private interests" and our personal conscious (or unconscious) motives and choices. Third, bearing in mind the postmodern attitude to history, Bart suggests that narcissism is not a shameful and reprehensible attitude, but a useful one, especially for certain social groups at a particular time.[556] The narcissistic self-awareness of postmodernism may prove to be a valuable solution in many ways. One of them is the controversial and perhaps even doubtful research strategy that brings together psychoanalysis, the Holocaust and postmodernism.

---

555 White, "Postmodernism and History." Cf. "Postmodernizm i historia," p. 36.
556 White, "Postmodernism and History." Cf. "Postmodernizm i historia," p. 40.

Chapter 12.
Styles of Reception of the Polish Holocaust Novel: Marek Bieńczyk and Andrzej Bart

> For Literature is like phosphorus: it shines with maximum
> brilliance at the moment when it attempts to die.[557]

The concept of the style of reception, as it took shape in Michał Głowiński's studies, understood as "norms of reading arranged in a certain system and determining the character of literary connotations characteristic of a given time,"[558] can be an extremely valuable tool in the analysis of the literary audience's understanding of Holocaust fiction. In this chapter, I will examine how expectations were formulated towards the "impossible form" (as for years the Holocaust novel was perceived by Holocaust studies) and what tasks were set for it. I am not going to be referring to all Polish novels – an endeavor that would require a separate, extensive study – but only to the reception of two which have been widely discussed, Marek Bieńczyk's *Tworki* (1999) and Andrzej Bart's *Fabryka muchołapek* (2008). Their critical reception reveals a significant change in the perception of the role of Holocaust fiction. At the turn of the millennium, readers were no longer interested in aesthetic categories of appropriateness and form or the notion of the impossibility of writing Holocaust fiction, absolutized in Holocaust studies. Instead, they became interested in what the novel has to say about history and its interpretations. As the case of Bart shows, the novel can and does become a subject on which historians express their views. They tend to read literary works the way they read historiography, and expect that it observe the criteria of objectivity and a multilateral assessment of the represented events backed up by research.

In reflections on the role of Holocaust fiction since the end of the war, the somewhat ambivalent attitude of the novel to documentary writing has been taken up. The open character of this literary form, as Roger Caillois claimed, makes everything possible. No *ars poetica* mentions the novel or prescribes laws

---

557 Roland Barthes, *Le Degré zero de l'écriture* (1953), p. 57; *Writing Degree Zero*, trans. Annette Lavers and Colin Smith (London: Jonathan Cape, 1967), p. 44. Qtd in Kazimierz Bartoszyński, *Kryzys czy trwanie powieści: studia literaturoznawcze* (Kraków: Universitas, 2004), p. 149.

558 Michał Głowiński, "Odbiór, konotacje, styl," in Michał Głowiński, *Dzieło wobec odbiorcy: szkice z komunikacji literackiej* (Kraków: Universitas, 1998), p. 129.

it must obey.[559] The French essayist juxtaposes here, of course, the novel with normative classicist poetics with its strict rules and rigid classification of genres. Meanwhile, the Holocaust novel has opted for literary forms convenient for the representation of facts; it favored witness accounts, displaying varying levels of their authors' education and cultural competence, but also prioritized freedom of expression on condition that elementary rules of storytelling were being observed.

Another problem in assimilating the novel by post-Holocaust culture has been the feature that some researchers call the novelistic. Marek Bieńczyk defined this feature drawing on Roland Barthes as persistent desire to record everyday events and to transform them into figures and rhetorical tricks (anacoluthon, aphorism, epiphany), understood as components of literariness.[560] These strategies make the novel independent of the concepts of form and genre, a category of ordering the world, imposing a top-down meaning on it and a certain vision or – as Bieńczyk described it in his essay "Rue des École" – "syntactic verification […], finding its syntax."[561]

In the first Polish article devoted entirely to the issue of Holocaust fiction, Michał Głowiński called, not the novel, but the short story the crowning genre of this type of literature. The reason for this opinion is the capacious and flexible format if the short story, its closeness to documentary forms of writing and the way in makes possible "the presentation of individual life stories in a concrete way, with no concern for complicated plot constructions, somehow inherently akin […] to report, factual account, a piece of reminiscence (if understood as a specific genre), and reportage."[562] Drawing on these strengths of the short story, one could – on the principle of opposition – draw up a similar description of the

---

559 Roger Caillois, *Siła powieści*, trans. into Polish by Tomsz Swoboda (Gdańsk: Wydawnictwo Uniwersytetu Gdańskiego, 2008), p. 21. *Puissances du roman* (1942).
560 Marek Bieńczyk, "Rue des Écoles" *Literatura na Świecie* (2004), nr 1/2, pp. 421–422. Katarzyna Chmielewska addresses the dual understanding of literariness in studies of Holocaust literature in an essay on "literariness as an obstacle and literariness as a possibility of expression." She notes here that "The unconditional rejection of poetry after Auschwitz and the notion of literature as blasphemy, as a reprehensible recreation of the Holocaust, which necessarily ends in failure, has repeated itself in various variants and has become the leitmotif in reflections on the Holocaust. This rejection, however, meets with an contrary tendency, one that manifests itself in the constant search for appropriate means of expression, in modifications of poetics and literary strategies, and, above all, in abundant literary creativity." Katarzyna Chmielewska, "Literackość jako przeszkoda, literackość jako możliwość wypowiedzenia," in Katarzyna Chmielewska, Michał Głowiński, Katarzyna Makaruk, Alina Molisak, and Tomasz Żukowski, eds., *Stosowność i forma: jak opowiadać o Zagładzie?* (Kraków: Universitas, 2005), p. 21.
561 Bieńczyk, "Rue des Écoles," p. 432.
562 Głowiński, "Wprowadzenie," in Chmielewska, Głowiński, Makaruk, Molisak, and Żukowski, eds., *Stosowność i forma*, p. 11.

novel, especially its Holocaust-related variant. Among its features we can name the following ones: high-level of fictionality, non-specificity, consisting in the dominance of anti-mimetic or grotesque style, as well as various other forms of expression based on conventionality, complex, multi-level plot construction, distance from popular non-fiction genres, such as reportage. The features essential to the short story, i. e., the reporting manner of handling events and the unsophistication of the language, which do not attract abundant critical attention, seem to be insignificant when it comes to the Holocaust novel. The following outstanding works are notable exceptions: Leopold Buczkowski's *Czarny potok*, Bogdan Wojdowski's *Chleb rzucony umarłym* and Jerzy Broszkiewicz's *Oczekiwanie*.[563] However, most of this fiction not only lacks an adequately transparent narrative, but, moreover, does not treat events and facts as the primary focus of the storytelling, while the general assumption is that historical truth should be the goal of any representation of the Holocaust. Only "real" narratives manage to achieve a balance between documentarism and fiction. Narrative coherence, specific primarily to documents, is much less likely to apply to the novel. As Berel Lang points out:

> Unlike the diary and the memoir, the novel is not usually conceived as a form primarily of historical writing; it is, furthermore, a more flexible genre than the diary or memoir in its openness to variation (e. g., in its more diverse possibilities of authorial point of view and of plot and character). It is the more significant, then, that in many novels about the Nazi genocide this potential for diversity is also constrained by the ideal of historical authenticity – a fact that is further accentuated in novels that otherwise closely follow the conventions of the genre.[564]

According to Lang, the anti-mimetic features of the novel, to be discussed presently in connection with the works of Bieńczyk and Bart, constitute its weakness and are responsible for what Lang calls "the disproportionate role of historical implication,"[565] which consists in alerting the reader too often to the historicity of the message, the truth of the reported events and the duties of literature, self-defined in terms of testimony, rather than an artistic artifact. The novel, agues Lang, is overanxious to hide its novelist nature, which is why it so insistently and definitively defends the truth, thus exposing its artificiality in the process. This is particularly evident in literary forms that imitate and rewrite the genres of personal document literature: diaries, memoirs, and autobiog-

---

563 Głowiński, "Wprowadzenie," p. 11.
564 Lang, *Act and Idea in the Nazi Genocide*, p. 133–134.
565 "The disproportionate role of historical implication which is most obvious in the conventional novels about the Nazi genocide also figures in works where historical reference more subtly and imaginatively shapes the literary structure." Lang, *Act and Idea in the Nazi Genocide*, p. 134.

raphies.[566] At their most extreme, such works conceal the truth and replace it with historical falsehoods.[567]

The fundamental doubt as to whether the genre in question can convincingly tell anything about the Holocaust, when confronted with the literary reality of hundreds of such texts, ceases to be surprising, even in relation to the examples cited at the beginning. Literary practice shows that, since the end of World War II, the novel has not only developed dozens of ways of talking about the Holocaust, but also some have been managed to effectively influence the way people think about history. In her article "Klęska powieści. Wybrane strategie pisania o Szoa" [The Defeat of the Novel. Selected Strategies of Writing about the Shoah], reflecting on the question "Are novels about the Shoah blasphemous?"[568] Katarzyna Chmielewska argues:

> The form of the novel is exceptionally capacious; therefore to answer this question in general terms makes no sense. It cannot be proclaimed that the novel as such is appropriate or not. Instead, one can *study individual strategies of the novel* and ask why some of them work while others fail. The first and fundamental task which the literary historian must tackle is to define what is appropriate and what is not.[569]

Following Chmielewska's clues, I want now to undertake a reconstruction of the reception of the two novels mentioned at the beginning, which – it will be recalled – are the most widely frequently discussed Holocaust-related works of

---

566 Lang, *Act and Idea in the Nazi Genocide*, p. 134.
567 Cf. Ruth Franklin, *A Thousand Darknesses: Lies and Truth in Holocaust Fiction* (2011); Sue Vice, *Textual Deceptions: False Memoirs and Literary Hoaxes in the Contemporary Era* (2014).
568 Katarzyna Chmielewska, "Klęska powieści? Wybrane strategie pisania o Szoa," in *Stosowność i forma*, p. 248. The problem of propriety (*decorum*) in Holocaust novels has been addressed relatively rarely by researchers. Despite the existence of many works devoted to abuses in literature, especially popular and genre literature, focused on pornographization and kitsch. Few studies have been devoted *expressis verbis* to this category. One of the most important is Alvin H. Rosenfeld's *A Double Dying: Reflections on Holocaust Literature* (Indiana University Press, 1980, pp. 221, 228), in which inappropriate representations of eroticism in William Styron's *Sophie's Choice* (1979) and inappropriate comedy in Leslie Epstein's *King of the Jews* (1979) are discussed. Sue Vice (*Holocaust Fiction*, p. 148) has commented on the inappropriateness in the presentation of the extermination of Ukrainian Jews and the Treblinka camp in relation to the controversial novel by H. Demidenko (H. Dale) *The Hand that Signed the Paper* and D. M. Thomas's controversial *The White Hotel*. Sławomir Buryła (*Wokół Zagłady*, pp. 97–98) considers A. Czerski's novel *Nieśmiertelni* (in relation to the manner of representing gas chambers) to be inappropriate, while Tomasz Mizerkiewicz (*Literatura obecna. Szkice o najnowszej prozie i krytyce*. Kraków: Universitas, 2013, p. 158) as violating the rules of decorum cites the scene of burning Jewish children in a locomotive, described by Krystian Piwowarski in the collection of short stories *Więcej gazu, Kameraden!* (I mention this example, even though it comes from a short story rather than a novel, to show that reflections on appropriateness are often brief remarks rather than extensive studies.)
569 Chmielewska, "Klęska powieści?" p. 249.

fiction in the 1990s and the 2000s. What allows us to see specifically in them a research-worthy object is not only the great number of reviews and studies written about them, but the sophistication and scope of problems they address. Added to the abundance of references to novel is the fact that they have been made in the most important literary journals in Poland (*Pamiętnik Literacki*, *Ruch Literacki*, *Teksty Drugie*, and others). My analysis here is based on the conviction that, from the reception of *Tworki* and *Fabryka muchołapek* we can distil preferred and rejected styles of writing about the Holocaust, styles that in Poland have met with either appreciation and rejection. The thus voiced opinions reflect the Polish literary audience's views on how narrating the past, especially in works of fiction, relates to historical knowledge and to philosophical concepts applicable to the subject of the Holocaust. Last but not least, these opinions touch on what is or should be branded as taboo, on what should not be discussed and should be consigned to concealment and oblivion.

As Głowiński argued in his essay "Konstrukcja a recepcja. (Wokół *Dziejów grzechu* Żeromskiego)" ["Between Construction and Reception: On Stefan Żeromski's *The Wages of Sin*"]:

> The study of the reception of literary works in a given epoch or in a given social or literary environment is usually the domain of unproblematic descriptions, as if this branch of literary history were by its very nature to be the province of pure factography. This, however, is a field that should also become the subject of theoretical reflection, because it poses many interesting and important issues for the literary historian.[570]

Complementing these assumptions, Chmielewska argues that the study of reception, understood as part of the history of literature, poses many problems for the researcher, such as the need to compile and study numerous individual opinions expressed on a particular literary work. The task may overwhelm the researcher:

> The impossibility to take into account the infinite diversity of audiences or individual readers condemns the project of a new literary history to inevitable arbitrariness, randomness and fragmentation, for historical audiences do not subscribe to a shared perspective. This problem is slightly more general. Theorists of reception tend to ignore the actual asymmetry of the author and the reader. To put it plainly, they forget that the author is one, and the readers are many, and receivers cannot be treated as a symmetrical reflection of the sender. Therefore, theoreticians here fail to see that if one takes as a starting point a real audience, a real reader or a potential extratextual addressee, it is impossible to obtain a homogeneous perspective, one that would allow us to grasp the history of literature as a whole.[571]

---

[570] Michał Głowiński, "Konstrukcja a recepcja. (Wokół *Dziejów grzechu* Żeromskiego)," in Głowiński, *Dzieło wobec odbiorcy*, p. 169.
[571] Katarzyna Chmielewska, "Ukryte założenia i aporie teorii recepcji," *Pamiętnik Literacki* 2001/4, p. 10.

Herman Kinder and Heinz-Dieter Weber have argued that the greatest diversity of interpretations is usually elicited by literary works which, no matter how lucid their parts, constitute a mystery when regarded as a whole. In such cases, individual interpreters will propose different modes of reading as a unity-bestowing experience and different ways of understanding the artistic principle of unity.[572]

Tworki and *Fabryka muchołapek* are good examples of such works. For, despite many accurate interpretations, they are still underread, polysemic novels, open various ways of decoding depending on the context. Although we are not capable of predicting with certainty what the impact the reading of a work will have,[573] preliminary assumptions can be made on this subject based on a context common to a specific group of readers. In the case of Bieńczyk and Bart, there is, on the one hand, the philosophical context, made up of famous and most frequently cited philosophical texts about the Holocaust (especially those by Jean-François Lyotard and Jean-Jacques Derrida) in the Poland of the years 1999–2013.[574] On the other hand, there is the cultural context. Following Anna Jarmuszkiewicz's reflections on the works of Harold Bloom, Maria Delaperrière and Stanley Fish, we can say that the latter context arises here within specific interpretative communities as a binder of their vision of the world and a fixed frame of reference. As such, it has the properties of cultural memory.[575]

> Reception is therefore a collection of […] interpretations created as historical readings (spread over time) and as traces of reading by interpretive communities that are being continuously and synchronously performed.[576]

---

572 Herman Kinder and Heinz-Dieter Weber, "Badania literaturoznawcze nad recepcją zorientowaną na działanie," trans. Waldemar Bialik, in *Współczesna myśl literaturoznawcza w Republice Federalnej Niemiec. Antologia*, ed. Hubert Orłowski (Warszawa: Czytelnik, 1986), p. 279.

573 H. Kinder and H.-D. Weber, "Badania literaturoznawcze nad recepcją zorientowaną na działanie," p. 286.

574 I designate and adopt this reception period after the internet dictionary *Polscy pisarze i badacze literatury przełomu XX i XXI wieku*, at http://www.ppibl.ibl.waw.pl, entries "Andrzej Bart" (http://www.ppibl.ibl.waw.pl/mediawiki/index.php?title=Andrzej_BART) and "Marek Bieńczyk" http://www.ppibl.ibl.waw.pl/mediawiki/index.php?title=Marek_BIE%C5%83CZYK) by Marlena Sęczek and Beata Dorosz, respectively, contain, besides the author's biographical notes, bibliography of publications on their work. *Fabryka muchołapek* is represented by 18 reviews and scholarly articles, *Tworki* by 30. Both entries are regularly updated ("Andrzej Bart" on 17.06.2019, "Marek Bieńczyk" on 8.02.2023).

575 Cf. Anna Jarmuszkiewicz, *Tropy Prousta. Problemy recepcji literackiej w literaturze polskiej po 1945 roku* (Kraków: Universitas 2019).

576 Anna Jarmuszkiewicz, "Współczesne badania nad recepcją literacką w kontekście literatury światowej oraz pamięci kulturowej," in *Mapy świata, mapy ciała: geografia i cielesność w literaturze*, ed. Aleksandra Jastrzębska (Kraków: Libron, 2014), p. 15.

An analysis of the reception of Bieńczyk's and Bart's novels will allow us to identify the dominant styles of reception of Holocaust fiction in recent years. At the same time, it will help us see why these two novels have become the subject of intense reflection of literary historians. *Tworki* and *Fabryka muchołapek* have turned out to be works capable of raising aesthetic doubts, but also ones about which a large part of Polish literary studies has felt compelled to express an opinion as a way of supporting or questioning their ideas as to how knowledge about the Shoah ought to be shared and narrated.

A listing of the titles of the studies of the two novels in the order in which they appeared will help us to reconstruct the cultural context of their reception. This list includes publications by Polish historians and sociologists as well as translations of historical studies published abroad since 1999: *Sąsiedzi* by Jan Tomasz Gross (2000), *"Szanowny panie Gistapo". Donosy do władz niemieckich w Warszawie i okolicach* by Barbara Engelking (2003), *"Ja tego Żyda znam!" Szantażowanie Żydów w Warszawie 1939–1943* by Jan Grabowski (2004), *"Jestem Żydem, chcę wejść". Hotel Polski w Warszawie, 1943* by Agnieszka Haska (2006), *Sprawcy, ofiary, świadkowie. Zagłada Żydów 1939–1945* by Raul Hilberg (2007), *"Moja żydowska dusza nie obawia się dnia sądu". Mordechaj Chaim Rumkowski. Prawda i zmyślenie* by Monika Polit (2012), and *Getto warszawskie. Przewodnik po nieistniejącym mieście* by Engelking and Jacek Leociak (2nd edition, corrected and expanded, 2013). Because contemporary novels about the Holocaust have been regarded as historical,[577] one should expect some transfer of knowledge to be taking place between writers, historians, and readers ready to accept those fictions not only as coherent factual truth, but above all as mental constructs, based on sources, references and footnotes.

The final assumption preceding the analysis concerns the adopted method of reconstructing the reception. Due to the fact that in the case of *Tworki* and *Fabryka Muchołapek* reception has developed in two waves – first under the influence of reviews and later scholarly studies – I feel obliged to consider in my analysis the fundamental differences between these two waves. My analysis is structured by two categories, propriety and form, considered by the editors of the book *Stosowność i forma* to be crucial for Holocaust-related discourse and superior to concepts such as hero/protagonist, narrator or plot, around which reflections devoted to the reception of the novel were previously conducted.[578]

In the eyes of the first reviewers of *Tworki*, the novel's language is a huge problem. They pointed out its impropriety, banality, exaggerated lightness and inadequacy to the represented events. According to Michał Witkowski, the mode

---

[577] This is Perry R. Anderson's position; see Fredric Jameson, *The Antinomies of Realism* (London and New York: Verso 2013), p. 259. See above, note 486 in Chapter 11.
[578] See Głowiński, "Konstrukcja a recepcja," p. 170.

of portrayal is nostalgic and occasionally "irritatingly sentimental."[579] He stresses the fictionality and textuality of the world of *Tworki* and points out that the meanings it conceals are not entirely clear. Mieczysław Orski, on the other hand, appreciates the boldness of Bieńczyk's literary imagination, praises him for choosing the form of the palimpsest and the allusions to *The Tales of One Thousand and One Nights*, while entirely ignoring the historical layer of the novel. He opines, for example, that the protagonists either belong to the Polish underground or are Jews hiding in the "tolerant German administration of the Tworki hospital."[580] A similar objection has been leveled at the melancholy tone of the novel, pointed out by Przemysław Czapliński and Piotr Śliwiński in *Megaron*. Agnieszka Czachowska in *Twórczość* spoke unfavorably about the way in which Bieńczyk's novel blows up details to the limit of acceptability. She has also objected to uninteresting and artificial emotional adventures of the protagonists and a poorly developed love story, unworthy of the author of *Terminal*. She concludes her review by stating that "[t]he banality of everyday life turns into the banality of tragedy."[581] Kazimiera Szczuka's evaluation of the novel's representation of history is similarly critical:

> Recreating the magical and soothing rhythm of the EKD railway station (nowadays WKD):... Reguły – Malichy – Tworki – Pruszków... Bieńczyk's novel returns to an authentic "chunk of history." In no way, however, could we guess at it in our encounter with the text itself, focused as it is on the ways of speaking and, by the author's license, enclosed within its own literariness.[582]

Yet Szczuka does appreciate the Langauge of *Tworki* for its refreshing specificity, characterized by a lack of trust in the existing rules, which she finds to be unsuitable for a Holocaust-related narrative:

> The talk-for-the-sake-of-talking kind of games with the language (as in raving, rhyming, repeating, jesting, sobbing, and so forth) do not let us forget about its own suspicious, ambiguous status. Allusions and various grim jokes undermine all attempts at making ourselves at home in the language...[583]

Unlike the earlier critics, Katarzyna Nadana expressed several decidedly favorable opinions about *Tworki* in a review published in *Res Publica Nowa*. Most of them concern the previously unobserved problem of Polish-Jewish relations

---

579 Michał Witkowski, "Majstersztyk," *Odra* 3 (2000), p. 125.
580 Mieczysław Orski, "O Jurku-ogórku głodnym przeżyć," *Nowe Książki* 1999, nr 11, p. 16. See also by this author *Opowieści dla dorosłych i opowiastki dla niedorosłych* (Wrocław: Atut Oficyna Wydawnicza, 2010), pp. 65–69.
581 Agnieszka Czachowska, "Dlaczego, psiakrew, polski?", *Twórczość* 1999, nr 12, p. 126.
582 Kazimiera Szczuka, "Miłość w czasach Zagłady," *Tygodnik Powszechny* 1999, nr 27, p. 14.
583 Szczuka, "Miłość w czasach Zagłady."

during the war. Nadana uses the phrase "the trauma of losing 'the same-other'"[584] to refer to them, meaning to capture also the friendship between Poles and Jews. The novel depicts this phenomenon by narrating protagonists' decisions to conceal their nationality by replacing their family names with first names, thus suggesting analogies between the fate of Poles and Jews.

In contrast to the reviews of Bieńczyk's novel, those of *Fabryka muchołapek* sound like a chorus of consistent praise, and tend to focus above all on the form of the novel. The reviewers find in it a new approach to the subject, tuned to discussion about history, capable of showing the narrator's profound longing for the Jewish Łódź and controversies around the leading figure of the Łódź ghetto, Chaim Mordechaj Rumkowski. Unlike Bieńczyk, Bart depicts events in a language that is relatively simple and occasionally ironic, thanks to which his novel has avoided being criticized the way *Tworki* has been. According to Sławomir Buryła, the author of *Rewers*

> [...] combines the truth of the document and the imagination. At the same time, the alternative to the documentary element is not a lie, but a message resulting from the artist's creative abilities. This creative aspect is not an unbridled force, but is subordinated, as far as possible, to historical truth.[585]

Buryła ascribes to irony an extremely important role in this respect. If it were not for irony, "one might wonder whether *Fabryka muchołapek* were anything except a well-crafted book for a not particularly fastidious audience."[586]

Maciej Robert, Krzysztof Cieślik and Włodzimierz Paźniewski emphasize the author's "good work," his high, if not always fully appreciated position in literature and the intentionality of his art[587] (they stress that *Fabryka muchołapek* is "a work of art which actually has something relevant to communicate [...]."[588]). Dariusz Nowacki is even more emphatic in stressing the novelty of Bart's work:

> It is an affirmative and lament-free journey through a city that Andrzej Bart genuinely loves [...]. *Fabryka muchołapek* could be shortlisted among Polish novels [...] with a fresh approach to the subject matter of the Holocaust. [...] one reads it with excitement and admiration.[589]

Some reviewers have identified the features of a postmodern fiction in *Fabryka muchołapek*, which has not prevented them from appreciating Bart's work or

---

584 Katarzyna Nadana, "U Pana Boga za piecem," *Res Publica Nowa* 1999, nr 7/8, p. 105.
585 Buryła, "Bez wyroku," p. 132.
586 Buryła, "Bez wyroku," p. 132.
587 Maciej Robert, *Notes Wydawniczy* 2009, nr 1; Krzysztof Cieślik, "Proces, którego nie było," *Polityka*, 28.11.2009; at http://www.polityka.pl/tygodnikpolityka/kultura/ksiazki/274600,1, recenzja-ksiazki-andrzej-bart-fabryka-mucholapek.read [accessed 14.10.2019].
588 Włodzimierz Paźniewski, "Trybunał Barta," *Przegląd Polityczny* 94 (2009), p. 157.
589 Dariusz Nowacki, "Z niezgody na nieobecność," *Tygodnik Powszechny* 48 (2008).

from considering the combination of postmodernism and the Holocaust as the right choice. For instance, Gustaw Romanowski has written:

> The postmodern convention used by this writer from the very beginning of his brilliant literary career allows him not only to mix historical layers and revive the dead, but also to embellish the main narrative thread of the novel with random quotations [...].[590]

Magdalena Górecka seems to be alone in expressing doubts as to the appropriateness of the form chosen by Bart: "Can one write about the Holocaust in this manner?" "Is the trial over the head of the Łódź ghetto a good topic for a postmodern novel?"[591] Paulina Małochleb dismisses such doubts:

> *Fabryka muchołapek* is perfect for not being yet another "Holocaust lipstick," the kind of story that is constantly published because it is in demand. There is no better recipe for a bestseller than to write a novel set in wartime... Meanwhile, Bart's novel is not a socially commissioned product.[592]

Scholarly studies of the two novels have gone in a direction opposite to that of reviews. While Bieńczyk has been appreciated, Bart's artistic strategy has been regarded with suspicion. The reasons for this discrepancy are not always immediately obvious, especially in view of the fact that in some cases the reviewer and the scholar is the same person. In one of the first articles devoted to *Tworki*, Maciej Leciński calls Bieńczyk's prose "a successful attempt to find a new language for the story of the Holocaust."[593] This statement could be regarded as symbolic. After years of doubts and hesitations as to whether a discourse capable of conveying the experience and memory of the Holocaust can be found, literature seems finally to have devised a fit mode of storytelling. This mode is not related to history, for in this respect *Tworki* has little to say, refusing to make the simplest extratextual references in the stories of Sonia, Jurek and Marcel or to lay out a context of the plots involving them. Rather, it is autonomously literary-artistic, for, as we have seen, Bieńczyk's "Rue des Écoles," indebted to Barthes, proposes an idea of the novel suitable for this purpose.

The researchers who studied *Tworki* focused their attention on several concepts prompted by philosophical, narrativist and psychoanalytic readings popular in the 2000s: language, its metonymic properties (Arkadiusz Morawiec after Frank Ankersmit),[594] fallacies and wilderness (Aleksandra Ubertowska),[595]

---

590 Gustaw Romanowski, *Proces bez wyroku. Powrót Rumkowskiego*, "Kronika Miasta Łodzi" 2009, z. 2, p. 271.
591 Magdalena Górecka, "Sprzedać duszę za złudę przetrwania," *Akcent* 2009, nr 3, pp. 138, 140.
592 Paulina Małochleb, "Murarz buduje, a ja majaczę," *FA-art* 2009, nr 1/2, p. 51.
593 Maciej Leciński, "'Likwidacja przewagi'. Praca żałoby i empatia w *Tworkach* Marka Bieńczyka," *Teksty Drugie* 1 (2001), p. 156.
594 Arkadiusz Morawiec, "Holokaust i postmodernizm. O "Tworkach" Marka Bieńczyka," in Morawiec, *Literatura w lagrze, lager w literaturze. Fakt – temat – metafora*, pp. 347–363.

mourning and melancholy (Leciński and Przemysław Czapliński),[596] narrative fetishism and posttraumatic culture (Katarzyna Bojarska),[597] inexpressibility in the postmodern novel (Maciej Płaza),[598] rhetoric of temporality (Jakub Muchowski),[599] the idyllic (Marek Zaleski),[600] post-memory (Marta Czemarmazowicz and Anna Mach),[601] messianism (Emilia Padoł),[602] love (Bartłomiej Krupa).[603] With the help of these categories, on the one hand, *Tworki* has been interpreted as a radical breakup with the Enlightenment tradition of writing about catastrophe (Zaleski). On the other, the novel has been seen as a violation of the boundaries of post-Enlightenment artistic practice, insulting its ethics and the memory of the victims (Ubertowska). Critics have emphasized that Bieńczyk has simultaneously created a novel about the language of the Holocaust and avoided talking about the Holocaust itself, thus rising to a major challenge of Holocaust fiction since its inception. "Bieńczyk decides to talk about the Holocaust by... not talking about the Holocaust," as Piotr Marecki put it.[604] Czapliński echoes this: "Bieńczyk's novel seems to be an attempt to show a specific language as the reason for misunderstanding the Holocaust."[605] "The novel does

---

595 Aleksandra Ubertowska, *Świadectwo - trauma - głos. Literackie reprezentacje Holocaustu* (Kraków: Universitas 2007), pp. 289–296.
596 Leciński, "'Likwidacja przewagi'. Praca żałoby i empatia w *Tworkach* Marka Bieńczyka."; Przemysław Czapliński, "Zagłada - niedokończona narracja polskiej nowoczesności," in *Ślady obecności*, ed. Sławomir Buryła and Alina Molisak (Kraków: Universitas, 2010), pp. 371–373.
597 Katarzyna Bojarska, "Historia Zagłady i literatura (nie)piękna. *Tworki* Marka Bieńczyka w kontekście kultury posttraumatycznej" [History of the Holocaust and (Non)Literature - Marek Bieńczyk's *Tworki* in the Context of Post-Traumatic Culture], *Pamiętnik Literacki* 2008/2, pp. 89–106.
598 Maciej Płaza, "Tekst doświadczenia, doświadczenie tekstu - narracje Marka Bieńczyka," in *Narracje po końcu (wielkich) narracji. Kolekcje, obiekty, symulakra*, ed. Hanna Gosk and Andrzej Zieniewicz (Warszawa: Dom Wydawniczy Elipsa, 2007).
599 Jakub Muchowski, "Figury czasowości w *Tworkach* Marka Bieńczyka" [The Figures of Temporality in Marek Bieńczyk's *Tworki*], *Teksty Drugie* 2006/3.
600 Marek Zaleski, *Echa idylli w literaturze polskiej doby nowoczesności i późnej nowoczesności* (Kraków: Universitas, 2007), pp. 277–310.
601 Marta Czemarmazowicz, "Podmiot literacki wobec doświadczenia (post)traumy. Reprezentacje Holokaustu w perspektywie postpamięci (na podstawie *Zagłady* Piotra Szewca, *Tworek* Marka Bieńczyka i *Każdy przyniósł, co miał najlepszego* Mieczysława Abramowicza," in *Podmiot w literaturze polskiej po 1989 roku. Antropologiczne aspekty konstrukcji*, ed. Żaneta Nalewajk (Warszawa Dom Wydawniczy Elipsa, 2011); Anna Mach, *Świadkowie świadectw. Postpamięć Zagłady w polskiej literaturze najnowszej* (Warszawa and Toruń: Wydawnictwo Naukowe Uniwersytetu Mikołaja Kopernika 2016).
602 Emilia Padoł, "Język i mesjanizm: (post)konteksty a problematyka żydowska w *Tworkach* Marka Bieńczyka," in Eugenia Prokop-Janiec, ed., *Polacy-Żydzi: kontakty kulturowe i literackie* (Kraków: Wydawnictwo Uniwersytetu Jagiellońskiego, 2014).
603 Krupa, *Opowiedzieć Zagładę*.
604 Piotr Marecki, "(Po)tworek Derridy," *Studium* 1999, nr 6 / 2000, nr 1, p. 180.
605 Czapliński, *Zagłada - niedokończona narracja*, p. 373.

not speak directly about the Holocaust, Jews, *szmalcowniki* [smugglers]...," observes Chmielewska,[606] while Krupa adds: "So the most important things happen – as all interpreters of the novel seem to agree – in the language itself."[607] Language here stands in opposition to something that does not exist or those who no longer exist. "It is better to stay in a human space, to end the story with a gesture of affirmation, than to fiercely keep exploring the absence," as Zaleski suggested.[608] Finally, Leciński again:

> Marek Bieńczyk's *Tworki* is a novel that restores faith in the meaningfulness of literature, because it shows that fiction can use the ability to empathize, to "listen" to another person, to identify one's own trauma and one's own loss. As for Bieńczyk the act of writing, which has long been considered therapeutic, so for the reader the act of reading may turn out to be a cure for the "disease of mourning." This is another piece of good news.[609]

It is worth noting that among the expressions of approval there has been no attempt at examining the novel in the context of historical knowledge. It is also worth repeating that *Tworki* was published in the late 1990s, that is to say, shortly before Jan Tomasz Gross's *Sąsiedzi: Historia zagłady żydowskiego miasteczka* was published (2000).[610] Gross's book opened a new era of discussion about the Holocaust in Poland, one focused on Polish agency and the tarnished image of Polish-Jewish relations during the war. Echoes of this debate, which continues to this day, are not heard in the articles discussed here. Otherwise, their tone, full of conviction that Bieńczyk managed to save humanistic values in the novel, would not have been so calm.

The studies of *Fabryka muchołapek* have explored areas entirely different than the reviews. What reviewers of the novel found praiseworthy (e.g., its complex structure), scholars regarded as repetitive, *déjà vu*, and artistically ineffective. In the words of Krystyna Pietrych, "the rich arsenal of intense text games [...] somehow fails."[611] This critic levels four other accusations against Bart's book: the novel is a collection of ready-made formulas; the trial over the protagonist is illusory (in fact, he is represented as a negative character); the ethical boundaries of creation have been violated: "Is it possible to speak from inside a moving truck when you can smell the exhaust fumes? The answer is not obvious to me. I feel,

---

606 Chmielewska, "Klęska powieści?" pp. 259–260.
607 Krupa, *Opowiedzieć Zagładę*, p. 332.
608 Zaleski, *Echa idylli*, p. 310.
609 Leciński, " 'Likwidacja przewagi'", p. 166.
610 Jan Tomasz Gross, *Neighbors: The Destruction of the Jewish Community in Jedwabne, Poland* (New York, NY: Penguin Books, 2002).
611 Krystyna Pietrych, "(Post)pamięć Holocaustu – (meta)tekst a etyka. *Fabryka muchołapek* Andrzeja Barta a *Byłam sekretarką Rumkowskiego* Elżbiety Cherezińskiej," in Andres and Pasterski, ed., *Inna literatura? Dwudziestolecie 1989–2009*, vol. 1, p. 214.

however, that in this case there the space of silence has been violated." Moreover, "somewhere along the way, the elaborate literary strategy launched by Bart dissipates the horror it was devised to produce in the reader."[612]

For Danuta Szajnert, Bart's narrative feats fail as a strategy for writing about the Holocaust:

> Problematic is not only the manifest metatextuality of *Fabryka muchołapek* or the self-defensive, ironic distance and tone, which are too light. They bring the novel close to the brink of propriety, if we consider the subject matter thus represented.[613]

Bart's novel has been considered a narcissistic show of sorts, performed by an author who lacks historical knowledge, who has neither mastered the rules of postmodern fiction[614] nor acquired accurate knowledge of the Litzmannstadt Ghetto. The sixth issue of the Yearbook IFiS PAN's Polish Center for Holocaust Research *Zagłada Żydów. Studia i materiały* initiated a discussion on *Fabryka muchołapek*. Justyna Kowalska-Leder criticized the cognitive layer of the novel in these words:

> To be sure, [the reader – M. T.] can admire the knowledge and artistry of Andrzej Bart, but his novel will not teach her anything new, nor will it be emotionally challenging for her. The problem lies in the fact that the author of *Fabryka muchołapek* does not undertake the most difficult and at the same time the most important task from the reader's perspective: an attempt to understand the conduct of Chaim Rumkowski, and thus to answer at least some of the questions that the figure has provoked.[615]

Jacek Leociak, for whom the main premise of Bart's novel is infelicitous, reduces its postmodern aesthetics to narcissistic counterfeiting of a document:

> Bart's novel is an example of what I would call narcissistic kitsch. It is halfway between fiction and non-fiction, a novel and a factual account, a testimony and the depiction of a dream. It blatantly manifests its "betweenness" as regards discourses, genres, truth and falsehood. Therefore, it perfectly fits the model of post-literature in postmodern times. As such, it can hardly surprise; its poetics is perfectly predictable, and painfully "post-traditional."[616]

A thorough analysis of the novel has been undertaken by Monika Polit. In the book already referred to, she calls *Fabryka muchołapek* "a lost opportunity, perhaps the last one, for a reliable and engaging novel about MChR as a man and

---

612 Pietrych, "(Post)pamięć Holocaustu," p. 216.
613 Szajnert, "Przestrzeń doświadczona, przestrzeń wytworzona," p. 22.
614 Izdebska and Szajnert ("The Holocaust – Postmemory – Postmodern Novel: *The Flytrap Factory* by Andrzej Bart, *Tworki* by Marek Bieńczyk and *Skaza* by Magdalena Tulli," p. 143) compare *Fabryka muchołapek* to a pocket dictionary and pill-dose knowledge.
615 Justyna Kowalska-Leder's review: A. Bart, *Fabryka muchołapek*, Warszawa 2010, *Zagłada Żydów. Studia i Materiały* 6 (2010), p. 322.
616 Leociak, *O nadużyciach w badaniach nad doświadczeniem Zagłady*, p. 14.

as the head of the Jewish Council in the Łódź ghetto to be published in Poland."[617] At the same time, referring to rare source materials and historical studies, she goes on to envision a would-be novel about Rumkowski, non-judgmental, factually truthful, and unambiguous.

The most significant researchers of the subject of the ghetto in Łódź have also penned the most extensive and severely critical studies of *Fabryka muchołapek*. Some of them, e.g., Agnieszka Izdebska, Pietrych and Szajnert, work at the University of Łódź, while others, Kowalska-Leder, Leociak, Polit, are associated with the Polish Center for Holocaust Research at the Polish Academy of Sciences. Generally, the opinion expressed by both these circles is that *"Fabryka muchołapek,* so eagerly awaited and praised, is a good piece of fiction as a novel about a particular place and its history, and as an expression of the artist's personal attitude towards them. Unfortunately, as a story about MChR [...] it is a failure."[618]

Despite obvious differences, the two novels have a lot in common. On the basis of the opinions quoted and discussed, we can conclude that in terms of their structural features, narrative solutions (such as the mixing of temporal planes) and philosophical references (to the Derridean concept of language or the category of the sublime understood by Lyotard as a strong and equivocal affect that combines pleasure with pain,[619] which evokes in the subject a feeling analogous to that experienced in situations of death and salvation[620]) they are similar, even though they justify different critical assessments. The approval of Bieńczyk's novel is related to an appreciation of the language, which ultimately has been considered appropriate for a literary treatment of the Holocaust.

On the other hand, the rejection of Bart's approach seems to have been caused by a poorly executed historical framework. The history of reception discussed here can be arranged in two groups. One, referring to *Tworki*, can be given the heading related to aesthetics: How is the Holocaust represented? The other, referring to *Fabryka muchołapek*, can be given the heading related to history: What is represented? What facts from Rumkowski's life has the author decided to represent? Did he rely on a sufficient number of historical sources to adequately

---

617 Monika Polit, *"Moja żydowska dusza nie obawia się dnia sądu". Mordechaj Chaim Rumkowski. Prawda i zmyślenie* (Warszawa: Stowarzyszenie Centrum Badań nad Zagładą Żydów, 2012), p. 203.
618 Polit, *Mordechaj Chaim Rumkowski. Prawda i zmyślenie*, p. 199.
619 "The sublime sentiment, which is also the sentiment of the sublime, is, according to Kant, a strong and equivocal emotion: it carries with it both pleasure and pain." Lyotard, "Answering the Question: What Is Postmodernism?" p. 77.
620 Jean-François Lyotard, "Wzniosłość i awangarda," trans. into Polish Marek Bieńczyk, *Teksty Drugie* 1996, nr 2/3, p. 182. Cf. "The Communication of Sublime Feeling (from *Lessons on the Analytic of the Sublime* (1991)," in *The Lyotard Reader and Guide*, ed. Keith Crome and James Williams (Edinburgh: Edinburgh University Press, 2006), pp. 254–265.

bring his vision of the past in line with historical truth? Understanding the reasons for the existing discrepant evaluations of similar artistic and formal devices and mental constructs can be facilitated by Ankersmit's narrative theory of historical representation, sublimity and trauma.

Increased interest of historians in the Holocaust in recent decades is due to the limitations of the linguistic turn, which has led to making language "the condition for the possibility of all historical knowledge and insight," but at the same time failed to understand the Holocaust itself. "It need not surprise us," Ankersmit explains, "[...] that the Holocaust was recognized as the greatest challenge to this linguistic transcendentalism." Indeed, it came as no surprise that "the linguistic turn in historical theory would encounter its *nemesis* in the representation of the Holocaust."[621] All linguistic representations of the past, including the novel, should be considered in terms of historical narratives, which are representations of the past, and thus "re-presentations" of absence. Admittedly, suggests Ankersmit, care should be taken to ensure that they credibly replace the absent past, but precisely because they are only substitutes for it, they cannot be judged as true or false (like propositions in logic).[622] Narrativization of history takes place through narrativization of trauma, that is, the inclusion of past events within the private experiences of the subject who decides to represent them. As a result, there is a separation of history and its representation, and the resulting experience of the sublime (which is a reaction to the movement of that separation). The past becomes part of the present, loses its sharpness, ceases to be threatening, and now the subject can exercise control over it.[623] This can be attained through countless personal narratives and testimonies, which shatter the monopoly of institutionalized history and prioritize memory ("privatized," "personalized") and counter-memories.[624]

The signals of control of the past as represented in *Tworki* are Bieńczyk's cultural allusions. Zaleski has written copiously about them, comparing the idyllic character of the novel with the melancholic paintings of Antoine Watteau and Jean Starobinski's *The Invention of Liberty*. Similarly relevant are Leciński's reading of *Tworki* as a reinterpretation of the Arcadian myth as well as Szczuka's and Ubertowska's critiques of the way in which Bieńczyk recalls the phantasm of

---

621 Franklin Ankersmit, "The Postmodern 'Privatization' of the Past," in Ankersmit, *Historical Representation*, pp. 160–161.
622 Franklin Ankersmit, "Wprowadzenie do wydania polskiego," trans. Ewa Domańska, in Franklin Ankersmit, *Narracja, reprezentacja, doświadczenie*, p. 32.
623 Franklin Ankersmit, "The Sublime Dissociation of the Past: or How to Be(Come) What One Is No Longer." *History and Theory* (October 2001): 295–323. "[...] by narrativizing a traumatic experience, by transforming it into a part of our personal history, we can hope to gain mastery of it and to rob it of its threatening features" (p. 316).
624 Ankersmit, "The Postmodern 'Privatization' of the Past," p. 164ff.

a beautiful Jewish woman. Relevant are also Bojarska's and Morawiec's interpretations of the figure of Anti-Plato and Platonic tradition in the novel. These critics have shown that Bieńczyk has managed to create a novel about the Holocaust *in line with our culture*; that he nevertheless found a way to describe the Holocaust using existing myths, tropes, and styles without questioning its most enduring principles and values. Published almost a decade later, *Fabryka muchołapek* has primarily been read from the perspective of the story it tells, although here too the critics have succeeded in identifying all the literary allusions and intertexts.[625] Bart is certainly closer to Linda Hutcheon's concept of the historiographical novel, with its liberal treatment of facts, crumbling form and understanding of the archive as a meeting place for history and literature.[626] And this must also mean that the author chose a style "uncomfortably present" in Poland, identified with fakery and entertainment, far from strengthening – despite the earlier deconstruction – the conviction of the importance of national culture.[627]

As this reconstruction of the reception of Bieńczyk's and Bart's novels has hopefully made clear, at the end of the 2000s the reflection on propriety and form was abandoned in favour of questions about history. The issues of ethical obligations of literature and its responsibility for settling accounts with the past, as well as the assessment of controversial attitudes of Poles and Jews during the war, keep returning. Although the number of historical studies is on the rise, this has found no reflection in scholarly publications on *Tworki*. The preferred style of reception of Holocaust-related fiction after 1989 tends to prioritize problems related to aesthetics, language, the functioning of rhetoric, conventions of the novel, the limits, ethical or otherwise, of representation and expression. The style associated with the postmodern approaches to and handling of history, as discussed in Linda Hutcheon's or Brian McHale's studies, has met with far less favorable reception. Parody and blunt distortion of facts[628] have been condemned as the novel's artistic weakness rather than being appreciated as its response to one of the challenges posed to literature by the Holocaust.

---

625 Cf. Bartosz Dąbrowski, "Postpamięć, zależność, trauma," in *Kultura po przejściach, osoby z przeszłością*, ed. Nycz.
626 Linda Hutcheon, "Historiographical Metanovel: Parody and Intertextuality of History," trans. Janusz Margański, in: *Postmodernizm*, p. 383.
627 Krzysztof Uniłowski, "Czym są fabulacje i dlaczego się je lekceważy?" in Krzysztof Uniłowski, *Prawo krytyki: o nowoczesnym i ponowoczesnym pojmowaniu literatury* (Katowice Wydawnictwo FA-art, 2013).
628 McHale, *Postmodernist Fiction*, p. 21.

Chapter 13.
Postmodern Realism, Abjection, Evaluation: The Benefits of Critical Reflection on Postmodernism and the Holocaust

1. "P.Cz.: ... Rabbi, what can be my attitude to historical obligation? You may have guessed. You may even know...
   Rabbi: I can only hope that my nephew does not leave this world as a provocateur." Piotr Czakański-Sporek, "Mówiąc tak między nami...", a short story published in *FA-art* 1993, nr 12–13, p. 122.
2. "At the beginning of the twenty-first century, it is difficult to treat postmodernism as a threat to history. It is easier not to notice it anymore. After all, its blade has evidently gone blunt." Tomasz Wiślicz, "Historiografia polska 1989–2009. Bardzo subiektywne podsumowanie" [Polish Historiography 1989–2009. A Very Subjective Summary]. *Przegląd Humanistyczny* 2010, nr 5–6, p. 39.
3. "But it is almost too easy to ridicule the postmodernism of the current New York art scene or of Documenta 7. Such total rejection will blind us to postmodernism's critical potential which, I believe, also exists, even though it may be difficult to identify." Andreas Huyssen, "Mapping the Postmodern," *New German Critique* No. 33, Modernity and Postmodernity (Autumn, 1984), p. 9.
4. "Finally, the art-critical version of postmodernism was sometimes seen to seal modernism in the formalist mold that we wanted to break. In the process the notion became incorrect as well as banal. But should we surrender it? Apart from the fact that the left has already conceded too much in this war, the notion may still possess explanatory, even critical power." Hal Foster, *The Return of the Real*, p. 206.

The year 2000 not only changed everything we had thought we knew about our own history. It also changed Polish postmodernism. A few years ago, wanting to understand the phenomenon of the influence of Jan Tomasz Gross's *Neighbors* on Polish society and Polish literature, I thought that it could be expressed along these lines: After Gross, it is impossible to write another *Tworki*. This was supposed to mean that confronting the massacre that Gross, who is also the author of *Fear: Anti-Semitism in Poland After Auschwitz* (2006; the Polish edition, *Strach: Antysemityzm w Polsce tuż po wojnie. Historia moralnej zapaści*, came out in 2008), forced us to do had permanently changed the existing Holocaust narratives, full of solidarity and sublimity, turning them into stories filled with cruelty and fear. The point of that statement was not so much to capture the excessive elegance or passivity of stories like Bieńczyk's, as to express the view that this type of writing had failed to pass the test of time, had gone stale and come to an end. Today I would shift emphasis from what followed Gross's publications to that fateful moment that stopped postmodernism in its tracks, centered as it was around the dramas of the first half of the twentieth century. In other words, I would stress, not *how Gross affected* postmodern aesthetics, but *what made postmodernism undergo this change in the first place.*

In this, I share Hal Foster's position on the deferred effects of certain actions, particularly those relating to art and cultural criticism.[629] However, instead of the avant-garde, I will refer them to postmodernism, assuming that it is also *nachträglich.* Besides, "rather than break with the fundamental practices and discourses of modernity, the signal practices and discourses of postmodernity have advanced in a *nachträglich* relation to them."[630] Foster's other inspiring insight concerns the critical and utilitarian potential of postmodernism, and as such I find it useful in reflections on valuation. Its value lies both in the basic dimension, referring to fundamental shifts within the critique of the entire trend of postmodernism (as follows from the mottos, seen today as a banal, unimportant, past, limited phenomenon, awaiting at most a recapitulation, suitable for a non-creative critic) and in the specific dimension as something that allows us to see in postmodernism a thought (or rather a weave of thoughts) no less involved in the life of the contemporary world than posthumanism. But the thing that makes it significantly more difficult to carry out this inference, Huyssen says, may be the complicated identification of these capabilities. As I do not intend to stop at the shaky assumptions rehashed in definitions of postmodernism,[631] I will briefly go over the postmodernization of the Holocaust and explain how I would like to combine my discussion of it with evaluation.

In the 1960s, with the publication of Leopold Buczkowski's *Pierwsza świetność,* the idea of a depiction of the Holocaust that would be radically different than documentary emerged in Polish literature. This new approach was expected to show that the document is not the exclusive form of communicating historical truth and that historical factuality does not have to be the final verdict when truthfulness is at stake. It is not difficult to imagine that this approach did not gain many supporters in Poland, despite the fact that in English-language literary studies it led to the creation of such outstanding books as Linda Hutcheon's *Historiographic Metafiction: Parody and the Intertextuality of History* and Amy

---

629 Hal Foster, *The Return of the Real. The Avant-Garde at the End of the Century* (Cambridge, Mass. and London: The MIT Press, 1996), xii.

630 Foster, *The Return of the Real,* p. 32; in the original the whole sentence is italicized.

631 They are discussed by Ryszard Nycz in *Tekstowy świat. Poststrukturalizm a wiedza o literaturze* (Kraków: Universitas 2000), pp. 161–171; Bogdan Baran, *Postmodernizm i końce wieku* (Kraków: Inter Esse, 2003), pp. 155–190; McHale, *Postmodernist Fiction,* pp. 3–11.

J. Elias's *Sublime Desire: History and Post-1960s Fiction*. Postmodernization of the Holocaust refers to several off-the-beaten-track narrative practices loosely relatable to each other. It involves the erasing and revealing of history, the politicizing of the place from which the writer speaks (it should be insignificant and visible or create an/a (o)position despised by others), protest against a purely aesthetic understanding of art, critical and political character of stories that deny neoconservatism, reflection on the legacy of modernism, etc. In Poland, these challenges have been formulated by Buczkowski, Anatol Ulman, Andrzej Kuśniewicz, Tadeusz Konwicki, Ewa Kuryluk, Marek Bieńczyk, Magdalena Tulli and Andrzej Bart. As a project that is now attaining completion, one can consider detaching it from history of literature conceived along traditional lines. Therefore, these writers should be compared with experimenting English, American or French authors, including Raymond Ferderman, Walter Abish, Jonathan Safran Foer, Nicole Krauss, Paul Auster and others, and their fictions should be seen in terms of phases roughly equivalent to decades. As a result, we have a string of narratives about the changing postmodernism and its impact on society and the state. This is the approach adopted by Foster, Huyssen and Grzegorz Dziamski.[632]

The project, called here "post-modernization of the Holocaust," does not end with this kind of arrangement if fiction in terms of succeeding phases. It also involves asking why several Polish novels have not attracted anyone's attention over the years and how much their assessment changes when we see them surrounded by ideologically strong foreign literary works representing the same decade. Showing Polish literature as a part of world literature radically changes its evaluation; for example, Ulman's novel, interpreted alongside the work of Federman or Georges Perec allows us to appreciate the idea of *sous rature* and to see the value of logical shifts in discussions on history. But it also restores the agency of postmodernism, making it a trend which welcomes subversive works of art, works which critics tend to consider problematic or which are left with no evaluation whatsoever and treated as incomprehensible due to the reader's lack of orientation in the development of avant-garde or neo-avant-garde art. For example, the creation of a network of influences and connections between the fiction of the 1980s by Walter Abish *(How German Is It)* or D. M. Thomas *(The White Hotel)* on the one hand, and the underrated *Nawrócenie* by Kuśniewicz allows us to see in the latter a critique of various forms of commemorating the past along with the ongoing process of *Historikerstreit* at that time and the reflection on nationalism and anti-Semitism in Polish literature. Another advantage of creating such a network is the initiation of an entirely new trend in

---

632 Grzegorz Dziamski, *Postmodernizm wobec kryzysu estetyki współczesnej* (Poznań: Wydawnictwo UAM, 1996), pp. 105–128.

Polish literature, which seems possible today and consistent with the idea of *Nachträglichkeit*.

Valuing, writes Foster, is an absolutely basic activity of anyone who creates and writes. It also depends on the "pathos of distance," which for Friedrich Nietzsche was synonymous with the tendency of critics to express "noble" intentions and "vile" resentment.[633] If there is no escaping valuation, one can at least loosen certain categories and make them useful. Useful evaluation is, I think, necessary for any critical study of postmodernism. It in turn results from obvious premises, as pointed out by Ewa Domańska: "the historical environment in Poland has not gone through a discussion on postmodern critique of history."[634]

Piotr Czakański's *Zimno* seems to be an ideal pretext for a reflection on the change that has taken place in postmodernism since 2000 and on the ongoing evaluation of Polish postmodern Holocaust-related novels.[635] Since both these phenomena are highly nuanced on the one hand and not very popular on the other, we must not assume that Czakański's novel will gain much from its inclusion in this type of research. I do not define valuation literally as "quick estimation of profit." Rather, I assume that it will be important in this case, for example, to weaken the impact of comments such as this:

> Placed among these works, *Zimno* reveals its distinctness. Namely, it shows that the Holocaust also included non-Jews, that in some cases others also shared the same fate, whose unique trauma similarly impacts subsequent generations despite the passage of time. Different from post-memory narratives is the Christian eschatology introduced at the end of this novel. It offers a positive perspective on the topos of Holocaust literature, which is that of being exiled from the myth (based on biblical images) and of being transferred into the midst of the drama of history.[636]

In the recent history of American literature, which admittedly supplies a natural context for an appreciation of *Zimno*, the 2000s was dominated by responses to the attacks of September 11, 2001. It was this event that set the tone for subsequent narratives, including those about the Holocaust, undermining its position of uniqueness and making it become part of postcolonial narratives about a synchronous type of terrorism, rather than hierarchical or clearly positioning

---

633 Foster, *The Return of the Real*, p. 225.
634 Ewa Domańska, *Historia egzystencjalna. Krytyczne studium narratywizmu i humanistyki zaangażowanej* (Warszawa: Wydawnictwo Naukowe PWN, 2012), p. 21.
635 "Ideal" mostly becuase this novel has met with almost no critical reception, with the exception of two reviews. In the opinion of the publishing house FA-art, to whose social circle the author of *Zimno* belongs, "the entity called writer Piotr Czakański-Sporek may not even exist" (Dariusz Nowacki's statement expressed in a private conversation).
636 Beata Gontarz, *Obrazy świata. Wizualne reprezentacje rzeczywistości w polskiej prozie współczesnej* (Katowice: Wydawnictwo Uniwersytetu Śląskiego, 2014), p. 132.

these events (as would be the case, for example, in Nicole Krauss's *The History of Love*, referring to the effects of the pogrom in Jedwabne, and indirectly to the events of 2001). The absence of hierarchy in the depiction of massacres is also a feature of the prose of Jonathan Safran Foer, whose 2002 novel *Everything is Illuminated* is worth comparing with *Zimno*.

Foer tells the story of an American Jew's search, in present-day Ukraine, for people who saved his ancestors from the Holocaust. However, Foer's manner of telling this story somewhat eccentric in that he uses two parallel narratives, the first of which concerns the search, while the other tells the history of a Jewish diaspora from the eighteenth century to the present day. In one of the episodes, Ukrainian Jews save a newborn child from an accident, when a carriage with a pregnant woman on board has fallen into the river. Actually, it is the child who is thus saved, born as a result of the shock and as it were as a consequence of the mother's death. The story is as improbable as it is cruel, while at the same time symbolic and, in a sense, foreshadowing the fate of the entire decade from which Foer's book originated. It seems that *the metaphor of supernatural birth* is primarily a *signum temporis* and reflects the character of narratives about the Holocaust in the 2000s. First of all, we need to note their generational character, closely related to the Holocaust (Foer and Krauss are representatives of the third generation, and their ancestors were born before the war in Poland, Belarus and Ukraine). Second, referring to the philosophy of the postmodernism of the 2000s, not limited to literary studies, the novels from this period form a great *abjectal statement about the real world*, a statement in which Czakański came to play a leading role.

When trying to understand the reasons for the fascination with trauma and jealousy of abject, Foster has noted that poststructuralist postmodernism rejected the Real, which then returned as the traumatic Real. I believe that this return has become possible primarily as a result of the philosophical, social and political reflection that took place around the events of 2000–2001 and unequivocally erased the previously binding ideology of realism, which incidentally may not have been the only such ideology. In the section "Realism" of the essay "Answering the Question: What Is Postmodernism?" (1986), Jean-François Lyotard argues that the realism of the 1980s arose as a result of the urgent desire to "liquidate the heritage of the avant-gardes"[637] and became motivated by the intention "to avoid the question of reality implicated in that of art,"[638] changing into a style limited on the one hand by academia ("academicism"), and on the other by kitsch.

---

637 Lyotard, "Answering the Question: What Is Postmodernism?" p. 73.
638 Lyotard, "Answering the Question: What Is Postmodernism?" p. 75.

> When power assumes the name of a party, realism and its neoclassical complement triumph over the experimental avant-garde by slandering and banning it, that is, provided the "correct" images, the "correct" narratives, the "correct" forms which the party requests, selects, and propagates can find a public to desire them as the appropriate remedy for the anxiety and depression that public experiences.[639]

One unquestionable merit of postmodernism is the dismantling of a strong, fascist subject, a subject which on the one hand tries to take power, while, and on the other, radically eliminates all that is alien. It is worth noting that theoreticians, e.g., Foster and Huyssen, are looking for a negative tradition for postmodernism in the form of establishing a canon of modernist thought in the 1940s and 1950s.[640] This opens up a wide field for many different revaluations that can help to create an ideological framework for the project of post-modernizing the Holocaust and to facilitate a closer look at some modernist traditions (Foster proposes to consider Lacan) and reject other, less useful ones.

An extremely important tradition, perhaps and unexpectedly also for Czakański himself, is to think about reality in terms of a wound with all the theoretical background of the concept of traumatic realism.[641] The category of trauma does not seem to be particularly popular among postmodernists writing about the Holocaust, because it imposes attitudes that limit the criticism of various political positions and their languages. When it appears, it is more as an opportunity for a volte-face and a counterattack than an invitation to a supportive description or acceptance.[642] In the case of *Zimno* and *Everything Is Illuminated*, however, we are dealing with a situation of a macabre wound, which on the one hand means a violent and unnatural birth, and on the other – a mutilated, orphan subject who becomes a rather unusual witness to everything she experiences later. "If there is a subject of history for the cult of abjection at all, it is not the Worker, the Woman, or the Person of Color, but the Corpse. This is not only a politics of difference pushed to indifference; it is a politics of alterity pushed to nihility. [...] Is abjection a refusal of power, its ruse, or its reinvention? Finally, is abjection a space-time beyond redemption, or the fastest route for contemporary rogue-saints to grace?"[643]

---

639 Lyotard, "Answering the Question: What Is Postmodernism?" p. 75.
640 For instance, Huyssen argues "that the age of Hitler, Stalin and the Cold War produced specific accounts of modernism, such as those of Clement Greenberg and Adorno." Huyssen, "Mapping the Postmodern," p. 26.
641 Cf. chiefly Michael Rothberg, *Traumatic Realism. The Demands of Holocaust Representation* (Minneapolis, MN, and London: University of Minnesota Press, 2000).
642 Cf. Joshua Hirsch, "Postmodernizm, drugie pokolenie i międzykulturowe kino posttraumatyczne" [Postmodernism, the second generation, and cross-cultural posttraumatic cinema], trans. Tomasz Bilczewski, Anna Kowalcze-Pawlik, w: *Antologia studiów nad traumą*, ed. Tomasz Łysak (Kraków: Universitas, 2015), pp. 253–284.
643 Foster, *The Return of the Real*, pp. 166–168.

Czakański's novel is based on well-known facts from the lives of the inhabitants of Markowa, Maria and Józef Ulma, who on March 24, 1944, died at the hands of Poles for offering shelter to Jews. Czakański writes about it in the first chapter entitled "April," but he immediately adds something from himself, because he uses first-person narration. Who is behind it? The seventh child of the Ulma family, absent from history, the six-fingered Zygmunt, carried away from the grave under the parish priest's cassock. Almost from the start, the narrative assumes the mode of confessions of a monster, a posthumous child or a living corpse, and as the plot evolves, more and more oddities come to light, including the protagonist's peculiar loneliness, adoption, terminal disease (*Chronic Lymphocytic Leukemia*), the tragic death of a doctor who might have been able to delay its development, and finally the perverse Catholicism of the last of the Ulmas. All this becomes much more important than the Holocaust itself, which is abandoned as early as the first chapter, having provided a convenient starting point, but not necessarily the best one. Czakański chooses not to follow in the footsteps of historians, Dariusz Libionka and Jan Grabowski, who in 2016 revealed that at the same time when the Ulma family and the Jewish families they were hiding were killed, many much more Jewish people were being murdered in the same area.[644] He is evidently satisfied with fresh and few studies available in 2006, chiefly those published by Józef Szarek and Mateusz Szpytma.[645] From those sources, Czakański extracts a poignant tale of the murder of six Poles described by a newborn child who survived the slaughter hidden in a grave. We are only a short distance away from stating this fact to admitting that *Zimno* is a psychotic fantasy by a Polish author on the theme of the Holocaust-related trauma of Polish society. What enforces this conclusion, I may add, is the impression that this may have been a strategy deliberately adopted by the author. First of all, in several places in the novel he lets his imagination run wild and imagines what would happen if Zygmunt's mother lived today and was persecuted because of many pregnancies; or what would happen if Maria and Józef's neighbor was called Abraham instead of Shlomo (suggesting that the salvation from the grave has the hallmarks of sacred story); and so forth. Secondly, at the end of the novel we find the caption "Maishofen 2006," referring to the name of an Austrian town which provides the setting for several chapters. What is the purpose of this caption? Is it perhaps to shift emphasis away from the Holocaust

---

[644] Jan Grabowski and Dariusz Libionka, "Bezdroża polityki historycznej. Wokół Markowej, czyli o czym nie mówi Muzeum Polaków Ratujących Żydów podczas II Wojny Światowej im. Rodziny Ulmów" [Historical Policy Gone Astray. What the Ulma Family Museum of Poles Saving Jews in World War II Fails to Discuss], *Zagłada Żydów. Studia i Materiały* 12 (2016), pp. 619–642.

[645] Mateusz Szpytma and Jarosław Szarek. *Ofiara sprawiedliwych. Rodzina Ulmów – oddali życie za ratowanie Żydów* (Kraków: Rafael, 2004).

and towards the incredible trauma of an alleged Polish witness, a trauma that cannot be questioned, but which may not be believed in.[646]

The redirection of attention and the shifting of focus achieved by Czakański, the author of *Ostatnia amerykańska powieść* [*The Last American Novel*], by means of *crossing the boundaries of empathy*,[647] are actually reserved only for people with similar experience, for example the Jewish people who were victims of persecutions and hunts around Markowa, described by Libionka and Grabowski. Based on negative affects such as anger or hatred, transgression leads the protagonist towards an increasingly ahistorical identification with Jews. This type of identification reaches a critical point in the likening of the Austrian sawmills, owned by Zygmunt on reaching adulthood, to the Citroën company:

> [...] when I learned from an article in a daily newspaper that a Polish Jew is the maker of Citroëns, I became eager to look at these cars. And so, over time, Citroëns were the only cars used in my company. Mr. Citroën himself was quite a discovery for me. I managed the company using the methods he invented. Like him, I decided not to own a house or an apartment. The money was in the company and the people. I spared no expense when it came to investments in technology. Everything and everyone had to work. Accuracy became our trademark. (Z 60)[648]

From an "incomplete witness" of the Holocaust and a "traumatic subject" the protagonist of *Zimno* turns into a common-mentality capitalist with limited expectations towards the world. He is mainly interested in markets, banks, transfers and in making his future financially secure. However, this largely incomprehensible transition from the description of the trauma of the Polish witness to the euphoria of the Austrian capitalist does not make the history of the Ulma family an object of manipulation. Rather, it is another example of what is common in contemporary fiction: stepping into other people's shoes. It is a contemporary Polish author's fantasy of impersonating an observer and an outsider, of experiencing the Holocaust from a bystander point of view.[649] Chakański has made his abjectal form of representation into a method of reaching for the new power. That power has been given him by capitalism in an alliance with the Polish parochial-type Catholicism, limited to the cult of so called *dewocjonalia*, items of devotion ("How about burying me with a picture of *Heil. Maria zu Piekar?*"; Z 74).

---

646 Foster, *The Return of the Real*, p. 168.
647 Anna Łebkowska, *Empatia. O literackich narracjach przełomu XX i XXI wieku* (Kraków: Universitas, 2008), pp. 85–104.
648 Quotations from the novel *Zimno* are from Piotr Czakański, *Zimno* (Katowice: FA-art, 2006) and marked with Z followed by page number.
649 On the meaning of these categories, see, among other publications, Karolina Koprowska's *Postronni? Zagłada w relacjach chłopskich świadków* (Kraków: Univrsitas, 2018).

In the last scene, which is a narcissistic variation on that fantasy, the protagonist is devising his funeral, not in a general way, but by being morbidly specific. We can say that he has chiselled every single detail to perfection, from the moment when he starts to die to when his grave gets overgrown with grass. What perverse desire does he gratify by indulging this fantasy?

> I will start dying by putting up the watercolor *Mother and Child* signed S. *10* by a twenty-year-old artist. It will be March again, and the year nineteen forty-four will still be a newcomer... mom turning senile; ice in puddles will crackle under the pressure of the hooves of gray horses. I will start running across a soggy field. The tiring awareness of the prohibition of crying will return. I will hear the hollow words of the sincere prayer of the rosary, chanted by the villagers for the peace of the souls of the murdered families. (Z 74)

The answer is, the perverse desire of being a little Jewish boy who runs along the Markowa fences in search of a place to hide. This interpretation is confirmed by the novel's last sentence, which is about the prayer for several (Jewish) families. It can be read as an indication that Czakański aligns narrative empathy with fantasies about a child in hiding, for whom Poles pray, without knowing anything about his or her fate.

In the case of *Zimno*, we are dealing with a pastiche of different types of narrative: the "adult infant," the Polish Righteous Person, the capitalist, and the Jew. But also with the pastiche of Thomas Bernhard's novel *Frost* (to which the motto refers). Taking into account Czakański's other works, including *Pierrot i Arlekin*, and his references to the Jewish tradition and culture,[650] we can call *Zimno* a surprising provocation rather than a psychotic narrative by a philo-Semite. Its critical potential lies primarily in the disarming of the fascist subject and the establishment of the Holocaust as the starting point for an extensive analysis of various deviations: from the mechanisms of projection and identification, related to writers' fantasies about participation in the Second World War as observers and witnesses, to the kitschy excess of misfortunes, referring to disability and the culture of the wound.

Postmodernism of the mid-2000s came up with critique of the state, the Church and capitalism. However, this critique was performed with the help of a few, barely noticeable narratives, which were relegated to banal or unsuccessful statements (as the case of Bart's *Fabryka muchołapek* demonstrates). Thus, what

---

650 These are mostly pastiches, parodies and paraphrase-rewritings of Franz Kafka (e. g., *Ostatnia powieść amerykańska* is a pastiche of Kafka's *Amerika*, while in *Pierrot i Arlekin* we can find allusions to a wartime episode in the life of Karl Jaspers and his Jewish wife). In this context, the short story "Mówiąc tak między nami..." (published by FA-art) is also important, being a conversation between a character who bears the author's name and his rabbi uncle. Importantly, this conversation is taking place in the Jewish cemetery in Kozielska Street 16 in Katowice, Silesia, Poland.

Foster has called (after Hilton Kramer) "the revenge of the philistines," "the vulgar kitsch of media hucksters," and "a new barbarism"[651] has not been restored to any type of social utility. Worse, the discussion of the critical possibilities of postmodernism was slammed shut like the lid of a piano. Postmodern realism, which eliminated the aesthetics of inexpressibility a dozen or so years before, became a project recognized superficially, abandoned and wasted. It would be necessary to return to its foundations, such as hyperrealism or criticism of morbid social behavior, as proposed by stories from more than a decade ago, in order to set back in motion the unfinished debate and see the usefulness of some of its aspects considered harmful in hasty and careless evaluations. The purpose of this return would be to consider the critical and political possibilities of postmodernism, the ones it was denied before the final reckoning.

As Ryszard Nycz put it, "[…] postmodern critique […] attacked the following targets: narrowly understood ('scientist') criteria of rationality; the concept of autonomous and objective science separated from both politics and morality; universal notions (unity, wholeness, the systemic); universally applicable criteria (including truth, reason, justice, objectivity, universality)."[652] Gross also struck at these stable foundations, giving rise to the critical trend of realistic postmodernism, which has produced literary fictions whose social impact is still awaiting reactivation.

---

651 Foster, *The Return of the Real*, 205.
652 Nycz, *Tekstowy świat*, p. 163.

Chapter 14.
Rien ne va plus?

Odd as it may seem, a conclusion turns out to be the hardest part of a book about postmodernizing the Holocaust. It is difficult to be sure which novel ends this trend. Indeed, it may not be possible to talk about the termination of this trend. Krzysztof Uniłowski, doubtful of the link between the commencement of postmodernism in Poland and the year 1989, used the term *"postmodernismus ante portas!"*[653] In an attempt to draw its boundary, he used a much less glamorous metaphor, that of a black hole.[654] Dreams of a black hole have repeatedly visited interpreters of Polish postmodernism, as in the case of the disappearance of Jews from the public discourse, in connection with the false mourning for Jews and in the context of Paweł Huelle's *Weiser Dawidek* (*Who Was David Weiser?*), whose eponymous hero, David, suddenly disappears, as though he had vanished into thin air.

The mystery of David Weiser's disappearance, a mysterious boy who for several months ruled over the souls of his friends, could be compared to the essence of post-modernization of the Holocaust as a trend that has been too weak to break through to wider waters, but with time, as a historical phenomenon, turned out to be a constellation of more stable and influential relations. Over time, this current, unsteady in its progress and trying out various directions, became much more visible. It has become a clear and intriguing perspective from which to see not only the narratives about the Holocaust, but also postmodernism itself.

The disappearance of Weiser David is some ways similar to what happens in Andrzej Bart's 2021 novel *Dybuk mniemany*. The unceasing monologue of Dawid Czarewicz, a survivor of the Warsaw Ghetto, becomes an opportunity to remind the reader of the author's previous work, from *Rien ne va plus* to *Fabryka muchołapek*. It also becomes an occasion for retrospection and reckoning. Bart is talking here about his artistic inattention, passes his verdict on Polish culture's

---

653 Uniłowski, *Skądinąd*, p. 31.
654 Uniłowski, *Skądinąd*, p. 219.

anti-Semitism, and is attempting to tell selected stories from the past with greater accuracy than before, among them the story of Marek Rudnicki, the protagonist of the documentary film *Hiob*. All this, however, pales in comparison to the most terrible story, that of the death of the daughter, Magdalena Bart. The author's statements in several interviews[655] make us see this story in terms of reality, not fiction. This in turn allows us to ask about the place of this story among other stories told by Bart, including above all the history of the Holocaust.

> But in *Dybuk mniemany* there are three sides of poignant prose, genuinely honest and genuinely personal. No curtains, no coquetry, no self-creation which tends to be so annoying. This passage is about the death of Magda, my daughter, tearing apart an intricately woven web of intertwining and unraveling narratives. And although Bart quotes Daniel's letter of consolation, he is left alone with his loss and pain. "There is a hell inside me that I can't handle in writing." This Bart is weak, clumsy, withdrawn, at a loss. It is a pity that we only get to see this part of him on three pages.[656]

Thus, suddenly, the post-modernization of the Holocaust also becomes an opportunity for private mourning, and the unbearably long and exhausting conversation that drives the narrative is primarily motived by the need to allow this mourning to take place. Everything else compared to Bart's confession becomes mere decorative reminiscence. What counts is his own experience. Also the "Job" figure in the film turns out to be a prefiguration of Bart's personal story, even though there are plenty of opportunities for him to act the jester, like Czarewicz.

The juxtaposition of *Dybuk mniemany* with *Weiser Dawidek*, and indirectly with postmodernism thanks to the shared motif of mysterious disappearance, also validates the assumptions of this book. The post-modernization of the Holocaust did not end at any specific historical moment, nor did it occur in one novel. Rather it needs to be seen as a practice that reflects the needs of many writers, especially the survivors. This practice has dispersed among many other literary practices, yet it has retained its ability to transform itself into causative actions, ones that accommodate other practices as well, including those related to care for the environment and for other people, including acts of personal mourning.

Postmodernism has brought humanism itself to an end. Moreover, it has revealed to mankind the end of the planet. Prophetically and tentatively, it has identified the Anthropocene (which is why, as noted in this book, there are so

---

[655] Irek Grin's interview with Andrzej Bart during the 2021 Bruno Schulz Festival, https://www.youtube.com/watch?v=WK3xzdSrqCU [access 10.08.2022]; Jacek Grudzień's interview with Andrzej Bart on 12.12.2021 in Dom Literatury in Łodzi, https://www.youtube.com/watch?v=MxF0dSQXDTk [access 10.08.2022].

[656] Jacek Leociak and Marta Tomczok, "Afektywny kicz holokaustowy – wprowadzenie" [Affective Holocaust Kitsch – An Introduction], *Zagłada Żydów. Studia i Materiały* 17 (2021), p. 38.

many ecocritical comments in the novels discussed here, expressing concern with land, air and the earth). As Ihab Hassan has stated in his remarkable essay "POSTmodernISM":

> We are, I believe, inhabitants of another Time and another Space, and we no longer know what response is adequate to our reality. In a sense, we have all learned to become minimalists – of that time and space we can call our own – though the globe has become our village. This is why it seems bootless to compare Modern with Postmodern artists, range "masters" against "epigones." The latter are closer to "zero in the bone," to silence or exhaustion, and the best of them brilliantly display the resources of the void.[657]

So where can we find postmodernism now? In a zone of silence and exhaustion, in the broad and flat band of white noise,[658] which at the same time soothes and heals, although it seems above all irritating and disturbing.

Disappearance combined with wide scale influence on subsequent formations of writers and their narratives, especially on posthumanism – as is perfectly visible in the evolution of the views of philosophers such as Rossi Braidotti – can be called a distinguishing feature of postmodernism. Like the disappearance of the protagonists of Paul Auster's *New York Trilogy*, the earliest and now-classic novel of this outstanding writer, translated into Polish in the 1990s,[659] which has inspired many Polish humanists,[660] among them the authors of *Weiser Dawidek* and *Dybuk mniemany*. To get a keener sense of this kind of disappearance, suffice it to look through the tables of contents in Krzysztof Uniłowski's books, the apostle of postmodernism in literary studies, to realize how nearly unrecognizable and unknown today are the novels he wrote about in the 1990s.[661] Finally, the disappearance of postmodernists themselves, like the sudden, unexpected death of Krzysztof Uniłowski in 2021, an event which, its drama notwithstanding, can also be understood as a point on the scale of significance of the entire movement, and thus making us aware of the extraordinary ability of postmodern interpenetration of the fate of people and literature. Postmodernism – one might say, recalling Lewis Carroll's *Through the Looking Glass* – does not accept the word "death." It allows its authors and characters to live in an invisible band of white noise. Perhaps what makes postmodernism a philosophy particularly close to writers interested in the Holocaust is its ability to produce friendly

---

657 Ihab Hassan. "POSTmodernISM: A Paracritical Bibliography," *New literary history* 3/1 (1971); *Postmodernism and the Contemporary Novel. A Reader*, ed. Bran Nicol (Edinburgh: Edinburgh University Press, 2002).
658 This is the title of Don DeLillo's 1985 novel, which is in part devoted to the Holocaust.
659 Paul Auster's *City of Glass* (1985), *Ghosts* and *The Locked Room* (1986) were originally published by Sun & Moon Press, Los Angeles. Paul Auster, *Trylogia nowojorska*, trans. into Polish Michał Kłobukowski (Warszawa: Noir sur Blanc 1996).
660 Maria Janion, first of all.
661 Cf. Uniłowski, *Skądinąd*.

and hopeful, though also ironic, fantasies. Auster bids farewell to his protagonist with these words: "He will be with me always. And wherever he may have disappeared to, I wish him luck."[662] Bart addresses Czarewicz in a similar fashion: "Daniel, wherever you are, hold on tight. Anything is possible. Good things too."[663] Doesn't this transformative narrative violate the drama of history? Doesn't it flatten that drama? It would seem that the capacity of softening the impact of history inherent in postmodernism turns out to be a convenient formula for reporting facts in a mode other than… reporting (or parallel to that mode). The trend of the post-modernization of the Holocaust, which eventually absorbed many outstanding novels, unequivocally contradicts the opinion that Polish postmodernism had to face for years – "fraud, mockery, something worthy of contempt."[664] It also unequivocally confirms the high position of the novel, a genre neglected for years by Holocaust research. For it is the novel and nothing but the novel that is able to carry, like a good and strong riverbed, this meandering current, which is disappearing in the distance but which may reappear and surprise us again someday.

---

[662] Paul Auster, "City of Ghosts," *The New York Trilogy* (London and Boston: Faber and Faber, 1987), p. 132.
[663] Andrzej Bart, *Dybuk mniemany* (Kraków: Wydawnictwo Literackie 2021), p. 406.
[664] Uniłowski, *Skądinąd*, p. 34.

Bibliography

Primary sources

Abish, Walter. *How German Is It (Wie Deutsch ist es)*. New York: New Directions Books, 1980 (1979).
Auster, Paul. *The Invention of Solitude* (non-fiction; 1982).
Auster, Paul. *The New York* Trilogy. London and Boston: Faber and Faber, 1987 (1985).
Auster, Paul. *In the Country of Last Things*. London and Boston: Faber and Faber, 1989 (1987).
Paul Auster, *Leviathan*. London and Boston: Faber and Faber, 1993 (1992).
Bart, Andrzej. *Fabryka muchołapek*. Warszawa: Wydawnictwo W.A.B., 2008.
Barth, John. *Lost in the Funhouse. Fiction for print, tape, live voice*. New York, Anchor Books, 1988.
Bieńczyk, Marek. *Tworki*. Warszawa: Sic! 1999.
Birenbaum, Halina. *Hope Is the Last to Die. A Personal Documentation of Nazi Terror*. Trans. from the Polish by David Welsh. Publishing House of the State Museum in Oświęcim, 1997 (first publication in English 1971).
Birenbaum, Halina and Barbara Bochenek. *Szukam życia u umarłych. Wywiad z Haliną Birenbaum*. Oświęcim: Wydawnictwo: Państwowe Muzeum Auschwitz-Birkenau, 2010.
Borges, Jorge Luis. *Labyrinths. Selected Stories and Other Writings*. Edited by Donald A. Yates and James E. Irby. London and New York: Penguin, 2000.
Borowski, Tadeusz. *Utwory wybrane*. Wrocław-Warszawa-Kraków: Ossolineum, 1991.
Borowski, Tadeusz. *"Here in Our Auschwitz" and Other Stories*. Translated by Madeline G. Levine. New Haven and London: Yale University Press, 2021.
Buczkowski, Leopold. *Black Torrent*. Trans. David Welsh. Cambridge, Massachusetts, and London, England: MIT Press, 1970.
Buczkowski, Leopold. *Pierwsza świetność*. Kraków: Wydawnictwo Literackie, 1978.
Buczkowski, Leopold. *Dziennik wojenny*. Edited by Sławomir Buryła and Radosław Sioma. Olsztyn: Wydaw. Uniwersytetu Warmińsko-Mazurskiego, 2001.
Cherezińska, Elżbieta. *Byłam sekretarką Rumkowskiego. Dzienniki Etki Daum*. Poznań: Zysk i S-ka, 2008.
Czakański, Piotr. *Zimno*. Katowice: Wydawnictwo FA-art, 2006.
Doctorow, Edgar Lawrence. *The Book of Daniel*. London: Picador, 1982.

Federman, Raymond. *Double or Nothing: a real fictitious discourse.* Chicago, IL: The Swallow Press Inc., 1971.

Raymond Federman, *The Voice in the Closet [a sad tale]* [1979]. Published by The United States Holocaust Memorial Museum Library. Available at Internet Archive, at https://archive.org/; and at http://www.federman.com/voice.htm (sites accessed 14.09.2023).

Federman, Raymond. *The Twofold Vibration.* Bloomington: Indiana University Press & Brighton: Harvester Press Ltd., 1982.

Federman, Raymond. *Smiles on Washington Square (A Love Story of Sorts).* New York: Thunder's Mouth Press, 1985.

Foer, Jonathan Safran. *Everything Is Illuminated.* Boston: Houghton Mifflin Harcourt 2002.

Foer, Jonathan Safran. *Wszystko jest iluminacją.* Trans. Michał Kłobukowski. Warszawa: W.A.B. 2003.

Foer, Jonathan Safran. *Extremely Loud, Incredibly Close* 2005; wyd. pol. *Strasznie głośno, niesamowicie blisko*, przeł. Z. Batko, Warszawa 2007).

Huelle, Paweł. *Who Was David Weiser?* Trans. Antonia Lloyd-Jones. London: Bloomsbury 1991.

Jabès, Edmond. *The Book of Yukel. Return to the Book.* Translated from the French by Rosmarie Waldrop. Middletown, CT: Wesleyan University Press, 1977 (1964 and 1965 for the originals, *Le Livre de Yukel* and *Le Retour au Livre*, respectively, being volumes 2 and 3 of the *Le Livre des Questions* trilogy).

Jabès, Edmond. *The Book of Questions. Yaël. Elya. Aely.* Translated from the French by Rosmarie Waldrop. Middletown, CT: Wesleyan University Press. 1983. (*Yaël, Elya* and *Aely* being vols. 4 through 6 of *Le Livre des Questions*, originally published in 1967, 1969 and 1972 respectively).

Jabès, Edmond. *From the Desert to the Book. Dialogues with Marcel Cohen.* Translated from the French by Pierre Joris. New York: Station Hill Press, 1990 (1980).

Koeppen, Wolfgang. *Jakob Littners Aufzeichnungen aus einem Erdloch.* Frankfurt am Main: Suhrkamp Verlag 1993.

Konwicki, Tadeusz. *Bohin Manor.* Trans. Richard Lourie. New York: Farrar, Straus and Giroux, 1990 (1989).

Krauss, Nicole. *The History of Love.* London and New York: Penguin Books, 2006.

Kuryluk, Ewa. *Century 21.* Normal, IL: Dalkey Archive Press 1992.

Kuśniewicz, Andrzej. *Nawrócenie.* Kraków: Wydawnictwo Literackie, 1989.

Kuznetsov, Anatoly. *Babi Yar: A Documentary Novel.* Translated by Jacob Guralsky. New York: Dell Publishing, 1967.

Michaels, Anne. *Fugitive Pieces.* London and Oxford: Bloomsbury, 1997 (rev. 2007).

Miłosz, Czesław. *The Collected Poems 1931–1987.* New York: The Ecco Press, 1988.

Mulisch, Harry. *The Assault.* Translated from the Dutch by Claire Nicolas White. New York: Pantheon Books, 1985 (1982).

Murdoch, Iris. *The Unicorn.* London: Vintage Books, 2000 (1963).

Perec, Georges. *W or the Memory of Childhood.* Translated by David Bellos. London: Vintage Books, 2011 (1975).

Perec, Georges. *Life: A User's Manual.* Trans. David Bellos. London: Vintage, 2003 (1978).

Rousset, David. *L'Univers concentrationnaire.* Éditions du Pavois, 1946; in English as *A World Apart* (1952).

Sebald, Winfried Georg. *Austerlitz*. Translated from the German by Anthea Bell. London: Penguin, 2001.
Szewc, Piotr. *Annihilation*. Translated into English Ewa Hryniewicz-Yarbrough. Normal: Dalkey Archive Press, 1999 (1997). Szewc, Piotr. *Zagłada*. Warszawa: Czytelnik, 1987.
Thomas, D. M. *The White Hotel*. London: Penguin Books, 1981.
Ulman, Anatol. *Cigi de Montbazon*. Warszawa: Iskry 1979.
Venezia, Shlomo. *Inside the Gas Chambers: Eight Months in the Sonderkommando of Auschwitz*. Translated by Andrew Brown. Cambridge, UK and Malden, MA: Polity Press in association with the United States Holocaust Memorial Museum, 2009.

Secondary sources

Abish, Walter and S. Lotringer. "Wie Deutsch Ist Es." *Semiotext(e)*, vol. IV, no. 2 (1982).
Andres, Zbigniew and Janusz Pasterski. *Inna literatura? Dwudziestolecie 1989–2009*. Vol. 1. Rzeszów: Wydawnictwo Uniwersytetu Rzeszowskiego, 2010.
Ankersmit, Frank. *Historical Representation*. Stanford CA: Stanford University Press, 2001.
Ankersmit, Frank. "The Sublime Dissociation of the Past: or How to Be(Come) What One Is No Longer." *History and Theory* (October 2001): 295–323.
Ankersmit, Frank. *Narracja, reprezentacja, doświadczenie. Studia z teorii historiografii*. Ed., wstęp Ewa Domańska. Kraków: Universitas, 2004.
Ankersmit, Frank. *Meaning, Truth, and Reference in Historical Representation*. Cornell, 2012.
Auster, Paul. *The Art of Hunger. Essays, Prefaces, Interviews and The Red Notebook*. New York: Penguin, 1993.
Auster, Paul. *Talking to Strangers. Selected Essays, Prefaces, and Other Writings*. New York: Picador, 2019.
Balbus, Stanisław. *Między stylami*. Kraków: Universitas, 1996.
Baran, Bogdan. *Postmodernizm i końce wieku*. Kraków: Inter Esse, 2003.
Barth, John. *The Friday Book. Essays and Other Nonfiction*. New York: G. P. Putnam's Sons, 1984.
Barth, John. *Lost in the Funhouse. Fiction for print, tape, live voice*. New York: Anchor Books, 1988.
Barthes, Roland. *Writing Degree Zero*. Translated by Annette Lavers and Colin Smith. London: Jonathan Cape, 1967 (1953).
Barthes, Roland. *Mythologies*. Selected and translated from the French by Annette Lavers. New York: The Noonday Press, 1991 (1957).
Bartoszyński, Kazimierz. *Kryzys czy trwanie powieści: studia literaturoznawcze*. Kraków: Universitas, 2004.
Baudrillard, Jean. *Simulacra and Simulation*. Translated by Sheila Faria Glaser. Ann Arbor: The University of Michigan Press, 1994 (1981).
Bauman, Zygmunt. *Modernity and the Holocaust*. Ithaca, NY: Cornell University Press, 2000.
Bellamy, Elizabeth J. *Affective Genealogies. Psychoanalysis, Postmodernism, and the "Jewish Question" after Auschwitz*. Lincoln and London University of Nebraska Press, 1997.

Benjamin, Walter. *Origin of the German Trauerspiel.* Translated by Howard Eiland. Cambridge, Mass. and London: Harvard University Press, 2019.

Benjamin, Walter. *Konstelacje. Wybór tekstów.* przeł. A. Lipszyc, A. Wołkowicz, Kraków 2012.

Bieńczyk, Marek. "Klucz francuski". *Kontrapunkt* (suplement to *Tygodnik Powszechny*) 2001, n. 3/4.

Bieńczyk, Marek. *Melancholia. O tych, co nigdy nie odnajdą straty.* Warszawa: Świat Książki, 2012.

Blanchot, Maurice. *The Sirens' Song. Selected Essays.* Edited by Gabriel Josipovici, translated by Sacha Rabinovitch. Bloomington: Indiana University Press, 1982.

Blanchot, Maurice. *The Book to Come.* Translated from the French by Charlotte Mandell. Stanford, CA: Stanford University Press, 2003.

Bloch, Ernst. *The Principle of Hope.* Translated by Neville Plaice, Stephen Plaice, and Paul Knight. Cambridge, Mass.: the MIT Press, 1986 (1959).

Błażejewski, Tadeusz. *Przemoc świata. Pisarstwo Leopolda Buczkowskiego.* Łódź: Wydawnictwo Uniwersytetu Łódzkiego, 2005.

Bojarska, Katarzyna. "Historia Zagłady i literatura (nie)piękna. *Tworki* Marka Bieńczyka w kontekście kultury posttraumatycznej" [History of the Holocaust and (Non)Literature – Marek Bieńczyk's *Tworki* in the Context of Post-Traumatic Culture], *Pamiętnik Literacki* 2008/2: 89–106.

Borowski. A. "Cesare Ripa czyli muzeum wyobraźni." In Cesare Ripa, *Ikonologia.* Translated into Polish by I. Kania. Kraków: TAiWPN Universitas.

Brenner, Rachel Feldhay. *Polish Literature and the Holocaust: Eyewitness Testimonies, 1942–1947.* Evanston, Illinois: Northwestern, 2019.

Buryła, Sławomir, Agnieszka Karpowicz, Radosław Sioma, eds., *...zimą bywa się pisarzem... o Leopoldzie Buczkowskim.* Kraków: Universitas, 2008.

Buryła, Sławomir. "Bez wyroku" *Więź* (2009), pp. 1–2.

Buryła, Sławomir and Alina Molisak, ed., *Ślady obecności.* Kraków: Universitas, 2010.

Buryła, Sławomir. "Topika Holocaustu. Wstępne rozpoznanie." *World of Texts. Rocznik Słupski* no. 10 (2012): 131–151.

Buryła, Sławomir. *Wokół Zagłady. Szkice o literaturze Holokaustu.* Kraków: Universitas, 2016.

Caillois, Roger. *Siła powieści.* Translated into Polish by Tomasz Swoboda. Gdańsk: Wydwnictwo Uniwersytetu Gdańskiego, 2008. (*Puissances du roman* 1942).

Cesarani, David. *Final Solution: The Fate of the Jews, 1933–1949.* New York: St. Martin's Press, 2016.

Chakrabarty, Dipesh. "The Climate of History: Four Theses." *Critical Inquiry*, Vol. 35, No. 2 (Winter 2009): 197–222.

Chmielewska, Katarzyna. "Ukryte założenia i aporie teorii recepcji." *Pamiętnik Literacki* 2001, z. 4.

Chmielewska, Katarzyna, Michał Głowiński, Katarzyna Makaruk, Alina Molisak, and Tomasz Żukowski, eds., *Stosowność i forma: jak opowiadać o Zagładzie?* Kraków: Universitas 2005.

Coussens, Catherine. 'Secrets of the Earth': Geology and Memory in Anne Michaels's *Fugitive Pieces, Annals of the University of Craiova*, Series: Philology, English, Year XI, No.2, 2010, pp. 73–87.

Crosthwaite, Paul. *Trauma, Postmodernism and the Aftermath of World War II*. Palgrave Macmillan 2009.
Czapliński, Przemysław. "Zagłada jako wyzwanie dla refleksji o literaturze". *Teksty Drugie* 2004, n. 5: 9–22.
Cuber, Marta. *Metonimie Zagłady. O polskiej prozie lat 1987–2012*. Katowice: Wydawnictwo Uniwersytetu Śląskiego 2013.
Czapliński, Przemysław. "Zagłada – niedokończona narracja polskiej nowoczesności." In: *Ślady obecności*, red. S. Buryła, A. Molisak, Kraków: Universitas 2010: 350–355.
Deleuze, Gilles and Félix Guattari. *A Thousand Plateaus. Capitalism and Schizophrenia*. Translated by Brian Massumi. Minneapolis and London: University of Minnesota Press, 2005.
Dellamora, Richard, ed., *Postmodern Apocalypse. Theory and Cultural Practice at the End*. Philadelphia: University of Pennsylvania Press, 1995.
Derrida, Jacques. "No Apocalypse, Not Now (Full Speed Ahead, Seven Missiles, Seven Missives)." Translated by Catherine Porter and Philip Lewis. *Diacritics* (Summer, 1984), Vol. 14, No. 2 (Nuclear Criticism): 20–31.
Derrida, Jacques. *Writing and Difference*. Translated, with an introduction and additional notes by Alan Bass. London and New York: Routledge, 2002.
Derrida, Jacques. *Sovereignties in Questions: The Poetics of Paul Celan*. Edited by Thomas Dutoit and Outi Pasanen. New York: Fordham University Press, 2005.
Derrida, Jacques. *Cinders*. Translated by Ned Lukacher; introduction by Cary Wolfe. Minneapolis and London: University of Minnesota Press, 2014.
Dessuant, Pierre. *Narcyzm. Przegląd koncepcji psychoanalitycznych* [*Le narcissisme*]. Translated into Polish by Zuzanna Stadnicka-Dmitriew. Gdańsk: Gdańskie Wydawnictwo Psychologiczne, 2007.
Di Leo, Jeffrey R., ed., *Federman's Fictions. Innovation, Theory, and the Holocaust*. New York: State University of New York Press, 2011.
Domańska, Ewa. *Historia egzystencjalna. Krytyczne studium narratywizmu i humanistyki zaangażowanej*. Warszawa Wydawnictwo Naukowe PWN, 2012.
Domańska Ewa. "Humanistyka ekologiczna" [Ecological Humanities]. *Teksty Drugie* 2013, nr 1–2: 13–32.
Dziamski, Grzegorz. *Postmodernizm wobec kryzysu estetyki współczesnej*. Poznań: Wydawnictwo UAM, 1996.
Eaglestone, Robert. *The Holocaust and the Postmodern*. Oxford: Oxford University Press, 2008.
Eaglestone, Robert. *The Broken Voice. Reading Post-Holocaust Literature*. Oxford: Oxford University Press, 2017.
Eco, Umberto. *O bibliotece* [*De Bibliotheca*]. Translated from the Italian by Adam Szymanowski. Wrocław: Ossolineum, 1990.
Elias, Amy J. *Sublime Desire. History and Post-1960s Fiction*. Baltimore and London: The Johns Hopkins University Press, 2001.
Fabiszak, Małgorzata and Marcin Owsiński, eds., *Obóz-muzeum. Trauma we współczesnym wystawiennictwie*. Kraków: Universitas, 2013.
Famulska-Ciesielska, Karolina and Żurek, Sławomir Jacek. *Literatura polska w Izraelu*. Kraków and Budapeszt: Austeria, 2012.

Federman, Raymond. *Critifiction. Postmodern Essays*. Albany N.Y.: State University of New York Press, 1993.
Foltz, Richard C. "Does Nature Have Historical Agency? World History, Environmental History and How Historians Can Help Save the Planet." *The History Teacher* 37 (2003) no. 1: 9–28.
Foster, Hal, ed. *Postmodern Culture*. London: Pluto Press, 1985.
Foster, Hal. *The Return of the Real. The Avant-Garde at the End of the Century*. Cambridge, Mass. and London: The MIT Press. 1996.
Foucault, Michel. *The Order of Things. An Archeology of the Human Sciences*. New York: Pantheon Books, 1970.
Franklin, Ruth. *A Thousand Darknesses: Lies and Truth in Holocaust Fiction*. New York and Oxford: Oxford University Press, 2011.
Freud, Sigmund. *The Interpretation of Dreams* (1913). Translated by Abraham Arden Brill. At https://en.wikisource.org/wiki/The_Interpretation_of_Dreams.
Gasztold, Brygida. "A Narrative Inquiry into Canadian Multiculturalism: *Fugitive Pieces* by Anne Michaels." *TransCanadiana* 2013, nr 6: 207–225.
Giddens, Anthony. *The Politics of Climate Change*. Cambridge and Malden, MA: Polity Press, 2009.
Gilloch, Graeme. *Walter Benjamin: Critical Constellations*. Cambridge, Oxford, Malden: Polity, 2002.
Głowacka, Dorota. *Po tamtej stronie: świadectwo, afekt, wyobraźnia*. Warszawa: Instytut Badań Literackich PAN, 2016.
Głowiński, Michał. *Dzieło wobec odbiorcy: szkice z komunikacji literackiej*. Kraków: Universitas, 1998.
Gołaszewska, Maria ed. *Estetyka w świecie. Wybór tekstów*. Kraków: Wydawnictwa Uniwersytetu Jagiellońskiego 1994.
Gontarz, Beata. *Obrazy świata. Wizualne reprezentacje rzeczywistości w polskiej prozie współczesnej*, Katowice: Wydawnictwo Uniwersytetu Śląskiego, 2014.
Gosk, Hanna and Andrzej Zieniewicz, ed.. *Narracje po końcu (wielkich) narracji. Kolekcje, obiekty, symulakra*. Warszawa: Dom Wydawniczy Elipsa, 2007.
Gosk, Hanna. *Przemoc w opowieści. Ze studiów postzależnościowych nad literaturą XX i XXI wieku*. Kraków: Universitas, 2019.
Grabowski, Jan and Dariusz Libionka. "Bezdroża polityki historycznej. Wokół Markowej, czyli o czym nie mówi Muzeum Polaków Ratujących Żydów podczas II Wojny Światowej im. Rodziny Ulmów" [Historical Policy Gone Astray. What the Ulma Family Museum of Poles Saving Jews in World War II Fails to Discuss], *Zagłada Żydów. Studia i Materiały* 12 (2016): 619–642.
Gross, Jan Tomasz. *Neighbors: The Destruction of the Jewish Community in Jedwabne, Poland*. New York, NY: Penguin Books, 2002.
Gross, Jan Tomasz. *Fear: Anti-Semitism in Poland after Auschwitz: An Essay in Historical Interpretation*. New York: Random House and Princeton University Press, 2006.
Grudzka, Anna. "Co nam zostało po Czarnobylu."
Grynberg, Henryk. *Monolog polsko-żydowski*. Wołowiec: Wydawnictwo Czarne, 2003.
Gumbrecht, Hans Ulrich. *After 1945: Latency as Origin of the Present*. Stanford, CA: Stanford University Press, 2013.

Gutmann, Yisrael and Michael Berenbaum, ed. *Anatomy of the Auschwitz Death Camp.* Washington, D.C.: United States Holocaust Museum; Bloomington and Indianapolis,Indiana University Press, 1994.

Gwóźdź, Andrzej and Piotr Zawojski, ed. *Wiek ekranów. Przestrzenie kultury widzenia.* Kraków: Rabid, 2002.

Handbook of Polish, Czech, and Slovak Holocaust Fiction: Works and Contexts. Ed. Elisa-Maria-Hiemer at al. Berlin-Boston: Walter de Gruyter GmbH, 2021.

Hassan, Ihab. "POSTmodernISM." *New Literary History* Vol. 3 (Autumn, 1971) No. 1, Modernism and Postmodernism: Inquiries, Reflections, and Speculations: 5–30.

Hirsch, Joshua. *Afterimage: Film, Trauma and the Holocaust.* Temple University Press 2003.

Holzer, Jerzy. *Historikerstreit. Spór o miejsce III Rzeszy w historii Niemiec.* London: Aneks 1990.

Hughes, Judith M. *The Perversion of Holocaust Memory: Writing and Rewriting the Past after 1989.* London: Bloomsbury Publishing, 2022.

Hewitt, Kenneth. *Regions of Risk: A Geographical Introduction to Disasters.* Harlow: Longman, 1997.

Hilberg, Raul. *The Destruction of the European Jews.* With a New Postscript by the Author. Chicago: Quadrangle, 1967 (1961).

Hundorova, Tamara. *The Post-Chornobyl Library: Ukrainian Postmodernism of the 1990s.* Translated by Sergiy Yakovenko. Boston: Academic Studies Press, 2019.

Hutcheon, Linda. "Subject In/Of/To History and His Story." *Diacritics* 16 (1), Spring 1986: pp. 78–91.

Hutcheon, Linda. *Narcissistic Narrative. The Metafictional Paradox.* New York and London: Methuen, 1984.

Hutcheon, Linda. *A Theory of Parody: The Teachings of Twentieth-Century Art Forms.* Urbana and Chicago: University of Illinois Press, 2000 (1985).

Hutcheon, Linda. *The Politics of Postmodernism.* London and New York: Routledge, 2001.

Hutcheon, Linda. *A Poetics of Postmodernism.* New York and London: Routledge, 2010.

Huyssen, Andreas. "Mapping the Postmodern." *New German Critique* No. 33, Modernity and Postmodernity (Autumn, 1984): 5–52.

Ibler, Reinhard. *The Holocaust in the Central European Literatures and Cultures since 1989 / Der Holocaust in den mitteleuropäischen Literaturen und Kulturen seit 1989.* Stuttgart: ibidem Press, 2014.

Jameson, Fredric. *Postmodernism, or, The Cultural Logic of Late Capitalism.* Durham: Duke University Press, 1991.

Jameson, Fredric. *The Antinomies of Realism.* London and New York: Verso, 2013.

Jarmuszkiewicz, Anna. *Tropy Prousta. Problemy recepcji literackiej w literaturze polskiej po 1945 roku.* Kraków: Universitas 2019.

Jarzębski, Jerzy. *Apetyt na przemianę. Notatki o prozie współczesnej.* Kraków: Znak, 1997.

Jastrzębska, Aleksandra, *Mapy świata, mapy ciała: geografia i cielesność w literaturze.* Kraków: Libron, 2014.

Kęder, Konrad C. *Wszyscy jesteście postmodernistami! Szkice o literaturze lat dziewięćdziesiątych XX wieku.* Katowice: FA-art, 2011.

Kember, Sarah. *Virtual Anxiety: Photography, New Technologies and Subjectivity.* Manchester and New York: Manchester University Press, 1998.

Kermode, Frank. *The Sense of an Ending: Studies in the Theory of Fiction*, with a New Epilogue. 2000 (1966). Oxford and New York: Oxford University Press, 2000. *Znaczenie końca.* Trans. O. i W. Kubińscy. Gdańsk 2010.

Kiślak, Elżbieta and Marek Gumkowski, eds. *Trzynaście arcydzieł romantycznych.* Warszawa: Instytut Badań Literackich Polskiej Akademii Nauk, 1996.

Kłosiński, Krzysztof. *Eros. Dekonstrukcja. Polityka.* Katowice: Wydawnictwo Naukowe "Śląsk", 2000.

Kolář, Stanislav. *Seven Responses to the Holocaust in American Fiction.* Ostrava: Ostravská univerzita, 2004.

Kolek, L. [review] "*The Fabulators*, Robert Scholes, New York 1967, Oxford University Press 1967, pp. X, 2 nlb., 180". *Pamiętnik Literacki* 65/1 (1974): 351–357.

Koprowska, Karolina. *Postronni? Zagłada w relacjach chłopskich świadków.* Kraków: Universitas, 2018.

Kowalska-Leder, Justyna. "Andrzej Bart, *Fabryka muchołapek.* Wydawnictwo W.A.B., Warszawa 2010" [review]. *Zagłada Żydów. Studia i Materiały* 6 (2010): 319–322.

Krupa, Bartłomiej. *Opowiedzieć Zagładę. Polska proza i historiografia wobec Holocaustu (1987–2003).* Kraków: Universitas, 2013.

Kurkiewicz, J. "Myszkin w czasach Zagłady". *Tygodnik Powszechny* 7 September 2003.

Kuryluk, Ewa. *Manhattan i Mała Wenecja. Rozmawia Agnieszka Drotkiewicz.* Warszawa: Wydawnictwo Zeszytów Literackich, 2016.

Kuśniewicz, Andrzej. *Puzzle pamięci. Z Andrzejem Kuśniewiczem rozmawia Grażyna Szcześniak.* Kraków: Eureka, 1992.

Kutnik, Jerzy. *The Novel as Performance. The Fiction of Ronald Sukenick and Raymond Federman.* Carbondale and Edwardsville: Southern Illinois University Press, 1986.

Lacan, Jacques, Jacques-Alain Miller and James Hulbert, "Desire and the Interpretation of Desire in *Hamlet.*" *Yale French Studies*, No. 55/56, Literature and Psychoanalysis. The Question of Reading: Otherwise. (1977), pp. 11–52.

Lacan, Jacques. *The Seminar of Jacques Lacan.* Book I. *Freud's Papers on Technique, 1953–1954.* Translated by John Forrester. Cambridge: Cambridge University Press, 1988.

Lacan, Jacques. *On the Names-of-the-Father.* Trans. Brice Fink. Cambridge and Malden, MA: Polity Press, 2013.

Lang, Berel. *Act and Idea in the Nazi Genocide.* Chicago and London: University of Chicago Press, 1990.

Langer, Lawrence *Holocaust Testimonies: The Ruins of Memory.* New Have and London: Yale University Press, 1991.

Lasch, Christopher. *The Culture of Narcissism: American Life in An Age of Diminishing Expectations.* New York and London: W. W. Norton, 1979. Rev. edition 1991.

Leciński, Maciej. "'Likwidacja przewagi.' Empatia i praca żałoby w *Tworkach* Marka Bieńczyka." *Teksty Drugie* 1 (2001).

Leder, Andrzej. *Był kiedyś postmodernizm… Sześć esejów o schyłku XX stulecia.* Warszawa: Wydawnictwo IFiS PAN, 2018.

Leggewie, Claus and Harald Welzer. *Koniec świata, jaki znaliśmy. Klimat, przyszłość i szanse demokracji.* Trans. into Polish by Piotr Buras. Warszawa: Wydawnictwo Krytyki Politycznej, 2012.

Leociak, Jacek. "O nadużyciach w badaniach nad doświadczeniem Zagłady" [On the Abuses in Research of the Holocaust Experience], *Zagłada Żydów. Studia i Materiały* 6 (2010): 9–19.

Leociak, Jacek and Marta Tomczok. "Afektywny kicz holokaustowy – wprowadzenie" [Affective Holocaust Kitsch – An Introduction], *Zagłada Żydów. Studia i Materiały* 17 (2021): 17–44.

Lipszyc, A. *Sprawiedliwość na końcu języka. Czytanie Waltera Benjamina.* Kraków: Universitas, 2012.

Lyotard, Jean-François. *The Postmodern Condition: A Report on Knowledge.* Minneapolis: University of Minnesota Press, 1984.

Lyotard, Jean-François. "Wzniosłość i awangarda". Translated into Polish by Marek Bieńczyk. *Teksty Drugie* 1996, nr 2/3.

Lyotard, Jean-François. *The Lyotard Reader and Guide.* Edited by Keith Crome and James Williams. Edinburgh: Edinburgh University Press, 2006.

Łuczewski, Michał, Tomasz Maślanka and Paulina Bednarz-Łuczewska, "Bringing Habermas to Memory Studies," *Polish Sociological Review* 01/183 (2013): 335–349.

Łukasiewicz, Małgorzata, ed., *Historikerstreit. Spór o miejsce III Rzeszy w historii Niemiec.* London: Aneks, 1990.

Łysak, Tomasz. *Antologia studiów nad traumą.* Kraków: Universitas, 2015.

Łysak, Tomasz. *Od kroniki do filmu posttraumatycznego. Filmy dokumentalne o Zagładzie.* Warszawa: Instytut Badań Literackich PAN, 2016.

Mach, Anna. *Świadkowie świadectw. Postpamięć Zagłady w polskiej literaturze najnowszej.* Warszawa and Toruń: Wydawnictwo Naukowe Uniwersytetu Mikołaja Kopernika, 2016.

Małochleb, Paulina. "Murarz buduje, a ja majaczę." *FA-art*, nr 1–2.

Małochleb, Paulina. "Iluzja i mistyfikacja. O powieściach Andrzeja Barta." [Illusion and Mystification. On Andrzej Bart's Novels] *Śląskie Studia Polonistyczne* 2012, nr 1/2 (2): 219–235.

Man, Paul de. *Aesthetic Ideology.* Minneapolis, MN, and London: University of Minnesota Press, 1996.

Marecki, Piotr. "*Tworki* Marka Bieńczyka jako powieść gatunkowa." [Marek Bieńczyk's *Tworki* as a Genre Novel], *Przestrzenie Teorii* 2012, no. 18: 101–133.

Markiewka, T. S., "Bruno Latour i 'koniec' postmodernizmu," *Diametros* 2012, n. 33: 101–119.

McHale, Brian. *Postmodernist Fiction.* London and New York: Routledge, 1987.

McHale, Brian. "The End." https://electronicbookreview.com/essay/the-end/ [accessed 16.09.2019].

McLean, Stuart. "Bodies from the Bog: Metamorphosis, Non-human Agency and the Making of 'Collective' Memory." *Trames* 2008, 12 (62/57), 3: 299–308.

Melchior, Małgorzata. *Zagłada a tożsamość. Polscy Żydzi ocaleni na "aryjskich papierach". Analiza doświadczenia biograficznego.* Warszawa: Instytut Filozofii i Socjologii PAN, 2004.

Milchman Alan and Alan Rosenberg, ed., *Postmodernism and the Holocaust.* Amsterdam and Atlanta, GA: Rodopi, 1998.

Milchman, Alan and Alan Rosenberg. *Eksperymenty w myśleniu o Holocauście. Auschwitz, nowoczesność i filozofia.* Translated into Polish by Leszek Krowicki and Jakub Szacki. Warszawa: Wydawnictwo Naukowe Scholar, 2003.

Mitchell, William J. *The Reconfigured Eye: Visual Truth in the Post-Photographic Era*. Cambridge, Mass.: The MIT Press, 1994.

Mizerkiewicz, Tomasz. *Literatura obecna. Szkice o najnowszej prozie i krytyce*. Kraków: Universitas, 2013.

Morawiec, Arkadiusz. *Literatura w lagrze. Lager w literaturze. Fakt – temat – metafora*. Łódź: Publikacje Wydawnictwa AHE w Łodzi, 2009.

Motte, Warren F. *The Poetics of Experiment: A Study of the Work of Georges Perec*. Lexington: French Forum Monographs, 1984.

Muchowski, Jakub. "Figury czasowości w *Tworkach* Marka Bieńczyka" [The Figures of Temporality in Marek Bieńczyk's *Tworki*], *Teksty Drugie* 3 (2006): 135–147.

Nabokov, Vladimir. *Pale Fire*. New York: Berkley Books, 1984.

Nalewajk, Żaneta, ed. *Podmiot w literaturze polskiej po 1989 roku. Antropologiczne aspekty konstrukcji*. Warszawa Dom Wydawniczy Elipsa, 2011.

Nicol, Bran, ed. *Postmodernism and the Contemporary Novel. A Reader*. Edinburgh: Edinburgh University Press, 2002.

Nowacki, Dariusz. "Czy Bart lektury wart?" *FA-art* 1993, no. 1 (11): 67–73.

Nowacki, Dariusz. "Pociąg do Hollywood. O prozie Andrzeja Barta." In *Skład osobowy. Szkice o prozaikach współczesnych*, cz. 2, ed. Agnieszka Nęcka, Dariusz Nowacki, Jolanta Pasterska. Katowice: Wydawnictwo Uniwersytetu Śląskiego, 2016.

Nycz, Ryszard. *Tekstowy świat. Poststrukturalizm a wiedza o literaturze*. Kraków: Universitas 2000.

Nycz, Ryszard, ed. *Kultura po przejściach, osoby z przeszłością: polski dyskurs postzależnościowy – konteksty i perspektywy badawcze*. Kraków: Universitas, 2011.

Owens, Craig. *Beyond Recognition. Representation, Power, and Culture*. Edited by Scott Bryson, Barbara Kruger, Lynne Tillman, and Jane Weinstock. Berkeley, Los Angeles and London: University of California Press, 1992.

Pascariu, Lucia-Hedviga. "Entropy and Loss: Paul Auster's *In The Country of Last Things*." *Procedia – Social and Behavioral Sciences* 92 (2013): 678–685.

Pearce, Fred. *The Last Generation. How Nature Will Take Her Revenge for Climate Change*, Eden Project Books 2006.

Pelekanidis, Theodor. *How to Write about the Holocaust. The Postmodern Theory of History in Praxis*. Abingdon and New York: Routledge, 2022.

Plato. *The Cratylus*. Trans. Benjamin Jowett. https://www.gutenberg.org/cache/epub/1616/pg1616-images.html.

Podraza-Kwiatkowska, Maria. *Symbolizm i symbolika w poezji Młodej Polski*. Kraków: Wydawnictwo Literackie, 1994.

Polit, Monika. *"Moja żydowska dusza nie obawia się dnia sądu". Mordechaj Chaim Rumkowski. Prawda i zmyślenie*. Warszawa: Stowarzyszenie Centrum Badań nad Zagładą Żydów, 2012.

Potocka, Maria Anna, ed. *Postmodernizm. Teksty polskich autorów*. Kraków: Bunkier Sztuki, Inter Esse, 2003.

Prokop-Janiec, Eugenia, ed. *Polacy–Żydzi: kontakty kulturowe i literackie*. Kraków: Wydawnictwo Uniwersytetu Jagiellońskiego, 2014.

Rabinovitch, Gérard. *Leçons de la Shoah. Nauki płynące z Zagłady*. Translated from the French by Grażyna Majcher. Warszawa: Wydawnictwo Dialog 2019.

Rachwał, Tadeusz and Sławek, Tadeusz. *Maszyna do pisania. O dekonstruktywistycznej teorii literatury Jacquesa Derridy.* Warszawa: "Rój," 1992.
Rauch, M. E. "Geologies of Silence." *The Nation* April 7, 1997: 35–38.
Reich, Wilhelm. *The Mass Psychology of Fascism.* Translated by Theodore P. Wolfe. New York: Orgone Institute Press, 1946; 3rd ed. https://www.bibliotecapleyades.net/archivos_pdf/masspsychology_fascism.pdf.
Reiter, Andrea. *Narrating the Holocaust.* Translated by Patrick Camiller. London and New York: Continuum 2005 (1995).
Robson, David. "Derrida, Pynchon, and the Apocalyptic Space of Postmodern Fiction." In: Richard Dellamora, ed., *Postmodern Apocalypse. Theory and Cultural Practice at the End.* Philadelphia: University of Pennsylvania Press, 1995: 61–78.
Rorty, Richard. *Contingency, Irony and Solidarity.* Cambridge: Cambridge University Press, 1999.
Rothberg, Michael. *Traumatic Realism. The Demands of Holocaust Representation.* Minneapolis, MN, and London: University of Minnesota Press, 2000.
Runia, Eelco. "Presence," *History and Theory* 45 (2006): 1–29.
Scholes, Robert. *The Fabulators.* New York: Oxford University Press, 1967.
Sendyka, Roma, Tomasz Sapota and Ryszard Nycz., ed., *Migracyjna pamięć, wspólnota, tożsamość.* Warszawa: Instytut Badań Literackich PAN, 2016.
Sicher, Efraim. *The Holocaust Novel.* New York and London: Routledge, 2005.
Scholem, Gershom. *Żydzi i Niemcy: eseje, listy, rozmowa.* Translated by Marzena Zawanowska and Adam Lipszyc. Sejny: "Pogranicze," 2006.
Sicher, Efraim, ed. *Breaking Crystal. Writing and Memory after* Auschwitz. Urbana and Chicago: University of Illinois Press, 1998.
Schütz, Alfred. "Terezjasz, czyli nasza wiedza na temat przyszłych zdarzeń". In *O wielości światów. Szkice z socjologii fenomenologicznej,* przeł. B. Jabłońska, Kraków 2008, p. 189–201.
Shostak, Debra. "In the Country of Missing Persons: Paul Auster's Narratives of Trauma." *Studies in the Novel* vol. 41, no. 1 (Spring 2009): 66–87.
Smith, Stephen D. *The Trajectory of Holocaust Memory: The Crisis of Testimony in Theory and Practice.* 2022.
Snyder, Timothy. *Black Earth: The Holocaust as History and Warning.* London: The Bodley Earth, 2015.
Spergel, J. *Canada's "Second History": The Fiction of Jewish Canadian Women Writers.* Hamburg: Verlag Dr. Kovač 2009.
Spinoza, Benedict de. *Ethics.* Ed. and trans. Edwin Curley. London: Penguin, 1996.
Staniczek, Paweł. *Arbeitslager Golleschau – dzieje podobozu.* Goleszów: 2015.
Steinlauf, Michael C. *Bondage to the Dead: Poland and the Memory of the Holocaust.* Syracuse, NY: Syracuse University Press, 1997.
Suleiman, Susan Rubin. *Crises of Memory and the Second World War.* Cambridge, Mass. and London: Harvard University Press, 2012.
Świerkocki, Maciej. *Postmodernizm. Paradygmat nowej kultury.* Łódź: Wydawnictwo Uniwersytetu Łódzkiego, 1997.
Swinden, Patrick. "D. M. Thomas and *The White Hotel*". *Critical Quarterly,* vol. 24, no. 4.

Smykowski, Mikołaj. *Ekologie Zagłady. Krytyczne studium z antropologii krajobrazu poobozowego na przykładzie Byłego Obozu Zagłady w Chełmnie nad Nerem.* Poznań: Wydział Historyczny, Uniwersytet im. Adama Mickiewicza w Poznaniu, 2019.

Szajnert, Danuta. "Przestrzeń doświadczona, przestrzeń wytworzona – literackie topografie Litzmannstadt Getto (rekonesans). Część druga" [The Space Experienced, the Space Created – Literary Topographies of Litzmannstadt Getto (reconnaissance). Part Two]. *Białostockie Studia Literaturoznawcze* 6 (2015): 7–25.

Szpytma, Mateusz and Jarosław Szarek. *Ofiara sprawiedliwych. Rodzina Ulmów – oddali życie za ratowanie Żydów.* Kraków: Rafael, 2004.

Tacik, Przemysław. *Wolność światel. Edmond Jabès i żydowska filozofia nowoczesności.* Kraków and Budapeszt: Wydawnictwo Austeria, 2015.

Taylor, Mark C. *Erring: A Postmodern A/theology.* Chicago and London: The University of Chicago Press,1987.

Taylor, Mark C. *Disfiguring. Art, Architecture, Religion.* Chicago and London: The University of Chicago Press, 1992.

The Oxford Handbook of Holocaust Studies. Ed. by Peter Hayes and John K. Roth. 2010.

Theweleit, Klaus. *Male Fantasies. volume 1: Women Floods Bodies History.* Translated by Stephen Conway in collaboration with Erica Carter and Chris Turner, foreword by Barbara Ehrenreich. Minneapolis: University of Minnesota Press, 1987.

Tippner, Anja. "Postkatastroficzne relikty i relikwie: los obrazów po Holokauście" *Poznańskie Studia Polonistyczne. Seria Literacka* 25 (45): 237–255.

Tomczok, Marta. "Alegorie Zagłady w *Tworkach* Marka Bieńczyka i *Wieku 21* Ewy Kuryluk." *Prace Filologiczne. Literaturoznawstwo* 2016, nr 6 (9): 157–170.

Tomczok, Marta. "Klimat Zagłady (w perspektywie powieści Pawła Huellego, Tadeusza Konwickiego, Andrzeja Kuśniewicza i Piotra Szewca)," *Teksty Drugie* 2017, nr 2: 147–165.

Tomczok, Marta. "Postmodernistyczne wymazywanie Zagłady (Raymond Federman, Georges Perec, Anatol Ulman)," *Poznańskie Studia Slawistyczne* 2017, nr 12: 299–315.

Tomczok, Marta. *Czyja dzisiaj jest Zagłada? Retoryka – ideologia – popkultura.* Warszawa: IBL PAN, 2018.

Ubertowska, Aleksandra. *Świadectwo – trauma – głos. Literackie reprezentacje Holocaustu.* Kraków: Universitas 2007.

Ubertowska, Aleksandra. "'Kamienie niepokoją się i stają się agresywne'. Holokaust w świetle ekokrytyki," *Poznańskie Studia Polonistyczne. Seria Literacka* 25 (45), Poznań 2015: 93–111.

Uniłowski, Krzysztof. "Postmodernizm w prozie a debaty krytyczne 1970–1987." In *Postmodernizm po polsku?* "Acta Universitas Lodziensis. Folia Scientae Artium et Litterarium", nr 8, ed. A. Izdebska, D. Szejnert, Łódź 1998: 35–52.

Uniłowski, Krzysztof. *Skądinąd: zapiski krytyczne.* Bytom: FA-art, 1998.

Uniłowski, Krzysztof. *Prawo krytyki: o nowoczesnym i ponowoczesnym pojmowaniu literatury.* Katowice Wydawnictwo FA-art, 2013.

Updike, John. "Sentimental re-education. The cerebral experimentalist gets personal." *The New Yorker*, 08.02.2004; accessed 29.08.2023.

Vice, Sue. *Holocaust Fiction.* London and New York: Routledge, 2000.

Vice, Sue. *Children Writing the Holocaust.* New York: Palgrave Macmillan, 2004.

Vice, Sue. *Textual Deceptions: False Memoirs and Literary Hoaxes in the Contemporary Era.* Edinburgh: Edinburgh University Press, 2014.
Welsch, Wolfgang. *Unsere postmoderne Moderne. Nasza postmodernistyczna moderna.* Translated from the German by Roman Kubicki and Anna Zeidler-Janiszewska. Warszawa: Wydawnictwo Oficyna Naukowa, 1998.
Welzer, Harald. *Climate Wars. Why People Will Be Killed in the Twenty-First Century.* Translated by Patrick Camiller. Cambridge and Malden, MA: Polity Press, 2012.
Wesseling, Elisabeth. "*In the Country of Last Things:* Paul Auster's Parable of the Apocalypse." *Neophilologus* 75 (1991): 496–504.
White, Hayden. *Proza historyczna.* Transletd by Rafał Borysławski et al., edited by Ewa Domańska. Kraków: Universitas, 2009.
White, Hayden. "Postmodernisme et histoire," in *Historiographies. Concepts et débats,* vol. II, eds. Christian Delacroix and François Dosse, et al. Paris: Gallimard, 2010: 839–844.
White, Hayden. *The Practical Past.* Evanston, IL: Northwestern University Press, 2014.
White, Hayden. *Przeszłość praktyczna.* Translated into Polish by Jan Burzyński, Agata Czarnacka, Tomasz Dobrogoszcz, Ewa Domańska, Emilia Kledzik at al., edited by Ewa Domańska. Kraków: Universitas, 2014.
Wiślicz, Tomasz. "Historiografia polska 1989–2009. Bardzo subiektywne podsumowanie" [Polish Historiography 1989–2009. A Very Subjective Summary], *Przegląd Humanistyczny* 2010, nr 5–6: 37–48.
Witek-Malicka, Wanda. *Dzieci z Auschwitz-Birkenau. Socjalizacja w obozie koncentracyjnym na przykładzie Dzieci Oświęcimia.* Kraków: Nomos, 2013.
Witko, Andrzej, ed. *Tajemnica "Las Meninas": antologia tekstów.* Kraków: Wydawnictwo AA, 2006.
Wolff-Powęska, Anna. *Pamięć: brzemię i uwolnienie. Niemcy wobec nazistowskiej przeszłości (1945–2010).* Poznań: Zysk i S-ka, 2011.
Wolf, Diane Lauren. *Beyond Anne Frank: Hidden Children and Postwar Families in Holland.* Berkeley, Los Angeles, London: University of California Press, 2007.
Wolff-Powęska, A. *Pamięć: brzemię i uwolnienie. Niemcy wobec nazistowskiej przeszłości (1945–2010).* Poznań 2011.
Young, James Edward. *Writing and Rewriting the Holocaust. Narrative and the Consequences of Interpretation.* Bloomington and Indianapolis: Indiana University Press, 1988.
Zaleski, Marek. *Zamiast. O twórczości Czesława Miłosza.* Kraków: Wydawnictwo Literackie, 2005.
Zaleski, Marek. *Echa idylli w literaturze polskiej doby nowoczesności i późnej nowoczesności.* Kraków: Universitas, 2007.
Zawadzki, Michał. "Teologia postmodernistyczna jako szansa dla religii chrześcijańskiej." *Diametros* no. 15 (2008): 97–101.
Zawilski, Apoloniusz. *Bitwy polskiego września.* Kraków: Znak, 2019.
Zawojski, Piotr, ed. *Teoria i estetyka fotografii cyfrowej. Antologia.* Trans. J. Kucharska, K. Stanisz. Warszawa: Narodowe Centrum Kultury, 2017.
Ziomek, Jerzy. *Retoryka opisowa.* Wrocław, Warszawa, and Kraków: Ossolineum, 2000 (1990).

Żychliński, Arkadiusz. *Laboratorium antropofikcji. Dociekania filologiczne.* Poznań: Wydawnictwo Naukowe Uniwersytetu im. Adama Mickiewicza; Warszawa: Instytut Badań Literackich PAN, 2014.

Index

Abish, Walter   89-93, 97, 99-101, 111, 199
Abramowicz, Mieczysław   191
Agamben, Giorgio   11
Amiel, Irit   16, 145
Amis, Martin   13
Andres, Zbigniew   168
Andersen, Hans Christian   62
Anderson, Perry R.   161, 187
Andrzejewska, Ewa   146
Ankersmit, Frank   13-15, 17, 19, 190, 195
Arendt, Hannah   10seq., 160, 169
Auster, Paul   25, 30seq., 33seq., 37, 46, 50, 53, 90seq., 101-109, 111, 199, 209seq.

Bakhtin, Mikhail Mikhailovich   57
Baran, Bogdan   198
Barańczak, Stanisław   36
Barnes, Djuna   128, 132
Bart, Andrzej   23, 149, 153, 159-171, 173-179, 181, 183, 186seq., 189seq., 192-194, 196, 199, 205, 207seq., 210
Barth, John   45, 114, 149-154, 171
Barthelme, Donald   45, 154
Barthes, Roland   101, 152, 181seq., 190
Bartoszyński, Kazimierz   181
Bass, Alan   30, 33
Bataille, Georges   9, 11, 177
Batko, Zbigniew   149
Baudrillard, Jean   164seq.
Bauman, Frank L.   53
Bauman, Zygmunt   91, 118, 120
Bednarz-Łuczewska, Paulina   121
Bellamy, Elizabeth Jane   12, 129
Benjamin, Walter   129seq., 132-136

Between, Quenette   72
Bialik, Waldemar   186
Bieńczyk, Marek   15seq., 18, 23, 97, 123seq., 128-130, 132-137, 159, 169seq., 181-183, 186-196, 198seq.
Biernacik, Dawid   85
Bird-David, Nurit   140
Birenbaum, Halina   23seq., 26-32, 34, 37, 42, 45seq., 57, 60, 65
Bismarck, Otto von   128
Blanchot, Maurice   9, 11, 33seq., 42, 66, 68
Błaszczak, Barbara   85
Błażejewski, Tadeusz   38seq.
Błoński, Jan   34, 71
Böcklin, Arnold   126
Bojarska, Katarzyna   18, 191, 196
Borges, Jorge Luis   45, 149-155
Borowski, Andrzej   132
Borowski, Tadeusz   29, 54
Braidotti, Rosi   209
Brill, Abraham Arden   177
Broszkiewicz, Jerzy   183
Brown, Andrew   94
Bruno, Latour   19
Buczkowski, Leopold   23-25, 28, 34-43, 45-47, 123, 183, 198seq.
Bulgakov, Mikhail   170
Buras, Piotr   86
Buryła, Sławomir   36seq., 71, 90, 92, 107, 161, 168seq., 184, 189, 191
Busse, Kristina   49-51

Calvino, Italo   45
Celan, Paul   135seq.

Cesarani, David 14seq., 20
Chagall, Marc 36
Chakrabarty, Dipesh 73
Chanter, Tina 10
Chereziṅska, Elżbieta 149, 153, 175
Ciaramelli, Fabio 10
Cieślik, Krzysztof 189
Cohen, Jeffrey Jerome 146
Cohen, Marcel 25
Coover, Robert 45
Coussens, Catherine 72, 140
Crome, Keith 194
Cuber, Marta (Tomczok, Marta) 23, 56, 90, 124, 169, 208
Curley, Edwin 117
Czachowska, Agnieszka 188
Czajkowska, Stella 173seq.
Czakański, Piotr 149, 153, 197, 200–205
Czapliński, Przemysław 10, 71, 78, 87, 89–92, 188, 191
Czemarmazowicz, Marta 191
Czernecki, Bartosz 85

Dąbrowski, Bartosz 169, 196
Deleuze, Gilles 158
DeLillo, Don 13, 209
Dellamora, Richard 90, 102
Demidenko, Helene 96, 184
Derrida, Jacques 9seq., 16, 30, 33seq., 67, 69, 102–104, 135seq., 186
Dessuant, Pierre 161
Di, Leo Jeffrey R. 45, 54
Dichter, Wilhelm 16
Dick, Philip K. 170
Diner, Dan 10
Doctorow, Edgar Lawrence 45seq., 48–53
Domańska, Ewa 8seq., 14, 17, 71, 87, 140seq., 144seq., 195, 200
Dostoevsky, Fyodor 57
Drabik, Lidia 34
Drotkiewicz, Agnieszka 128, 130
Dürer, Albrecht 128
Dutoit, Thomas 136
Dziamski, Grzegorz 199

Eaglestone, Robert 11seq.
Eco, Umberto 149, 153seq.
Ehrenreich, Barbara 100
Eichengreen, Lucille 172seq.
Elias, Amy 101seq., 199
Elżbieta, Kiślak 135
Engelking, Barbara 187
Epstein, Leslie 184

Fabiszak, Małgorzata 118
Farat, Ryszard 85
Federman, Raymond 13seq., 16, 23seq., 30, 33, 37, 45–49, 53–59, 61, 64–70, 90seq., 111–114, 116–121, 151–154, 199
Ferdinand of Aragon 104
Fessenden, Tracy 10
Filipiak, Janusz 85
Fink, Brice 165
Foer, Jonathan Safran 149, 153, 199, 201
Foltz, Richard C. 75
Forecki, Piotr 71
Forrester, John 165
Foster, Hal 8, 132, 197–202, 204, 206
Foucault, Michel 9, 11, 52, 166seq.
Frank, Anna 120
Franklin, Ruth 153, 184, 195
Freud, Sigmund 54, 92, 95, 98, 139, 141, 161, 165, 175, 177
Fried, Gregory 10
Froment-Meurice, Marc 10

Gallus, Jan 18
Garbo, Greta 128
Gass, William Howard 42, 45
Gasztold, Brygida 140
Gibbons, Alison 7
Gierowski, Stefan 21
Gilda, Nandor 118
Glaser, Sheila Faria 164
Gleich, Teddy 128
Głowacka, Dorota 100
Głowiński, Michał 16, 64, 130, 168seq., 181–183, 185, 187
Godard, Jean-Luc 163
Goethe, Johann Wolfgang 35seq., 128, 131seq., 176

Gontarz, Beata 200
Górecka, Magdalena 190
Gosk, Hanna 8, 191
Grabowski, Jan 187, 203seq.
Graeme, Gilloch 134
Gross, Jan Tomasz 14, 187, 192, 197seq., 206
Grudzka, Anna 83
Grynberg, Henryk 15, 72
Guattari, Félix 158
Gumbrecht, Hans-Ulrich 77, 86
Gumkowski, Marek 135
Gwóźdź, Andrzej 164seq.

Haan, Ido de 120
Habermas, Jürgen 121
Haska, Agnieszka 187
Hassan, Ihab 209
Heidegger, Martin 11, 67, 99
Hewitt, Kenneth 75, 90
Hilberg, Raul 15, 120, 156, 187
Hitler, Adolf 50, 81, 103, 202
Holzer, Jerzy 119
Hryniewicz-Yarbrough, Ewa 73
Huelle, Paweł 71-73, 78seq., 89seq., 108, 207
Hundorova, Tamara 108
Hutcheon, Linda 36, 51, 54, 94-96, 104seq., 161, 166, 170-172, 196, 198
Huyssen, Andreas 8, 17, 20, 197-199, 202

Ibler, Reinhard 169
Ingold, Tim 140, 143, 145seq.
Isabella I of Castile 104
Izdebska, Agnieszka 89, 169, 193seq.

Jabès, Edmond 23-26, 28, 30-34, 42, 45-47, 53
Jakusik, Ewa 73, 85
Jameson, Federick 8, 105-107, 161, 187
Jarmuszkiewicz, Anna 186
Jarzębski, Jerzy 78, 89
Jastrzębska, Aleksandra 186
Josipovici, Gabriel 42
Jowett, Benjamin 135
Jung, Carl Gstav 98, 141

Ka-Tsetnik 13
Kafka, Franz 74, 170, 172, 174, 205
Kantaris, Sylvia 97seq.
Karpowicz, Agnieszka 36
Kasprowicz, Tomasz 85
Katz, Menke 45
Kember, Sarah 163
Kermode, Frank 101, 103seq.
Kinder, Herman 186
Klejnowski, Krzysztof 85
Kłobukowski, Michał 149, 209
Kłosiński, Krzysztof 66seq.
Koeppen, Wolfgang 153
Kofman, Sarah 10
Kohany, Miriam 128
Kolek, Leszek 126
Kołyszko, Piotr 30, 47
Konopnicka, Maria 98
Konwicki, Tadeusz 23, 71-73, 78seq., 81seq., 84, 89seq., 108, 111, 199
Kosiński, Jerzy 15
Kowalska-Leder, Justyna 168seq., 193seq.
Krajny, Ewa 85
Krauss, Nicole 149, 153-158, 199, 201
Krowicki, Leszek 10
Krupa, Bartłomiej 71seq., 191seq.
Kubiak-Sokół, Aleksandra 34
Kubicki, Roman 99, 103
Kubryń, Zofia 18
Kurkiewicz, Juliusz 15
Kuryluk, Ewa 23, 123seq., 128, 130seq., 133-137, 199
Kuśniewicz, Andrzej 23, 71-75, 83seq., 89-91, 93, 108, 111, 199
Kutnik, Jerzy 53, 114
Kuznetsov, Anatol 94-96

Lacan, Jacques 54seq., 161, 165, 175-178, 202
Lacoue-Labarthe, Philippe 9seq.
Lang, Berel 124seq., 128, 183seq.
Langer, Lawrence L. 137
Lankosz, Borys 161, 163seq., 172-174
Lanzmann, Claude 71
Lasch, Christopher 159
Lavers, Annette 152, 181

Leciński, Maciej 190-192, 195
Leder, Andrzej 7seq.
Leggewie, Claus 86seq.
Lejeune, Philippe 60seq.
Leociak, Jacek 168, 178, 187, 193seq., 208
Leśny, Jacek 85
Levin, David Michael 10
Levinas, Emanuel 9seq.
Libionka, Dariusz 203seq.
Limanówka, Danuta 85
Lipszyc, Adam 129, 137
Lloyd-Jones, Antonia 73
Lorenc, Halina 86
Lotringer, Sylvére 92
Lyotard, Jean-Francois 9, 16, 159seq., 186, 194, 201seq.
Łabędzki, Leszek 85
Łebkowska, Anna 204
Łuczewski, Michał 121
Łukasiewicz, Małgorzata 121
Łysak, Tomasz 163, 202

Mach, Anna 18, 71, 87, 191
Makaruk, Katarzyna 130, 182
Malarecka, Bogumiła 19
Małczyński, Jacek 74, 146
Małochleb, Paulina 162, 168seq., 190
Man, Paul de 11, 26, 126, 129
Márai, Sándor 170
Marecki, Piotr 18, 191
Margański, Janusz 196
Markiewka, Tomasz Szymon 19
Markowski, Michał Paweł 33
Márquez, Gabriel García 45
Martel, Yann 150
Maślanka, Tomasz 121
Massumi, Brian 158
McCaffery, Larry 45
McEwan, Ian 13
McHale, Brain 7seq., 24, 35, 42, 49, 52seq., 55, 61, 69, 93seq., 196, 198
McLean, Stuart 139seq., 142
Melchior, Małgorzata 133, 136seq.
Mengele, Josef 29
Michaels, Anna 13, 19seq., 56, 72, 139-145
Milchman, Alan 9-12, 15

Miłosz, Czesław 146
Mitchell, William J. 163
Mizerkiewicz, Tomasz 184
Molisak, Anna 71, 90, 130, 182, 191
Morawiec, Arkadiusz 15, 79, 130, 136, 190, 196
Muchowski, Jakub 191
Mulisch, Harry 14, 111, 113-121
Murdoch, Iris 126-128, 135

Nabokov, Vladimir 42, 45
Nadana, Katarzyna 188seq.
Nalewajk, Żaneta 191
Nancy, Jean-Luc 10
Nasalska, Anna 81
Nowacki, Dariusz 161seq., 167-170, 189, 200
Nycz, Ryszard 26, 146, 169, 196, 198, 206

Orłowski, Hubert 186
Orski, Kazimierz 188
Ośródka, Leszek 85
Ostachowicz, Igor 146
Outi, Pasanen 136
Owczarek, Bogdan 36
Owens, Craig 123
Owsiński, Marcin 118

Padoł, Emilia 191
Pasterski, Janusz 168, 192
Paźniewski, Włodzimierz 189
Perec, Georges 23seq., 33, 37, 45seq., 48, 53, 55seq., 59-65, 67seq., 70, 199
Perechodnik, Calek 26
Peukert, Helmut 10
Pietrych, Krystyna 168, 192-194
Piwowarski, Krystian 184
Plato 127, 135, 196
Płaza, Maciej 191
Podraza-Kwiatkowska, Maria 126
Polit, Monika 168, 187, 193seq.
Prager, Emily 13
Pronicheva, Dina Mironovna 94-96, 98seq.
Pyrc, Robert 85

Rabinovitch, Gérard 11
Rabinovitch, Sacha 42
Rachwał, Tadeusz 157
Rauch, Molly E. 140
Rawicz, Piotr 14–16
Regis, Durand 142, 160
Ricardou, Jean 54
Ripa, Cesare 132
Robbe-Grillet, Allain 54
Robert, Maciej 189
Robin, Régine 53
Rogula-Kozłowska, Wioletta 85
Romanowski, Gustaw 190
Rorty, Richard 97
Rosenberg, Alan 9–12, 15, 49seq.
Rosenfeld, Alvin H. 184
Różewicz, Tadeusz 16, 42
Rubens, Peter Paul 128
Rudnicki, Marek 163, 208
Rumkowski, Mordechaj 160–162, 166, 168–170, 172–178, 187, 189, 193seq.
Runia, Eelco 76seq., 82
Rutkowski, Krzysztof 79
Rykiel, Sonia 177
Rymkiewicz, Jarosław Marek 16, 78

Sachs, Benjamin 101seq.
Santner, Eric 12
Sapota, Tomasz 146
Schlink, Bernhard 13
Scholem, Gershom 170, 174
Scholes, Robert 123, 125–128, 130, 135seq.
Schulz, Bruno 132, 208
Schütz, Alfred 82
Schwitters, Kurt 104
Sebald, Winfried Georg 13, 56, 76
Sendyka, Roma 146
Shakespeare, William 103, 170
Sheffler, Manning 10
Shostak, Deborah 102seq., 107
Sicher, Efraim 12–14, 78, 102
Sioma, Radosław 36
Sławek, Tadeusz 157
Smith, Colin 126, 181
Smykowski, Mikołaj 144

Sobol, Elżbieta 34
Spergel, Julie 40
Spinoza, Benedict de 115–117
Stadnicka-Dmitriew, Zuzanna 161
Staniczek, Paweł 142
Steinlauf, Michael C. 71
Styron, William 13, 184
Sukenick, Ronald 7, 45, 54, 114
Suleiman, Susan Rubin 46, 54–57, 59–61
Świerkocki, Maciej 114, 151–154
Swinden, Patrik 92
Szacki, Jakub 10
Szarek, Jarosław 203
Szczuka, Kazimiera 188, 195
Szczypiorski, Andrzej 78, 87
Szejnert, Danuta 89
Szeman, Sherri 13
Szewc, Piotr 16, 71–73, 78–80, 84, 89seq., 108
Szymanowski, Adam 154

Tacik, Przemysław 33
Taylor, Mark C. 10
Themerson, Stefan 128
Theweleit, Klaus 99seq.
Thomas, D.M. 13, 89–100, 102, 111, 139, 141, 184, 199, 205
Tippner, Anja 108seq.
Tokarczuk, Olga 23
Tokarska-Bakir, Joanna 146
Tomaszewska, Agata 71
Tomczok, Marta 23, 169, 208
Tulli, Magdalena 169, 193, 199
Tylor, Marian 10, 126

Ubertowska, Aleksandra 16, 18seq., 74, 76, 135, 190seq., 195
Ulma, Józef 203
Ulma, Maria 203seq.
Ulman, Anatol 23–25, 45seq., 48, 64–70, 89, 112, 199
Ulmer, Gregory L. 132
Uniłowski, Krzysztof 64–67, 69seq., 89, 196, 207, 209seq.
Updike, John 92seq.
Urban, Grzegorz 85

Venezia, Shlomo   93seq.
Vice, Sue   56seq., 95seq., 98, 184
Vonnegut, Kurt   45

Waldrop, Rosmarie   26, 32, 34
Warszawski, Dawid   17
Watson, R. James   10
Weber, Heinz-Dieter   186
Welsch, Wolfgang   99, 103seq.
Welzer, Harald   74–76, 82, 86seq.
Werner, Andrzej   29
Wesseling, Elisabeth   104, 106
White, Hayden   9, 13–15, 17, 20, 160, 164, 171, 175, 178seq.
Wibig, Joanna   73, 85
Williams, James   194
Wilner, Joshua   136
Wiślicz, Tomasz   197
Witek-Malicka, Wanda   27
Witko, Andrzej   166
Wójcik, Ryszard   85
Wojdowski, Bogdan   183
Wolf, Diane Lauren   100, 120

Wolff-Powęska, Anna   119
Wolski, Paweł   169
Wrocławski, Bronisław   172
Wyka, Kazimierz   33

Yakovenko, Sergiy   108

Zagajewski, Adam   16
Zaleski, Marek   18, 68, 124seq., 191seq., 195
Zawadzki, Michał   10
Zawilski, Apoloniusz   38
Zawojski, Piotr   165
Zeidler-Janiszewska, Anna   99, 103
Żeromski, Stefan   185
Ziębińska-Witek, Alina   118
Ziemiański, Michał   85
Zieniewicz, Andrzej   191
Zimand, Roman   72, 84
Ziomek, Jerzy   69, 128, 131
Żukowski, Tomasz   130, 182
Żychliński, Arkadiusz   157